CONTENTS

PREFACE

In writing this book, I wanted it to be 'alive' in the sense that, while it gives a clear and comprehensive overview of the major debates in sociology, it also involves the students as much as possible, getting them to find out information and then to express their own opinions on sociological issues. The information and exercises in the book are really only a starting point for students to get out of the classroom and discover more for themselves.

The source material is meant to generate discussion and it is not intended that students should work through the exercises individually, rather that they should tackle work informally in small groups. The ideas that emerge should form the basis of the student enquiries required for the GCSE examination.

Stephen Moore
June 1987

ACKNOWLEDGEMENTS

My grateful thanks to Richard Wadge and his staff at Southend College of Technology library, to Hatti and Tuan of Solidisk Technology Ltd, to Roger Cutting, Carlo Caruso and Chris Evans.

Sarah and Claudia insist on being thanked too, though I can't for the life of me see why fighting, screaming, falling over, standing on my word-processor, being sick (amongst other things) on the floor of the study, falling down the stairs, ripping my books, stealing my pens, eating page four of *Social Trends*, singing endlessly (out of tune), pestering me to go to Peter Pan's Playground, demanding food and drink at the times of heaviest concentration, and generally making my life sheer hell, deserve thanks. But there you are.

Stephen Moore

The authors and publishers are grateful to the following for permission to reproduce previously published material:

Associated Book Publishers Ltd for extracts from *Coal is our Life* by N Dennis, F Henriques and C Slaughter, Tavistock, 1969 (p 113); *The Family* by A Wilson (p 98); table from *Power Without Responsibility* by J Curran and J Seaton (p 258); and adapted material from *Age and Generation* by M O'Donnell (p 85) ● Basil Blackwell Ltd for extracts from *The Sociology of Housework* of A Oakley (pp 15, 59, 115) and adapted material form *Girl Delinquents* by A Campbell (p 217) ● The British Psychological Society for adapted material from 'Self-reported delinquency among schoolboys and their attitudes to the police' by H B Gibson, *British Journal of Social and Clinical Psychology*, 6 (p 217) ● John Calder Ltd for adapted material from *The Assembly Line* by R Linhart, translated by M Crossland, 1981, originally published by Editions de Minuit, Paris (p 176) ● The Careers Research and Advisory Centre (CRAC), Cambridge for figures used in diagram on p 55 ● Centre for Contemporary Culture for extracts by P Cohen (p 193) ● Collins Publishers for an extract from *The Home and the School* by J W B Douglas (p 162) ● Comedia Publishing Company Ltd for extracts from *The British Media* by M Grant (pp 260, 267) ● David and Charles for extracts from *View from the Boys* by H Parker (pp 23, 25) ● Alan Dunn for an article in *The Guardian* 13.2.86 (p 262) ● *The Economist* for an extract from issue of 1.3.86 (p 268) ● The Council of the Eugenics Society for the graph of serious illness (p 32) ● Faber and Faber Ltd, for adapted material from *Married Life in an African Tribe* by I Shapera (p 106) ● Gower Publishing Company Ltd for extracts from *British Social Attitudes* by P Jowell and S Witherspoon (pp 20, 24); *Police and People in London* by D Smith and J Gray (p 70); and *Sex, Gender and Society* by A Oakley (p 50) ● Jane Gregory on behalf of Pluto Projects (a division of Visionslide Ltd) for material from *The State of the nation* by S Fothergill and J Vincent, Pan Books (pp 67, 142, 197, 235) ● *The Guardian* for material from various issues (pp 96, 109, 232) ● William Heinemann Ltd for an extract from *The Grapes of Wrath* by John Steinbeck (p 9) ● Help the Aged for an extract from *People not Pensioners* (p 90) ● David Henke for articles written for *The Guardian*, 10.10.86 and 19.6.86 (pp 96, 109) ● The Controller of Her Majesty's Stationery Office for Crown copyright material, including figures from Office of Population Censuses and Surveys, Labour Force Survey, *Employment Gazette*, Department of Employment New Earning Survey, British Crime Survey, Royal Commission on the Distribution of Income and Wealth (pp 32, 43, 56, 68, 95, 121, 122, 131, 142, 161, 171, 197, 208, 214). HMSO ask us to point out that more up-to-date information is now available. ● Hodder & Stoughton Educational for an extract from *Sociology* by S Moore and B Hendry (pp 18, 185) ● *The*

Independent for an extract from issue of 31.1.87 (p 275) ● Eileen Krige for an extract from *The Realm of a Rain Queen* by J and J D Krige, Juta & Co Ltd, South Africa (p 158) ● Longman Group Ltd for an extract from *Health and Illness* by S Taylor and L Jordon (p 251) ● Macmillan Publishers Ltd for an extract from *The ABC of Sociology* by M Slattery (p 206) and for an extract from *Sociology in Context* by J Nobbs (p 28) ● Mail Newspapers plc for material from *The Mail on Sunday* (pp 30, 39) ● Manchester University Press for an extract from Hightown Grammar by C Lacey (p 164) ● William Morrow & Co Inc for an extract from *Male and Female* by Margaret Mead, Greenwood Press, 1977 (p 5) ● New Internationalist Publications Ltd for adapted material from *The New Internationalist* (pp 78, 89) ● New Scientist Syndication for an adapted material from *New Scientist*, 18.10.84 (p 148) ● *New Society* for material from various editions (pp 41, 43, 94, 99, 117, 124, 137, 138, 142, 144, 167, 182, 196, 198, 220, 236, 270) ● *New Statesman* for an extract from issue of 8.7.83 (p 233) ● *The Observer* for material from various editions (pp 65, 82, 199, 231, 232) ● Octopus Books Ltd for 'Dominic's Curls' from *50 Five Minute Tales* (p 52) ● Penguin Books Ltd for extracts from *Sociology: A Biographical Approach* by P L and B Berger © 1976 P & B Berger (p 182); *Double Identity: The Lives of Working Mothers* by S Sharpe © 1984 S Sharpe (p 123); *Clever Children in Comprehensive Schools* by A Stevens, Pelican Books © 1980 A Stevens (p 155); *Just Like a Girl: How Girls Learn to be Women* by S Sharp © 1976 S Sharp (p 166); and *Working for Ford* by H Beynon, first published as Penguin Education 1973, © 1973, 1984 H Beynon (p 185) ● Laurence Pollinger Ltd on behalf of Colin Turnbull for extracts from *The Mountain People* (pp 2, 77) and *The Forest People* (pp 6, 116), Jonathan Cape Ltd ● Andrew Rawnsley for an extract from an article from issue of 27.5.86 of *The Guardian* (p 152) ● Rex Features for an extract from issue of 13.1.86 of *The Sun* (pp 262–3) ● Routledge and Kegan Paul for extracts from *Family and Class in a London Suburb* by P Willmott and M Young (pp 113, 190); *World Revolution and Family Patterns* by W J Goode (p 124); *Social Class and the Comprehensive School* by J Ford (p 155) and *Human Societies* by G Hurd *et al* (p 106); and from issue of 20.6.69 of *The British Journal of Sociology* (p 280) ● Sylvia Secker for an extract from *The Ragged Trousered Philanthropists* by R Tressell, Panther, 1965 (p 275) ● Professor Shorrocks of Essex University for figures on wealth (p 43) ● *The Social Science Teacher* for adapted material from 'A New Deal for British Youth' by D Finn, Vol 13, No 2 (p 157) ● Thames Television Ltd for an extract from *Our People* (p 66) ● Times Newspapers Ltd for material from *The Times Educational Supplement* (p 161) ● Unwin Hyman Ltd for extracts from *Gender* by E A Clarke and T Lawson (p 56); *Topics in Sociology* by P Trowler, (p 21); *Poor Britain* by J Mack and S Lansley (pp 240, 243); and *Youth and Leisure* by K Roberts (p 192) ● John Wiley & Sons Ltd for an extract from *All things bright and beautiful?* by R King (p 53) ● Woman's Own for material from *Woman's Own*

We are grateful to the following for permission to reproduce illustrations and for providing prints:

Mike Abrahams/Network (pp 26, 75, 134, 219 left, 278 centre) ● Katalin Arkell/Network (p 173 bottom right) ● Associated Press Ltd (p 278 left) ● David Austin/Mail Newspapers plc (p 36) ● Janis Austin/Photo Co-op (p 43 centre right) ● Steve Benbow/Network (p 278 right) ● John Cole/Network (p 201) ● Comedia Publishing Company Ltd (p 145) ● Countryside Properties plc (p 91) ● Chris Davies/Network (pp 135, 179, 218) ● The Elim Pentecostal Churches (p 287) ● Geoff Franklin/Network (p 92) ● Gina Glover/Photo Co-op (pp 187, 219 centre) ● Hill Samuel Investment Services (p 11) ● Crispin Hughes/Photo Co-op (p 254) ● Nils Jorgensen/Rex Features (p 1) ● Monash Kessler/Photo Co-op (p 238) ● Barry Lewis/Network (p 43 right) ● Mail Newspapers plc (pp 29–30, 266 left) ● Edward McLachlan/Punch (p 73) ● New Internationalist (p 72) ● NSPCC (p 109) ● A D Peters & Co Ltd (from Posy Simmonds, *Very Posy*, Jonathan Cape, 1983 (p 59) ● Geof Rayner/Photo Co-op (p 61) ● Rex Features (pp 43 left, 126, 173 top right, 174, 272) ● Sarah Saunders/ Photo Co-op (pp 12, 202) ● Laurie Sparham/Network (pp 146 left, 173 top left). ● John Sturrock/Network (pp 43 centre left, 146 right and centre, 173 bottom left, 219 right, 246, 266 right, 268) ● Helen Tann/Photo Co-op (p 150) ● Topham Picture Library (p 143) ● Vicky White/Photo Co-op (pp 48, 139, 169)

Every attempt has been made to contact copyright holders, but we apologise if any have been overlooked.

INTRODUCTION

Once upon a time, there was a factory guard and a worker on the night shift. One morning at the end of the shift, the worker came out pushing a wheelbarrow full of straw.

'There's something fishy here,' thought the security guard.

'Alright, let's have a look at this lot, then.' Well, he searched and searched, but there was nothing he could find inside the straw. 'OK, on you go,' he said. The next morning the same thing happened, a wheelbarrow full of straw, a search and nothing found.

For the next few weeks the guard would regularly search the straw, sometimes leaving the worker for a few days to lull him into a false sense of security and then pouncing, but he never caught him out.

Finally, in despair, because it was driving him mad, the factory guard said to the worker. 'Look, if I promise not to tell anybody, please would you tell me what on earth you're stealing?'

'Wheelbarrows!', replied the worker.

Sometimes the most obvious things are those we overlook. Because everybody lives in society and experiences life daily, they seem to think that it is so obvious as not to be worth studying. Yet the sheer power of society in shaping our lives should not be ignored. Everything we are, every thought we have, our hopes and aspirations, these are all strongly influenced, if not actually formed, by society.

Sociology studies the way that society shapes our lives, by refusing to take for granted the most obvious day-to-day experiences of people. With a fresh mind and an outlook unclouded by bias, it pulls apart all those excuses and myths about the world that flow around us. Unfortunately, many of the answers it arrives at upset people, because the truth is not what they would like to believe. In particular, what sociology does is to relate individual experience, of whatever kind, to the nature of the wider society.

I can therefore only understand myself if I see myself as part of a wider society.

CHAPTER ONE
SOCIALISATION AND CULTURE

Instinct versus learning . . .

Culture . . .

Socialisation . . .

Social control . . .

Social roles . . .

Beliefs, values and norms . . .

Instinct versus learning

What makes us act the way we do?

There are two views about what makes us do things. The first of these is the common sense approach that is always being put forward. It is the belief that people are born with natural desires and uncontrollable **instincts**. So when men rape women, it is a result of their uncontrollable sexual desire. When women cuddle babies, it is the response to their natural mother instinct. When wars are fought, it is the natural result of man's aggressiveness. Theft is the result of our instinct to possess.

Sociologists are very doubtful about this explanation. The first, and major, objection is that if people's behaviour is natural then it ought to be, by and large, the same all over the world, just as their physical abilities are. Most human beings all over the world have the same physical needs such as eating and sleeping, and the same physical abilities such as walking, running and lifting. But *desires*, *attitudes* and *patterns of behaviour* vary tremendously from one society to another.

Culture

Colin Turnbull studied a tribe in the north of Uganda in the 1950s. The Ik tribe had traditionally been hunters. The Ugandan government, however, decided that their hunting lands should become a game reserve and resettled them in a mountainous region, where there were few animals to hunt and inadequate rainfall to grow crops. In effect they had been sentenced to death. The Ik gradually developed a culture to cope with their new and horrifying circumstances.

The quality of life that we hold as necessary for survival, love, the Ik also dismiss as idiotic and highly dangerous. . . .

So we should not be surprised when the mother throws her child out at three years old. She has breast-fed it, with some ill humor, and cared for it in some manner for three whole years, and now it is ready to make its own way. I imagine the child must be rather relieved to be thrown out, for in the process of being cared for he or she is carried about in a hide sling wherever the mother goes, and since the mother is not strong herself this is done grudgingly. Whenever the mother finds a spot in which to gather, or if she is at a water hole or in the fields, she loosens the sling and lets the baby to the ground none too slowly, and of course laughs if it is hurt. . . . Then she goes about her business, leaving the child there, almost hoping that some predator will come along and carry it off. This happened once while I was there – once that I know of, anyway – and the mother was delighted. She was rid of the child and no longer had to carry it about and feed it, and still further this meant that a leopard was in the vicinity and would be sleeping the child off and thus be an easy kill. The men set off and found the leopard, which had consumed all of the child except part of the skull; they killed the leopard and cooked it and ate it, child and all. . . .

Hunger was indeed more severe than I knew, and the children were the next to go. It was all quite impersonal – even to me, in most cases, since I had been immunized by the Ik themselves against sorrow on their behalf. But Adupa was an exception. Her stomach grew more and more distended, and her legs and arms more spindly. Her madness was such that she did not know just how vicious humans could be, particularly her playmates. She was older than they, and more tolerant. That too was a madness in an Icien world. Even worse, she thought that parents were for loving, for giving as well as receiving. Her parents were not given to fantasies, and they had two other children, a boy and a girl who were perfectly normal, so they ignored Adupa, except when she brought them food that she had scrounged from somewhere. They snatched that quickly enough. But when she came for shelter they drove her out, and when she came because she was hungry they laughed that Icien laugh, as if she had made them happy. . . .

Finally they took her in, and Adupa was happy and stopped crying. She stopped crying forever, because her parents went away and closed the *asak* [compound] tight behind them, so tight that weak little Adupa could never have moved it if she had tried. But I doubt that she even thought of trying. She waited for them to come back with the food they promised her. When they came back she was still waiting for them. It was a week or ten days later, and her body was already almost too far gone to bury. In an Ik village who would notice the smell? And if she had cried, who would have noticed that? Her parents took what was left of her and threw it out, as one does the riper garbage, a good distance away.

Source: Adapted from C Turnbull, *The Mountain People* (Picador, 1974)

1 What are the main values of the Ik, do you think?

2 Why did these values develop in your opinion?

3 Why was Adupa different?

4 Do you think the women in the Ik tribe have a maternal instinct? Give a reason for your answer.

5 Sociologists argue that no behaviour is natural to mankind; goodness, evil, love are all products of society. Having read the extract, what is your opinion? Discuss in small groups then appoint one person to report back to the class.

What is culturally normal in one society may be rather unusual in another

Take the case of language, for example; everybody has the ability to talk, i.e. the ability to make sounds, yet there are thousands of different languages throughout the world. The English language is not 'natural', it is really just an agreement that certain sounds mean certain things. Language is a **social creation**. But so too are manners. In Bedouin society, for example, it is regarded as polite to 'burp' after a meal, to show that you have found the meal satisfying and tasty. It is regarded as extremely bad manners in Britain. It could be argued in reply that, of course, certain unimportant things are not natural, but all the important ones are, such as sex drives, the mother instinct, the instinct of personal survival, and so on. But this is not true. Society is so powerful that it can swamp these drives with ease. Take the instinct for personal survival; can this explain the actions of Japanese kamikaze pilots at the end of the Second World War (1939–45) who deliberately flew their planes, packed with explosives, into American ships? They were not forced to do it, they were proud to volunteer. In the Japanese culture of that time, it was a wonderful, heroic gesture to die for one's country and emperor. A similar thing is happening in Iran at the time of writing, with 'revolutionary guards' who are prepared to go to almost certain death in their country's war with Iraq.

What about people who starve and beat their own children, do they have parental instincts? As for the sex drive, there are countless examples of men and women who choose to become priests or nuns, and so never make love.

What happens to people isolated from human contact in childhood?

The simplest way to prove the importance of **learning** as opposed to instinct is to look at examples of people who have lived their first few years without other human company. The results have always been the same; the person does not have the abilities which we recognise as normal amongst humans. In the case of the 'wild boy of Aveyron' in France, he was found running on all fours and surviving on nuts and berries, living in exactly the same way as the animals with whom he had spent his first formative years. His instinct may have been to survive, but how he behaved was a result of learning.

When people tell us that our actions are the result of nature, they are certainly wrong. Wrong because we know that virtually all human behaviour is the result of learning and, as societies vary in what they consider normal, people learn different things. Sociology says that by understanding the real causes of problems in society, we can learn to control them.

Role models and socialisation

Human beings act in the way they do through copying others around them. The following extract described how a boy, who had been brought up by wolves, was found.

He heard some squealing, crept up, and saw the boy playing with four or five wolf cubs. He was most emphatic they were wolves.

The boy had very dark skin, finger-nails grown into claws, a tangle of matted hair and callouses on his palms, elbows and knees. He ran rapidly on all fours, yet couldn't keep up with the cubs as they made for cover.

The mother wolf was not in sight. The thakur caught the boy and was bitten. But he did manage to truss him up in his towel, lash him to the bicycle and ride home.

At first Shamdev cowered from people and would only play with dogs. He hated the sun and used to curl up in shadowy places. After dark he grew restless and they had to tie him up to stop him

following the jackals which howled round the village at night. If anyone cut them-selves, he could smell the scent of blood and would scamper towards it. He caught chickens and ate them alive, including the entrails. Later, when he had evolved a sign language of his own, he would cross his thumbs and flap his hands: this meant 'chicken' or 'food'.

Eventually the thakur weaned him off red meat. He forced rice, dal and chappatis down his throat, but these made him sick. He took to eating earth, his chest swelled up and they began to fear for his life. Only gradually did he get used to the new diet. After five months he began to stand: two years later he was doing useful jobs like taking straw to the cows.

Source: The *Sunday Times Magazine*, 30 July 1978

1 When the boy was caught by the thakur what did his behaviour resemble?

2 Could you suggest any reason why he behaved like this?

3 Why did he want to eat only raw red meat?

Culture

What is a culture?

As we have just seen, what is regarded as normal behaviour varies from one society to another. This leads us to the concept of **culture**. A culture is the whole set of beliefs and guidelines as to how people ought to behave in any society, which people regard as natural and normal. Each society has a different culture: Expectations of behaviour in Britain are very different from those in China, for instance.

Cultures vary over time (the values and expectations of Victorian England compared with today) and by country and area (Tanzania compared with France). Within cultures, groups can vary considerably in their agreement with the main culture; for example many people argue that youth is a period when young people are likely to rebel and to reject the normal values of society. Sociologists call distinctive sets of values within cultures **subcultures**.

What is a sub culture?

The important point to realise is that cultures are made by people in the first place to give a framework and a meaning to life. There is no such thing as 'normal' behaviour or 'abnormal' behaviour for all human beings. When-ever you study another society, rather than thinking how weird/silly/strange their behaviour is, you should realise that it is as sensible and normal as our own seems to us.

Socialisation

How is culturally approved behaviour learned?

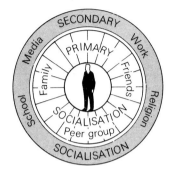

The new-born baby lying in the cot is the centre of attention of her parents and family. They play with her, they smile at her, eventually she learns to smile back. Months later she learns from tones of voice which actions are not to be done and which actions please her parents. After her parents have constantly repeated words like 'mummy' and 'daddy' to her, she learns that by saying these 'magic' words, she gets a kiss or a drink, or some reward. As time progresses, the child learns more words, and more rules of behaviour. Eventually, the little girl will have learned all the behaviour expected of her in most situations, and of course she will regard this behaviour as perfectly natural. As the girl grows up, through playing games with her friends, through the example of her parents and later through the official learning at school, the girl will come to learn all the appropriate behaviour expected of girls and women in our society.

Everyone passes through this **socialisation** process and emerges with similar expectations of behaviour. It is only as a result of this that society is possible, otherwise there would be chaos with people doing exactly what they wanted.

In modern societies, sociologists distinguish between **primary** and **secondary socialisation**. Primary socialisation is the learning of social behaviour from those closest to you, such as family and friends. Secondary socialisation is the learning of social rules that takes place in school and at work, and very importantly, in the mass media (television, radio, newspapers).

Socialisation and personality

This extract describes child-rearing in two societies.

The Arapesh treat a baby as a soft vulnerable precious little object, to be protected, fed and cherished. Not only the mother, but the father also must play this over-all protective role. ... When the mother walks about, she carries the child slung beneath her breast ... whenever it is willing to eat even if it does not show hunger, it is fed gently and with attention. Through the long protected infancy, the child is never asked to perform tasks that are difficult or exacting.

The Mundugumor women actively dislike child-bearing and they dislike children. Children are carried in harsh baskets that scratch their skin, high up on their mother's shoulders, well away from the breast. Mothers nurse their children standing up, pushing them away as soon as they are the least bit satisfied. Here we find a character developing that stresses angry, eager greed.

Source: Adapted from M Mead, *Male and Female* (Penguin, 1962)

1 Give two words which would describe the Arapesh view of children, and two to summarise the Mundugumor attitude.

2 What sort of personalities do you think the Arapesh children will have when they grow up?

3 What sort of personalities do you think the Mundugumor children will have?

4 What does the extract tell us about the relationship between child-bearing and adult personalities?

Socialisation: Learning the skills

The pygmies were mainly hunters who travelled through the forest, only staying in one place for a short time (nomadic). The extract shows how the children learn the skills necessary to survive as adults in the forest.

Like children everywhere, pygmy children love to imitate their adult idols, and this is the beginning of their schooling, for the adults will always encourage and help them. What else do they have to be taught, except to grow into good adults? So a fond father will make a tiny bow for his son, and arrows of soft wood and with blunt points. He may also give him a strip of a hunting net. The mother will delight herself and her daughter by weaving a miniature carrying basket, and soon boys and girls are 'playing house'. They solemnly collect the sticks and leaves, and while the girl is building a miniature house the boy prowls around with his bow and arrow. He will eventually find a stray plantain or an ear of corn which he will shoot at and proudly carry back. With equal solemnity it is cooked and eaten, and the two may even sleep the sleep of innocence in the hut they have made.

They will also play at hunting, the boys stretching out their little bits of net while the girls beat the ground with bunches of leaves and drive some poor, tired, old frog in towards the boys. If they can't find a frog they go and awaken one of their grand-parents and ask him to play at being an antelope. He is then pursued all over the camp, twisting and dodging amongst the huts and the trees, until finally the young hunters trap their quarry in the net, and with shouts of delight pounce on him, beating him lovingly with their little fists. Then they roll over and over in a tangle with the net until they are exhausted.

For children life is one long frolic interspersed with a healthy sprinkle of spankings and slappings. Sometimes these seem unduly severe, but it is all part of their training. And one day they find that the games they have been playing are not games any longer, but the real thing, for they have become adults. Their hunting is now real hunting, their tree climbing is in earnest search of inaccessible honey, their acrobatics on the swings are repeated almost daily, in other forms, in the pursuit of elusive game, or in avoiding the malicious forest buffalo. It happens so gradually that they hardly notice the change at first, for even when they are proud and famous hunters their life is still full of fun and laughter.

Source: C Turnbull, *The Forest People* (Picador, 1976)

1 Suggest three skills needed by pygmies to survive in the forest (no jokes about height, please!) and show how they learn these skills through socialisation as described in the extract.

2 How do people learn skills and knowledge in our society today? List five skills all children learn in our society.

Social control

How do societies ensure that people conform?

If people act in a way which does not conform to the expectations of society, then they are punished in some way, either by being regarded as odd and perhaps having no friends, or, in extreme cases, being branded as criminals. This is known as **social control**.

There are two types of social control, **formal** and **informal**. Formal social control is when the rules of society are expressed in law and they are backed up by official agencies such as the police and the courts. Informal social control is where there are certain expectations of behaviour which are not formally written down, but most people take for granted. When people break these 'rules', then others show their disapproval.

So, people learn the expectations and values of society (culture) through socialisation and if they do not follow the guidelines of society, then they are punished in some way (social control). (For a more detailed discussion of social control, see pages 203–5.)

Social roles

How do the activities of people fit together if people are all individuals?

Do you remember playing with Lego kits as a child, where you put the pieces together to make houses or robots? Each piece of the Lego was fitted together to make the final construction. If the pieces had not fitted, then the house or robot would not have held together.

The situation is exactly the same for society. All society consists of is a number of people acting in predictable ways that fit together into a pattern. The pieces of our 'social Lego' are known as **roles**. A role is a pattern of behaviour that is associated with a particular position (or **status)** in society. For example, the role of father is someone who is supposed to love his children, to teach them manners and punish them when they are naughty, to look after them and to do his best for their future. The same person may also be a teacher and this role involves passing on information to students, being fairly strict, showing an interest in the students, joining in with games after school, and so on.

The important point for society about roles is that the role of father/teacher remains the same even if different people fill those roles. Thus a degree of predictability and order is made possible in society.

Learning the roles

How do we learn social roles?

Children play games, and the very first ones are usually of the 'playing at being Mum and Dad' type, and then they develop into playing team games. For sociologists, these games are very important, for they help the children to be aware of how other people see the world, which they need to take into account in order to behave normally themselves. For example, when a group of children play football, each person needs to know just what the other person has to do in order to understand his/her own part in the team. Gradually the child builds up an awareness of what other people expect and how they will react to his/her actions. This process of learning what is appropriate behaviour continues throughout our lives, although the most important period of learning is in the first five years.

To simplify this incredibly difficult task of having to live in everybody else's mind as well as our own, the number of social roles are restricted. People do not behave just as they wish, they conform to what is generally considered to be the correct behaviour for a particular role. By and large, the behaviour of students is predictable, so is that of teachers, of shop assistants and policemen. We all know what these people ought to do, and it does not matter too much which individual fits into the role, they will behave roughly the same. So, I fit my role (for example, at the moment as writer and teacher) to your role (as reader and student).

Role conflict

What happens if our roles place different demands upon us?

All of us play more than one role in society. The teacher, for example, may also be a wife, a mother, a best friend, a keen fan of Liverpool Football Club, a member of a church, and a local government councillor. Sometimes, these roles conflict and when they do so then the person has to try to balance one against the other. Generally the culture gives us a 'nudge' to help us to choose which role is more important than another. In the example above it is usually stressed, in our society, that the role of mother is the most important.

Roles

The following extract comes from the classic novel of poverty in the USA of the 1930s, *The Grapes of Wrath* by John Steinbeck. Here a tractor driver has been sent to destroy the crops of a farmer who is to be evicted with his family. The farmer has no money and nowhere to go. Although it is a novel, it is based upon fact.

The extract illustrates, among other things, the role of sociology in the world. Like the farmer in the extract, we find that the world is far more complicated than we imagine when we try to understand our problems. We give up and just accept that most of the things that happen to us are caused by 'fate' or 'bad luck', and so resign ourselves to accepting our situation. The farmer finally understands that society and its problems, such as crime, unemployment and poverty, are made by people and so if we can truly understand how our situation was created we can strive to change it. This is the whole point of sociology.

'Why, you're Joe Davis's boy!'

'Sure,' the driver said.

'Well, what you doing this kind of work for – against your own people?'

'Three dollars a day. I got damn sick of creeping for my dinner – and not getting it. I got a wife and kids. We got to eat. Three dollars a day, and it comes every day.'

'That's right,' the tenant said. 'But for your three dollars a day fifteen or twenty families can't eat at all. Nearly a hundred people have to go out and wander on the roads for your three dollars a day. Is that right?'

And the driver said: 'Can't think of that. Got to think of my own kids. Three dollars a day, and it comes every day. Times are changing, mister, don't you know? Can't make a living on the land unless you've got two, five, ten thousand acres and a tractor. Crop land isn't for the little guys like us any more. You don't kick up a howl because you can't make Fords, or because you're not the tele-phone company. Well, crops are like that now. Nothing to do about it. You try to get three dollars a day some place. That's the only way.'

'Nearly a hundred people on the road for your three dollars. Where will we go?'

'And that reminds me,' the driver said, 'you better get out soon. I'm going through the door-yard after dinner.'

'You filled in the well this morning.'

'I know. Had to keep the line straight. But I'm going through the door-yard after dinner. Got to keep the lines straight. And – well you know Joe Davis, my old man, so I'll tell you this. I got orders wherever there's a family not moved out – if I have an accident – you know, get too close and cave the house in a little – well, I might get a couple of dollars. And my youngest kid never had no shoes yet.'

'I built it with my hands. Straightened old nails to put the sheathing on. Rafters are wired to the stringers with baling wire. It's mine. I built it. You bump it down – I'll be in the window with a rifle. You even come too close and I'll pot you like a rabbit.'

'It's not me. There's nothing I can do. I'll lose my job if I don't do it. And look – suppose you kill me? They'll just hang you, but long before you're hung there'll be another guy on the tractor, and he'll bump the house down. You're not killing the right guy.'

'That's so,' the tenant said. 'Who gave you orders? I'll go after him. He's the one to kill.'

'You're wrong. He got his orders from the bank. The bank told him: "Clear those people out or it's your job." '

'Well, there's a president of the bank. There's a board of directors. I'll fill up the magazine of the rifle and go into the bank.'

The driver said: 'Fellow was telling me the bank gets orders from the east. The orders were: "Make the land show profit or we'll close you up." '

'But where does it stop? Who can we shoot? I don't aim to starve to death before I kill the man that's starving me.'

'I don't know. Maybe there's nobody to shoot. Maybe the thing isn't men at all. Maybe, like you said, the property's doing it. Anyway, I told you my orders.'

'I got to figure,' the tenant said. 'We all got to figure. There's some way to stop this. It's not like lightning or earthquakes. We've got a bad thing made by men, and by God that's something we can change.' The tenant sat in his

doorway, and the driver thundered his engine and started off, tracks falling and curving, harrows combing, and the phalli of the seeder slipping into the ground. Across the door-yard the tractor cut, and the hard, foot-beaten ground was seeded field, and the tractor cut through again; the uncut space was ten feet wide. And back he came. The iron guard bit into the house-corner, crumbled the wall, and wrenched the little house from its foundation so that it fell sideways, crushed like a bug. And the driver was goggled and a rubber mask covered his nose and mouth. The tractor cut a straight line on, and the air and the ground vibrated with its thunder. The tenant man stared after it, his rifle in his hand. His wife was beside him, and the quiet children behind. And all of them stared after the tractor.

Source: J Steinbeck, *The Grapes of Wrath* (Heinemann, 1939)

There are two people in the extract who fill different roles, the tractor driver and the farmer.

1 What behaviour is associated with the role of the driver?

2 What other roles does the driver fill in his life?

3 What behaviour do you think is associated with this?

4 There is evidence of 'role conflict' in the extract. Find this role conflict and describe it.

5 List at least four roles that you play in life. Is there any role conflict?
Take one example and show how you cope with it.

6 Although the two characters in the extract are arguing they share at least one value in common. What is it?

Beliefs, values and norms

Cultures develop in order to make sense of the world around us: they provide us with order and meaning, and as societies' circumstances vary, so do their cultures. The main component parts of cultures are **beliefs**, **values** and **norms**.

Beliefs

These are very vague, general feelings or opinions about the world. They are rarely very clear, or organised, but they provide us with the general framework of our understanding about the world. So most people believe that they are 'free' in our society, exactly what that means is unclear, but it is constantly referred to in newspapers and on the television, 'a free society', the 'freedom of the individual'. This belief in freedom is powerful enough to explain why people ought to go to war – they go to 'defend freedom'.

Values

Values are the ideas about correct and just behaviour that come from beliefs. For example, Western values stress that it is generally wrong to harm or kill others.

Norms

These are normal, expected patterns of behaviour in everyday life. Norms include things like maintaining the correct distance from someone when talking to them, not asking personal questions of people we do not know too well, and saying thank you. Norms guide us in our everyday existence.

Norms are expected patterns of behaviour. Those who differ in some way are treated as 'odd' and face exclusion from 'normal society'

Norms vary over time

Values

What are the values
of British society?

1   What was your answer to the question posed in the advertisement?

2   The advertisement illustrates a fundamental *value* of British culture. What is it?

3   Examine a selection of newspapers. What other values of British society are illustrated in them?

CHAPTER TWO
SOCIOLOGICAL RESEARCH

The practice of sociology

What is the difference between sociology and journalism?

The aim of sociology is to uncover the rules of society that govern our everyday lives, which we take for granted. This involves exploring people's experiences, describing their lifestyles and understanding their feelings. But sociologists are not alone in this work: novelists and journalists along with a host of other people do a very similar thing. But there is a difference. Whereas novelists and journalists may embroider their stories, or make their accounts of what happens more exciting in order to sell a few more copies, sociologists must simply, clearly and accurately describe and explain the social world for the sole purpose of advancing our knowledge.

If you watch an expert craftsman at work, you will notice that he uses the very best tools and follows rules of workmanship that have developed over years of training and experience. If sociologists want to perform their work accurately, then they too must have excellent tools and rules of workmanship. This chapter is devoted to studying these.

Do all sociologists use the same sorts of methods in their studies?

There is a division among sociologists between **positivists** and **subjective sociologists**.

Positivists

Positivists follow, very broadly, the same sorts of research methods as natural scientists (physicists, biologists, etc) and believe this is the very best way to understand society. The methods used include **surveys**, official published **statistics** (such as the crime rates which are published every year), **historical sources** (such as diaries and war records) and **experiments**.

Subjective sociologists

These sociologists are not convinced that borrowing the methods of the natural sciences is the best way to understand social life. They prefer to try to put themselves in the minds of people whose behaviour we may find unusual or criminal. For instance, to understand why certain young people commit acts of vandalism or fight at football matches, they will join them to try to discover just how they think. The method used, as described above, is known as **participant** observation.

The aim of sociology is to go beyond appearances and uncover the reality of social life

Surveys

What is a survey?

The most commonly used research method in sociology is the **survey** and the most well-known example of the survey is the **opinion poll**, often used to predict the results of elections. A survey is simply a series of questions which are given to a cross-section of the group of people you wish to study (known as a **population** in sociology). For example, when the opinion poll companies want to predict the outcome of a general election, they ask a cross-section of British voters which party they intend to vote for. They add the results together and then make their prediction. Of course sociologists will want to carry out surveys on all different groups on a wide range of opinions.

What different types of survey are there?

There are different types of survey which are useful for different sorts of studies. The main problem with the ordinary **cross-sectional survey** just described above is that it only gives people's opinions at the exact time of the survey. It cannot tell you about changes of viewpoint. Sociologists may therefore use **longitudinal surveys**, which are surveys of groups of people lasting a number of years. A well-known example of this is the 'Seven Up' series of television programmes which have broadcast an update of the lives of a group of people every seven years since they were seven, in order to explore the influence of social class on their lives. The main problem with longitudinal surveys is the number of people who decide to drop out of the survey, or who the researchers lose contact with. If too many people are 'lost' it may make the survey unreliable.

Making sure surveys cover a cross-section of the population

Why do sociologists sample?

There are about 56 million people in Britain. Finding out everybody's views would be terribly expensive and complicated to do. Only the government has the resources to carry out a survey of every household in Britain (this is the **census**) and there are so many problems that even the government only does it once every ten years. In order to find opinions and get information, sociologists have to rely upon taking an accurate cross-section of people, known as a **sample**, and hope that the opinions of this sample represent the opinions of everyone in the population under study. Clearly, if the sample is not a true cross-section of the people then the whole study will be inaccurate.

Pilot surveys

No matter how able the researcher, he/she will not be able to foresee how people are going to interpret the questions asked in the interview or questionnaire, nor what words they may find difficult to understand. Furthermore, the people chosen for interviewing may not be the correct ones for the purpose.

The interview schedule or questionnaire should be given a trial run before being used for the main survey. This testing exercise is called the 'pilot survey'.

1 What is a pilot survey?

2 Give three reasons why sociologists use pilot surveys?

Sampling

How do you find your sample?

The source of the sample

The sample must be taken from some source; it could be every third person walking down the street, or it could be a random selection of names from the list of voters in a town (a list of local voters can be found in the main library of any town), or a selection from the names of people enrolled in an evening class. Each of these is an example of a **sampling frame**, which can be defined as the source from which a sample can be drawn. If the sampling frame is poor then the sample, and the survey, will be of little use. For instance, it is no use taking names at random from a list of 12-year-olds if the purpose of the survey is to find how people intend to vote in the next election.

Sampling frames

In *The Sociology of Housework*, Ann Oakley studied the attitudes of housewives with young children. This is how she found her sample.

The main sample of forty women were selected from the practice lists of two general practitioners (doctors) in London – one in a predominantly working class area, one in a predominantly middle class area. The names of the potential respondents were selected from the lists on an alphabetical basis. Two names were selected for each letter of the alphabet – the first two names occurring of married females born between 1940 and 1950 with at least one child under 5.

Source: A Oakley, *The Sociology of Housework* (Martin Robertson, 1974)

1 What is a sampling frame?

2 What was Ann Oakley's sampling frame?

3 Why did she use one list from a working-class area and another from a middle-class area?

4 Can you suggest one other sampling frame a person could use who wanted to interview mothers of young children?

5 Suggest appropriate sampling frames for the following:
   a survey of people over 18;
   a survey of pupils in a comprehensive school;
   a survey of football fans;
   a survey of Conservative Party members;
   a survey of plumbers.

Method of sampling

What types of sampling method are used?

There are basically two ways in which sociologists ensure that their sample of the population is accurate: through **random sampling** and through **quota sampling**.

Random sampling

This is based on the idea that if you select entirely randomly (as when you throw a dice, the result is random), then you are likely to end up with a sample which is a mirror of the population, as each person has an equal chance of being picked. For example, you could put all the names of the people in your class at school/college in a hat and then select eight at random.

There are some variations on this basic idea. For instance you may first divide up the population into groups based on some important characteristic, such as social class, and then choose at random within social class groups. This may give greater accuracy. This is known as **strata sampling**.

Sometimes the population you wish to interview is scattered over a wide area. In this case you could select only a few places at random, and then randomly select a number of people within *these* places. In this way you keep the people you wish to interview within a few clusters. This is known as **multi-stage** or **cluster sampling**.

Finally, you may wish to go back after your original survey and ask more detailed questions of some of the people. To do this, you choose a few of your original sample at random and interview them. This is known as **multi-phase sampling**.

Quota sampling

This form of sampling is used by most commercial market research companies, as it is accurate and very cheap. Basically, it is the same as strata sampling; each interviewer is told to go out and interview an exact number of particular groups of people in direct proportion to their existence in the population as a whole. For instance, we know that about half the population is female, so half the sample must be female, we also know the proportion of women in each age group, so the interviewers are told to find women in the correct proportion of ages to mirror the population, and so on.

The main problems with this sort of sampling are that firstly, it only works when you know a lot about the population you wish to study, and secondly, it relies upon interviews correctly spotting the 'right' type of person to fit their quota.

There are numerous forms of sampling. Some techniques are more accurate than others

Asking questions: Questionnaires and interviews

In order to find out what people actually think, sociologists have to ask them questions. There are two ways of doing this: you can either write down the questions and leave people to answer them by themselves, a **questionnaire** or you can simply ask them face to face, an **interview**.

Asking questions

When sociologists do research, they have to phrase their questions very carefully – they must be clear and straightforward and have only one possible meaning to the respondent; they must also be expressed in clear English and they ought to 'force' the respondent to give a clear answer. Finally, it must be possible for the researcher to be able to put all of the information obtained into a clear summary.

Here are six questions; imagine you are going to ask them to 20 people. Indicate which are useful for sociological research and which are not. Give the reasons for your answer. Try asking someone these questions.

1 What do you think about nuclear weapons?
2 How many hours' homework do you do each night?
   a) less than one hour
   b) one hour to two hours
   c) more than two hours
3 Why do you think people commit crime?
4 Do you agree or disagree with the following statement: 'It is wrong to eat meat'?
5 The idea of transubstantiation seems very important to Catholics. What is your view?
6 Which political party do you support?
7 Could you please explain why anybody would possibly vote for the Conservative Party?
8 Wouldn't you agree that Liverpool is the best football team in Britain?

1 If you only wanted to obtain the views of two people, would it alter your opinion on the usefulness of any of the questions?

2 Sociologists distinguish between open and closed questions. Indicate which of the above are 'open' and which are 'closed' (see the section on Questions on page 18).

Questionnaires

What are the uses and limitations of questionnaires and interviews?

Researchers ought to be aware that some people seem to dislike being questioned

These are usually posted or handed out to people. The essence of a good questionnaire is that it asks exactly the right questions to uncover the information you want to find in as clear and simple a manner as possible and that it is as short as possible.

Questionnaires are very useful for reaching a widely spread group of people (as you can simply put them in the post), and are cheap, as they only need the cost of an envelope and postage stamp. Sometimes people will reply to rather embarrassing questions contained in a questionnaire, which they would not answer if faced by an interviewer.

The disadvantages are that very often people cannot be bothered to send a questionnaire back, so the **response rate** is very low. This can make a survey useless, as you do not know if the few who replied are typical in their views of all those who did not reply. A second problem is that it is difficult to go into depth in a questionnaire, because the questions need to be so clear and simple. Finally, you can never be sure that the person you want to fill in the form actually does so.

Interviews

If the subject of enquiry is complex, or a survey needs to be done quickly, then sociologists generally use interviews. They can be very tightly organised, with the interviewer simply reading out questions from a prepared questionnaire, or they can be very open, with the interviewer being given scope to ask extra questions or rephrase difficult ones. In the first case, the interview is said to be **structured** and in the second case it is described as **unstructured**.

Apart from being useful for examining complex issues, the interviewer can compare his/her own observations with the answers of the respondent, to check if they are telling the truth. Also, there is a much higher response rate than when questionnaires are used.

The disadvantages are that the interviewer may influence the replies of the respondent in some way. For instance, a black interviewer asking a white respondent about racial prejudice has been found to receive very different replies than a white interviewer. And, of course, hiring trained interviewers is expensive.

Interviewing

Howard Newby studied the attitudes of farmers and farmworkers in Suffolk. He felt that it was necessary to play different roles with either group.
'With the farmowners this meant convincing them that I was a serious researcher, with the necessary stage props to prove it – briefcase, printed questionnaire and formal manner. Farmers were more difficult to handle than their employees. Some questioned my questions. In addition my own personal dislike of the views of most farmers meant that I was consciously playing a role' [to hide his feelings].
And with the farm workers:
'Here my main concern was to understate the elements of formality and professionalism ... leave the briefcase in the car, appear casually to jot down notes on a piece of paper, laugh, crack jokes.'
Incidentally, Newby wore a suit when interviewing the farmers and took off his jacket and tie when interviewing the farmworkers.

Source: S Moore and B Hendry, *Sociology* (Hodder and Stoughton, 1982)

1 Briefly describe the different ways Newby portrayed himself to farmers and farmworkers.

2 Why do you think he acted differently with each group?

3 Do you think the outcome of the research would have been different if he had not hidden his feelings of dislike of the farmers' views?

4 Three interviewers go to ask questions of male, middle-aged, white teachers. One is young and black, a second female and white, a third middle-aged and white. Will the outcomes of the interviews be different, do you think?

5 What if one of the interviewers was much more talkative than the others and expressed his/her opinions forcibly?

6 Now devise a few simple questions on an area such as feminism or race and test whether different types of interviewer influence the sort of responses obtained.

Questions . . .

Which is the best style of question?

If you wish to find out people's views in some depth, then you ask **open-ended** questions, for example, 'What is your opinion ... ?', which requires the respondent to give his/her views on the matter in some detail. If you wish to obtain short, very clear replies then **closed** questions are asked, for example, 'Would you agree or disagree with the following statement ...'. In this case the respondent has merely to say yes or no.

And answers

Once the answers are obtained and collected together then there has to be some way of **codifying** them. This involves somebody sitting down and sifting through all the answers and, usually today, putting them into a computer. For example, Do you think sociology is an interesting subject?

Yes, very interesting	1
Quite, interesting	2
No, not very interesting	3
Don't know	4

If the answer is 'yes, very interesting', then the number 1 is put into the computer, if 'no, not very interesting', then number 3. The computer then categorises all the replies and prints a summary.

The construction of sociological information

When you read a sociology book it usually contains a number of tables which summarise people's attitudes or behaviour. Here is an example of how one table was constructed. The aim of the questions was to understand people's fears of which country in the world posed the greatest threat to world peace.

Stage 1: People were asked the following questions by an interviewer:

- Which of the phrases on this card is closest to your opinion about threats to world peace?
- America is a greater threat to world peace than Russia
- Russia is a greater threat to world peace than America
- Russia and America are equally great threats to world peace
- Neither is a threat to world peace
- Don't know

Stage 2: As a result the researchers produced the following table, which contains some rather surprising information considering that Britain is a close ally of the United States and is politically opposed to many of the policies of the Soviet Union:

America is a greater threat to world peace than Russia	11%
Russia is a greater threat to world peace than America	26%
Russia and America are equally great threats to world peace	54%
Neither is a threat to world peace	5%

Stage 3: The researchers decided to go further and study how replies varied by political party. They therefore asked the following questions:

Generally speaking, do you think of yourself as a supporter of any one political party?

(If the reply was Yes, the interviewer asked question (a) below; if the reply was No, the interviewer asked (b).)

a) Which one?

b) If there were a general election tomorrow which political party do you think you would be *most likely* to support?

Conservative
Labour
Liberal
SDP/Social Democrat
(Alliance)
Scottish Nationalist
Plaid Cymru

Stage 4: Putting the two tables together they arrived at the following results:

	Conservative identifiers %	Alliance identifiers %	Labour identifiers %
America greater threat to world peace than Russia	8	9	17
Russia greater threat to world peace than America	34	20	20
Russia and America equally great threats	50	64	56
Neither a threat	6	3	4

The researchers felt able to comment: 'Over one half of the sample regarded the United States as being as much a threat to world peace as the Soviet Union. . . . Alliance supporters were much more likely than those in other parties to think that the two superpowers were equally great threats to world peace, while Conservatives were, not surprisingly, more likely to feel that the Soviet Union was a greater threat. Labour supporters by contrast were more likely to name the United States as a greater threat, though this view was held by only a small minority of them.'

Source: Adapted from R Jowell and S Witherspoon (ed.), *British Social Attitudes* (Gower, 1985)

Construct a table containing two separate pieces of information. If you wish you can ask the same questions, or devise some of your own. The researchers in the example above had a computer – you probably have not got immediate access to one.

To collect the information, you will need three sheets of paper: one for Labour supporters, one for Conservative supporters and one for Alliance supporters.

Each sheet ought to look like this for the example above:

Political Party . . . .
Threat to world peace comes from:
  America . . . .
  Russia . . . .
  Both . . . .
  Neither . . . .

Tick the appropriate line according to the answer you receive. You can then work out your own conclusions.

Experiments

Why do sociologists only rarely use experiments?

These are not often used by sociologists, because it is the job of sociologists to study people as they behave naturally in their everyday lives. If people were put into an artificial situation in order to see their responses, they would not act naturally. To compensate, sociologists often compare the behaviour of different groups in similar situations, to see the differences there are between them which makes them act differently.

Sociologists rarely use experiments as it is extremely difficult to fit people into test-tubes

Secondary sources

Can sociologists make any use of information collected by non-sociologists?

These include all statistics and information not collected directly by a sociologist engaged in research, but which have been collected by other people. For example: **government statistics** on crime, births, deaths, marriages, etc: **historical documents** such as diaries, church records, descriptions of important events and court documents **newspaper and television stories;** **factually-based novels** and **autobiographies**.

Sometimes, research is based entirely on these, particularly if the people being studied are dead, acting illegally or are difficult to trace, but generally sociologists are very wary about using secondary sources. More often sociologists use secondary sources as 'background information' to help them understand their own study better.

The problems with secondary sources are that they have generally been collected for specific reasons, by people who have varying motives. A diary, autobiography or novel may reflect the values and prejudices of the writer. How much therefore can be believed? Statistics on crime are less a reflection on how many crimes are committed a year, more a reflection of how many of the crimes are actually reported to the police (and we know the majority are not) and how many of these the police take seriously.

Secondary sources

Official statistics must always be treated with caution by sociologists, as they may not be what they seem.

Whenever a person dies in Britain, a medical certificate must be obtained from a doctor stating the cause of death. Based on this information the government produces statistics each year on the causes of death in the population as a whole. Nothing could be simpler or clearer . . . you would think.

When the doctor writes 'cause of death' on a death certificate in the case of an old person, it is a toss up which [one of several existing conditions] the doctor will choose to write on the death certificate. In a person dying at the age of 70, there are quite likely to be 12 or 13 separate and possible causes of death. . . . Because of this coincidences of ailments [various things wrong with them], they are also likely to be taking several different courses of drugs which can confuse diagnosis – and the patient – still further by their muddle of side effects.

Source: P Trowler, *Topics in Sociology* (Bell and Hyman, 1984)

1 We can see from the extract above how difficult it is for a doctor to decide the exact cause of death, so making 'causes of death' in official statistics rather unreliable.

2 Using the cartoon on the right, what comment can you make about suicide statistics?

Accident? Suicide? Murder?

Participant observation

Isn't it better to actually join people in their activities than simply to ask questions?

The methods we have examined so far are generally associated with sociologists who believe that sociology ought, as far as possible, to follow the methods of the natural sciences such as chemistry or physics. The survey is seen as the substitute for the experiment. However, other sociologists argue that the best way to understand people is to try to get as close to them in their daily lives as possible. These sociologists stress the usefulness of **observational methods**.

Observational techniques are particularly useful for studying people in circumstances where they would not normally reply to a questionnaire or interview. For example, in a study of delinquents or of groups of violent football supporters, it would hardly be possible to ask them to stop fighting for ten minutes while they answered a few questions!

What normally happens in observational studies is that the sociologist joins a group which he/she wishes to study in depth. He/she then has a number of decisions to make.

Does the sociologist become a full member of the group (perhaps the group is engaged in criminal activities)? This is known as **participant observation**. Or does the sociologist follow them around, simply observing, rather like a 'fly on the wall'? This is known as **non-participation observation**.

Sociologists who use the participant observation approach like to blend in unobtrusively with the group under study

If the sociologist becomes a full member of the group, the advantage is that he/she will readily get to see things the way the group does, but may be influenced so much by this that the research becomes too biased in favour of the group or prejudiced against them.

If the sociologist acts as a 'fly on the wall', the advantage is that there is far less risk of getting too drawn into the group, so that greater objectivity (seeing things as they really are) results. But there is less chance of fully understanding things as the group under study do, as the researcher is not really one of them.

Whether the researcher engages in participant or non-participant observation, a crucial problem which he/she must solve is the extent to which the mere presence of an observer influences the group's actions. People just do not act naturally, if they know they are being observed.

Should the sociologist tell the group that they are being studied?

In certain circumstances sociologists may prefer to pretend to be a member of the group. James Patrick did this in *A Glasgow Gang Observed*, where he joined a violent gang, and pretended to be an active gang member, joining in their fighting and stealing. This has the advantage of really being treated as a full gang member. This is known as **covert observation**.

On the other hand, Howard Parker told the gang of petty criminals in his study, *View from the Boys*, exactly what he was doing. This is known as **overt observation**. Firstly, this was morally better as he was not deceiving anyone.

Secondly, he found that gang members would confide things in him that they would be embarrassed to tell other gang members, just because he was a trusted outsider.

Participant observation

Howard Parker decided to study the lives of a group of adolescents in inner Liverpool who were generally regarded as delinquents by the police because they regularly stole car radios. Parker felt that the best way to explain their delinquency was to try to see the world through their eyes. He adopted the method known as participant observation, so he could really get to know and understand them. But the problem was to gain their acceptance – after all, they were 16 years old and he was 22, a middle-class researcher with a degree.

My hanging around 'all the time' period came in the autumn of the second year of my research, when most of the boys were unemployed and were spending their days knocking around the neighbourhood and standing on the corner. The evenings were generally spent in the pubs.

No doubt everyone was aware that I spoke differently and 'posher' than they did.

This was not a problem. It was more important to be able to understand 'scouse' than to speak it . . . as time went on, or when drunk, I found myself swearing a lot more and using local words and phrases – divvy, tart, gear, busies, come'ed, bevvy. . . .

My position in relation to theft was well established. I would receive 'knock off' and say nothing. If necessary I would 'keep dixy' [keep watch] but I would not actually get my hands dirty. . . . There were occasions when I actually interfered with car-radio theft and suggested to those about to get involved that given the situation and their strategy someone was likely to get caught. My advice was always taken. This reaction on my part could be seen as 'bad' participant observation since it was interfering in normal group behaviour. . . . It was during the first half of year three that I found myself as accepted as I ever would be, in the thick of things and at my most functional. Due to my regular court attendance I was regarded as something of an expert in such matters and was able to give advice from time to time.

Source: H Parker, *View from the Boys* (David and Charles, 1974)

The aim of participant observation is to observe groups as they are naturally and, by becoming accepted and close to the group members, to gain a close understanding of how the group under study really does see the world.

1 There are two major problems which all sociologists who adopt participant observation face: that their presence influences the activities of the group and so they do not act as they would have done without the sociologist and, secondly, that they become so drawn into the group that they lose their ability to describe in a clear and objective way just what is going on. Is there any evidence in the extract that these problems existed for Parker?

2 The advantage of participant observation is that by becoming accepted by the group the researcher can find out far more than any outsider. Do you think that there could have been any other way a researcher could have found out about the lifestyle of 'the Boys'?

Which method of research is the best?

None of them!

A sociologist chooses the method which seems most appropriate to the circumstances and aims of the research. Usually surveys are preferred if the aim is to find out opinions of large numbers of people. Secondary sources are used to provide background information or to uncover evidence when there is nobody able or willing to answer questions. Participant observation is used to study small groups and/or deviant groups where simply asking them questions would not uncover the reasons for their behaviour.

Choosing the method of study

There is no single *best* method of finding the people you want to ask questions of. It depends upon the amount of money available, the size of the group you wish to study (the whole population, or male delinquents in Southend, for example), and the information you wish to find (political attitudes, or number of crimes committed, for example).

The following are very brief summaries of the sampling methods used to cope with the different circumstances of the study.

A national random cross-sectional survey

In *British Social Attitudes*, Jowell and Witherspoon wanted to find out the views of the whole of the British population. In order to do so they did a national random sample.

The survey was designed to yield a representative sample of people aged over 18 living in Britain....

Names were selected from the electoral registers [lists of all the voters in Britain] in 103 of the 552 constituencies in England and Wales, and 11 local authority districts in Scotland....

Twenty-two addresses were selected at random in 114 polling districts [a smaller part of the constituencies], which gave 2508 addresses. Inter-viewers then went to these houses to request an interview with the elector selected.

In all 70 per cent of those selected agreed to be inter-viewed

Source: P Jowell and S Witherspoon, *British Social Attitudes* (Gower, 1985)

A longitudinal survey

D J West wished to find the reasons why certain working-class youths are more likely than most to engage in delinquent acts. By studying the boys over a number of years (a longitudinal survey), West claimed he could isolate the particular influences which affected the lives of delinquent boys compared to non-delinquent ones. He was able to clearly record all the important influences on a young boy's life.

In order to show that delin-quents really are different from their fellows ... they must be studied from an early age, using regular interviews ... before they begin to appear in court ... to show that their delinquency is not due to the effects of police action and court labelling.

The study was based on 411 boys. They represented an unselected sample of local schoolboys living in a tradi-tional working class area of London. They were intensively studied from eight to ten years and have been subsequently followed up till the age of 19.

Source: D J West and D P Farrington, *Who becomes delinquent?* (Heinemann, 1974)

A participant observation study of a group of 'tough' youths

In this second extract from *View from the Boys* (on the following page), Parker describes how he gradually widened his network of connections, known as the **snowball method** – as he 'rolled along' he gained more and more contacts.

It was working as a residential community worker at a country holiday centre for Liverpool 'street kids' that I first encountered The Boys. They came and stayed whenever they could. We went on camping trips and day trips, had parties, discos and arguments. It was only because I got on with and enjoyed being with The Boys and The Girls that this study developed. My acceptance into the network would have been highly unlikely if my credentials hadn't been checked in the highly favourable atmosphere here. By the time I came down-town I was established as OK – that is boozy, suitably dressed and able to play football, as well as 'knowing the score' about theft behaviour and sexual exploits.

Once accepted locally by a few of The Boys, I was able to move slowly into a wider acceptance until I could join any combination of the network when I had the time.

Source: H Parker, *View from the Boys* (David and Charles, 1974)

A covert participant observational study of the police

Simon Holdaway decided to study his own colleagues in an attempt to show the way that the police force really operates. However, as other policemen so strongly objected to his research, he had to do it in secret (covert observation), unlike Howard Parker in the earlier extract who explained his situation and aims to The Boys.

I found I was fortunate because I was in a unique position to carry out research: before I studied sociology and during the course of my undergraduate and graduate work I was a police officer.

Source: S Holdaway, *Inside the British Police* (Blackwell, 1984)

1 What is the aim of doing a 'random survey'?

2 What method did the researchers choose to find people over 18?

3 How many people were chosen to be interviewed in all?

4 Do you think that Jowell and Witherspoon did all the interviewing themselves?

5 Can you think of any problems that might occur when you have a large number of interviewers going around collecting information?

6 What percentage of people agreed to be interviewed? If only 25 per cent of people had agreed, would it have been important

7 What is meant by a 'longitudinal survey'?

8 Why did D J West think that a longitudinal survey was the best way to explain why certain youths are more likely to commit delinquent acts

9 Howard Parker tried another way of explaining delinquent behaviour. What was this?

10 Why did he do this instead of asking questions like D J West?

11 What was the term used to describe the method by which he enlarged his network of delinquent friends?

12 In Parker's study all the Boys knew that he was a university researcher, yet Holdaway in his study of the police chose a 'covert' course of study. What does this mean and why did he choose it?

13 Can you suggest another situation in which Holdaway's covert method would be the most appropriate to gain maximum information. Why? Are there any potential dangers in this approach?

14 Which type of research strategy would you use if you were studying
    a) the Mafia?
    b) a group of school students' attitudes towards teachers in your own school?
    c) the views of the headmaster of a local state school on the existence of private schools?
    d) the behaviour of a group of young people at a party?
    e) the attitudes of the British population on the extension of pub opening hours?

CHAPTER THREE
SOCIAL CLASS

Social Divisions

Divisions other than social class

What are the major divisions between people?

This chapter explores the **social class** divisions which have an important influence on our lives. However, before we examine social class in detail, we need to look at other types of social divisions.

Divisions in British society today

On meeting somebody for the first time, you will notice a number of things about them. Almost certainly, three of these things will be their **sex**, their **ethnic group** and their **age**. The category in which you place the person (for example, middle-aged, black and male) will influence very strongly how you will behave towards him.

In Britain, although social class remains a very powerful influence on our lives, sociologists have increasingly turned their attention to these forms of social divisions. For example, *within* each social class, people of different sexes, of different ages and of different ethnic backgrounds have very different experiences. Women are more likely to be found in routine office jobs, and rarely in the senior management positions (76 per cent of clerks are female). Blacks are heavily over-represented in manual work. Young people are far more likely to be unemployed than the middle-aged. These divisions have to be looked at alongside social class. As they are so important, each of the divisions of age, of sex and of ethnic group are studied in more detail in their own chapters.

Divisions in the past

There have been two particularly important forms of social divisions in history: **estates** and **caste**.

Estates

In **feudal** societies, which existed in Europe until the late sixteenth century, people were divided into estates, which were based upon ownership of land. Individuals swore allegiance to the king, who rewarded them with land. In turn, followers of these landholders swore allegiance to them and were rewarded with portions of the land. The distribution of land ended with tiny plots being given to peasants, who swore allegiance in exchange for giving a portion of the produce from their land, plus occasional military service. Each level was known as an estate. The divisions between the estates were very marked, with great stress laid on the lower estates giving the higher estates higher status. It would have been unthinkable for a person from one estate to marry a person from a higher estate.

Caste

The caste system developed in India. It is based upon the Hindu religion, which preaches that people have more than one life and that they are born into a particular caste in a life according to their behaviour in their previous lives. Someone who has been extremely wicked will be born into the lowest caste and the good person into the highest caste. The fact that one's caste is determined by God means in essence that it is extremely difficult to change caste and move upwards, no matter how much money or land a person acquires. There are rigid lines between the castes and no form of social mixing is allowed, indeed a person of a higher caste who touches a person of a lower caste regards himself as being contaminated. Sociologists describe a situation where one's social position is determined at birth as **ascription**.

The caste system

Castes

Brahmins	priests
Kshatriyas	soldiers
Vaishyas	traders
Shudras	servants and labourers
Harijan (untouchables)	the worst work, refused by others

A man is born into a *jati* [a division of a caste] and this is the only way of acquiring membership. The Hindu doctrine of 'karma' teaches the young Hindu that he is born into a particular sub-caste because that is where he deserves to be born. His life is governed by principles of pollution which rigidly enforce the separation of castes. If a Brahmin, for example, ate food cooked by an untouchable, the resulting pollution would be thought to be so great that he would be thrown out of his caste.

Each caste is traditionally associated with a particular occupation.

Caste membership is linked to status: not only houses, but clothes, customs and manners become symbols of status for those who share a common culture.

1 Which is
   a) the lowest layer?
   b) the highest layer of the caste system?

2 How does a person enter a particular caste?

3 Would it be possible for members of different castes to be friends?

4 How would people recognise those from a different caste?

5 How would you recognise someone from a different social class in modern Britain?

6 What three differences can you think of between caste and social class?

Source: Adapted from J Nobbs, *Sociology in Context* (Macmillan Education, 1983)

Social class

Social class is the main form of **social stratification** in British society. People are graded according to economic and status differences. Some people are wealthier than others and some receive greater prestige than others. The differences between social classes are not clearly marked and they merge into one another.

Although many people are in the same social class as their parents, this is not true for everybody. Social class is 'open' and people move up or down the 'ladder' of social prestige. This movement is known as **social mobility**.

Draw a diagram or cartoon which illustrates the differences between estates, caste and social class.

Images of class

This is a light-hearted look at class taken from a national newpaper.

Everything has class over-tones, from sexual habits to taste in flowers.

The things people think of as most natural, spontaneous, unclassifiable, reflect background, achievements, values, aspirations – *class* – in shining lights.

Take the people in the pictures. You can practically tell their life stories from what they're wearing and how they are standing.

Upper middle

Caroline and Henry are saying, 'Will that do – you won't keep us *too* long, will you?'

They are upper middle class. He's tall, she's rather lean and everything about them, from their hair to their shoes, says exactly what they are: fairly conformist, mainstream.

Signals

Take the hair. It's very natural and pushed back, long but reasonably disciplined, meaning in order but relaxed. Henry's is a little foppish, curling over the ears in a way that's slightly cavalier.

Caroline's plain pearl stud earrings make it clear she is not a free thinker.

And their coats are a uniform. They could just as well be officer's coats with all the signals of rank, they're so clear. Henry's is a covert (pronounced 'cover') coat and other ranks simply don't wear them. It's a staple of the City, barristers' chambers and smart law firms.

His striped trousers and black tassel loafers (Brooks Brothers, New York? Church's?) are also standard City No 1 kit. The only thing arty is his horizontally-banded woollen tie.

Caroline is Sloaney but there's something so trim and lean about her and her well-cut navy blue coat – it *has* to be navy blue – as to be almost American, almost Preppie and almost careerist. Perhaps she's a business analyst and works in the City, too.

Thinking middle

Roger and Sarah are middle class – but not just any old middle class.

They are the thinking, caring, *higher-educated* middle class of the late Sixties, early Seventies, and they work in some kind of job that reflects that set of attitudes: teaching, writing or social work, not mainstream industry.

Sympathy

The message this couple is giving out is 'We're interesting, travelled people with our sympathies in the right places.'

Practically everything they are wearing is a declaration of sympathy for something outside their own world or experience.

They are both *scarfists*, crazy on hand-knitted scarves made by some sort of folk-persons and they are knotted in a style that suggests they both liked films where people wore mufflers and cloth caps, though there is nothing 'cloth-cap' about them.

Sarah's jeans are aggressively worker/urban guerilla with turn-ups. But her boots are the biggest statement of all, signalling armchair revolutionary by loudspeaker.

Such boots are worn only by higher-educated women of a certain type in places like Camden, London.

And they show their wearer's heart is in the right place – right behind the women's movement, the labouring classes and freedom fighters.

Upper working

Jim and Jean are modern, upper-working class.

They are smartly dressed and well turned-out in a way that ought to be classless but somehow isn't.

They are well-fed people who know their rights and what's available but the look isn't middle class.

Healthy

For casual clothes, these are a bit too unrelaxed and new for traditional middle class taste.

And though they are healthy, they are both finding it hard to keep the excess pounds off.

Jean knows she ought to serve fish or chicken more often but Jim likes a good steak now he can afford it.

As for Jean's hairstyle, there's a bit too much of the 'big blonde' bouffant about it for a middle class taste – a carry-over from her teenage years in the early Seventies, like the full-length leather coat, a modern working class prosperity symbol.

And her dark stockings and high-heeled patent courts are more formal and sexy than middle class women would wear with this outfit.

Jim's clothes are very Top Man-ish and rather too smart for the weekend, suggesting he wears casual or working clothes the rest of the week, not the other way around.

And his two-tone shoes might also be judged too 'flash' by traditional middle class types.

Older working

Doris and Ron are more basic or traditional working class.

Two things say it all here.

Ron's nylon anorak is standard older man's factory gate gear.

And he's cupping his cigarette behind his hand, an old working class habit dating from the forces or very strict 'no smoking at work' rules.

Practical

Doris is smoking, too, and smoking is now a rather lower class habit.

Ron's open-necked shirt – it's not deliberately casual, it *should* have a tie with it – and canvas shoes with dark check trousers are so accidental, so unconsidered, that you suspect they never had enough money when they were young for him to learn how to shop for clothes.

It's basic and practical body-covering all the way.

The purse at the ready suggests Doris does all the food shopping, perhaps the money from a part-time job like a school dinner lady.

Unlike the other three couples pictured here, their clothes aren't trying to declare anything but are simply clean, decent and practical.

But it *is* 1985 and Doris can afford to have her hair done nicely, probably on her own money again.

Source: The *Mail on Sunday*, 18 August 1985

1 Do you recognise the sorts of people portrayed in the photographs?

2 Design a simple table using the headings:
clothes, income, typical occupations, type of house, area of town lived in, leisure patterns, educational level (GCSE/O-levels, A-levels, degree, etc) plus two more categories which you have thought of yourself. Then comment on social class differences.
As a group compare your answers. What similarities and differences emerge?

3 As a result of your research, do you think class is important in our lives?

The importance of social class

In what ways does class influence our lives?

Social class is probably the most important influence on our lives:

- Birth – children of unskilled working-class parents are three times more likely to die within a year of birth than the children of professionals;

- Health – working-class people are three times more likely to have a serious illness than middle-class people. They are six times more likely to get arthritis and rheumatism;

- Family life – working-class people marry younger, have slightly larger families and are more likely to divorce than middle-class people;

- Housing – eighty-five per cent of the upper middle class own their own houses compared to 25 per cent of the unskilled working class;

- Income – the higher up the social classes you climb the larger your income;

- Education – the middle classes are more successful in the education system and 60 per cent of the upper middle class have been to university or polytechnic;

- Politics – the higher your social class, the greater the chance you vote Conservative;

- Death – a man with a professional job can expect to live seven years longer on average than a man with a labouring job.

Social class, life . . . and death

A   Infant deaths within a year of birth
(Rate per 1000 births)

	Professional	White-collar	Skilled manual	Unskilled manual
1981	7.7	8.5	10.3	15.8

B   Deaths from cancer by social class*

Social class	1	2	3n	3m	4	5
1971	75	80	91	113	116	131
1981	99	97	99	113	113	116

C Serious illness by social class*

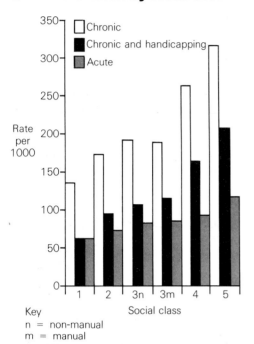

Key
n = non-manual
m = manual

Source: M Blaxter, 'Social Class & Health Inequalities' in
         C O Carter and J Peel, *Equalities and Inequalities
         in Health* (Academic Press, 1976)

D Accidents at work by social class*

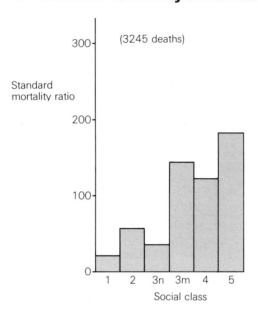

Source: *Occupational Mortality: 1970–2* (HMSO, 1978)

E Death-rates for 16–64-year-old age groups*

Socio-economic group	1921–3	1930–2	1949–53	1959–63	1970–2
Professional	82	90	86	76	77
Managerial and lower professional	94	94	92	81	81
Skilled manual	95	97	101	100	104
Semi-skilled manual	101	102	104	103	113
Unskilled manual	125	111	118	143	137

Source: *Social Trends* (HMSO, 1985)

F And what your are paid for it . . .

	Average weekly wage, 1984	
	Male	Female
Manual workers	£152.07	£ 93.50
Non-manual workers	£209.00	£117.20

Notes: (i) For social class gradings 1–5, see the Registrar-General's classification on page 36. (ii) Tables B, D and E, are all based on the idea of a 'Standard mortality ratio': this means that the figure 100 stands for the average; if a social class has a figure above this, it means they have more deaths than average; below means fewer deaths.

Sociologists argue that social class strongly influences our life chances (the quality of a person's life).

1 What is the rate of infant deaths (table A) for
    a) the children of professional parents?
    b) the children of unskilled manual parents?

2 Is there any relationship between parents' occupations and infant deaths?

3 An illness like cancer is natural and one would expect it to strike people of every class equally (table B). Is this true?

4 Which classes have
    a) the highest?
    b) lowest rates of chronic illness (table C)?

5 The first three classes in table D have low rates of accidents at work, the next three classes have much higher rates. Could you suggest any reason(s) for this?

6 The death rates in 1970–2 (table E) were
    a) higher for which group?
    b) lower for which group?

7 Over time all social classes have had changes in their death rates, but are the changes the same? Explain your answer.

8 Look at the wage rates in table F. What clear differences emerge in wages by
    a) class?
    b) sex?

Give three examples of how these can influence a person's style of life.

The nature of social class

How have sociologists explained the origins and basis of social class?

Although it is agreed that social class influences our lives in many ways, there is less agreement about what social class actually is and what its origins are. The two sociologists who first discussed social class in the last century, Max Weber and Karl Marx, have left behind quite distinct sociological traditions. Marxists see society as fundamentally divided into two groups, while those influenced by Weber see society as consisting much more of a 'ladder' of different groups, with only small differences between them.

The Marxist view

The Marxist view of social class is that in every society one group emerges which gains control of the economy (in Britain today, industry and commerce; in pre-industrial Britain, it was the land). Marx calls these the **bourgeoisie**, and they arrange society to their own benefit using their enormous wealth and power. They are only a tiny fraction of the whole population, no more than five per cent. Everyone else in society works for these people, making them richer.

Of course, there are massive differences between those people who work for the bourgeoisie, some are managers earning very high salaries, others may be manual workers who earn very little. However, they all share one fundamental link. They do not own in any significant way the industry or the commercial institutions. These people are called the **proletariat**.

Marxists today stress that there are many superficial distinctions between the various groups in society, but point out the enormous concentration of wealth in the hands of very few people in contemporary Britain. In order to understand our society with its social problems and great differences in wealth and quality of life, Marxists point to the power of the bourgeoisie to manipulate the rest of the population to work for them and to accept this situation as being quite correct.

Critics of Marx have pointed out firstly that it is possible to be socially mobile and to become successful in 'capitalist' society. Secondly, they have pointed to communist societies which claim to follow Marx's ideas, such as the USSR where those in power appear to control the population for their own benefit in a far more ruthless way than in capitalist Britain. Thirdly, they have argued that modern society has developed in a more complex way than Marx foresaw, writing a hundred years ago, and the idea of there being only two classes, bourgeoisie and proletariat, is simply inaccurate.

Weber's view

Weber's view of stratification comes from this last criticism. For him, to divide society into two groups on the basis of ownership of the economy or not was just too simple. He suggested instead that social class was based on three elements: **economic factors**, such as how much money a person earned or inherited from parents; **status**, such as the prestige we give to a person based on such things as accent, style of dress and level of education; **power**, the amount of influence a person has to affect important social decisions.

It is by balancing these three elements together that we arrive at our judgement of where a person belongs in society. A scrap metal dealer may earn far more than a doctor, yet it would generally be agreed that in some way the doctor is of a higher social class than the dealer. Weber's view of social class is that it is constantly changing, depending on people's opinions of the worth of a particular occupation. Ownership of property is important, as Marxists argue, but it is only one of a number of elements that link together to form our **life chances**, by which Weber means the chances of being successful in life. In Britain today, for instance, the chances of success for the son of a wealthy banker, who attends public school, are clearly very high.

1 Name the two sociologists who first discussed social class.

2 Who are
        a) the bourgeoisie?
        b) the proletariat?

3 How many classes are there in the Marxist analysis of the class system?
    To which do you belong?

4 What do critics of Marx say concerning his division of society into two groups?

5 According to Weber, of what three elements does class consist?

6 What does the term 'life-chances' mean?

7 Draw a diagram to summarise Marx's and Weber's divisions of society.

The measurement of social class

How do we categorise people into social class?

In actual research projects, sociologists need to measure social class. Generally, they find the easiest way to do this is to grade people by **occupation**. There are a number of reasons why they do this. First of all, because information on people's occupations is simple and quick to obtain, but also because occupation is related to a number of very important social differences, such as:

- differences in earnings;
- differences in the standard of education;
- differences in accent and styles of dress, because these in turn reflect differences in education and occupation;
- differences in values and patterns of behaviour, again reflecting education;
- differences in how people are ranked by others and given prestige, so the doctor receives greater prestige than the estate agent.

Measuring people's social class can be difficult

Given that occupation is important and useful, we need to group similar occupations together to form a classification. There have been a number of such classifications. The simplest is the division of **manual work** from **non-manual work**. Jobs which require physical labour of some kind, such as in a factory or on a building site, are divided from those which involve working at a desk. This is mainly because considerable differences have been found in the level of skill, of earnings, of working conditions, of social attitudes and social prestige attached to manual and non-manual occupations.

Source: The *Mail on Sunday*,
11 August 1985

Registrar-General's classification

The most commonly used classification is the **Registrar-General's classification** which groups all jobs into five general categories as follows:

Class

1   Professional and higher administrative, such as lawyers, architects and doctors

2   Intermediate professionals and administrative personnel, such as shopkeepers, farmers and teachers

3   Skilled
    a) Non-manual, such as shop assistants and clerical workers in offices
    b) Manual, such as electricians and miners

4   Semi-skilled, such as bus conductors, farm workers

5   Unskilled, such as labourers on building sites

The division of class three between manual and non-manual workers reflects the importance of the differences mentioned earlier, even if earnings are broadly similar.

According to the Registrar-General's model there are no rich people, as class 1 is mainly composed of professional and managerial workers. Also, self-employed people who have very different opportunities and conditions from employed people are not distinguished as a separate group.

Goldthorpe's classification

Occupational group	*Percentage of workers*
Service class	
1 Higher grade professionals, administrators and owners of companies (the 'bosses')	7.7
2 Lower-grade professionals, administrators and managers, high level technical staff (For example, teachers)	6.0
Intermediate class	
3 Clerical, sales and rank and file service workers (sales assistants and clerks)	7.4
4 Owners of very small firms and the self-employed (such as a small builder)	12.6
5 Lower grade technicians and foremen	11.3
Working class	
6 Skilled manual workers in industry (such as an electricial in a factory)	27.2
7 Semi-skilled and unskilled workers in industry (such as assembly line workers) and agricultural workers	27.8

In a study of social mobility in the early 1970s, a sociologist at Cambridge University, J Goldthorpe, decided that the Registrar-General's classification had too many flaws and so he devised a modernised and refined version.

This model has seven groupings with distinctions made between those who give orders and those who take them, between self-employed and employees, and between agricultural workers and industrial workers. Furthermore, the occupations are classified into three classes which enjoy broadly similar life chances.

In sociological research you will see these classifications used to explain differences in earnings, educational success, levels of home ownership, standards of health and a host of other social differences.

Place the following occupations in their groups according to:
a) the manual/non-manual division;
b) the Registrar-General's classification;
c) Goldthorpe's classification.

a teacher	a plumber working for a large
a shopkeeper	building contractor
the owner of a large manufacturing	a self-employed plumber
company	an agricultural labourer

The class structure in Britain

In what ways has social class changed in the last forty years?

We have seen that social class exists in Britain and exerts considerable influence over our lives. It is important to remember, however, that social class divisions are fluid and change over time. The differences between the classes, as shown by the ownership of cars, houses and consumer goods which were so great in the 1950s, have narrowed considerably with the spread of affluence to much of the nation. For instance, almost 70 per cent of the population now own their own homes compared with only 30 per cent in 1945, and whereas less than 10 per cent of the population had cars then, today the figure is 60 per cent.

A second change has been the move from manual work to white-collar work, this means that today more than half the workforce is engaged in jobs traditionally regarded as middle-class. Whereas a decent education was once only possible for the middle and upper classes, today it is possible for most of the population, and this has allowed many children from working-class backgrounds to enter professional jobs, such as medicine and accountancy.

In sum, therefore, there have been considerable changes in the class structure of Britain. Let us look first at the changes using Goldthorpe's division into working, intermediate and service classes, and then move on to examine the extremes of wealth and poverty.

The working class

What evidence is there to show the existence of 'affluent workers'?

In the 1950s the working class formed two-thirds of the workforce, and consisted of manual workers in manufacturing industries. Wages were low and so were living standards. Attitudes towards education and the family were very different from the middle class. However, by the 1960s the differences between the middle and working class seemed to be disappearing and some sociologists claimed that a process of **embourgeoisement** (that is, the working class becoming middle class) was taking place. The argument was that the spread of affluence had reached certain higher paid workers, that these were able to afford middle-class standards of living and that they were abandoning their traditional support for the Labour Party.

In a famous research project in the mid-1960s, Goldthorpe and Lockwood studied a group of so called 'affluent workers', mainly production line workers at the Vauxhall factory in Luton, to see if they were becoming middle-class. They concluded that there were still significant differences in terms of:

● income – the affluent workers earned less than white-collar workers unless they did considerable overtime;

● values – the affluent workers had very different views on the nature of society from white-collar workers and disliked their jobs far more;

● lifestyles – the affluent workers had no adopted middle-class leisure patterns (for instance giving dinner parties) although they had changed from traditional working-class lifestyles by having a much closer family life.

This study was, however, 20 years ago and much has changed since then. Many of the traditional working-class jobs have disappeared with the decline in the manufacturing industries and so the younger generation of workers have moved into white-collar work. Consequently the actual numbers of manual workers has declined. Those who do remain have changed their patterns of consumption, with foreign holidays, house ownership and high spending on consumer goods such as cars and videos, all funded by credit. Traditional middle-class sports, such as golf and squash, have now been adopted in a large way by the working class and the loyalty of the working class to the Labour Party is under great threat. The result then is not necessarily the disappearance of class, or the embourgeoisement of the working class, but the narrowing of the great gulf of the past.

One more point has been made by researchers into the working class – that more divisions have appeared *within* the working class over the last 20 years. Important divisions have appeared between the employed and the unemployed, those in secure jobs and those in the declining manufacturing industries, between those living in the New Towns and overspill estates and those living in the traditional close-knit working-class communities of the inner cities and the mining villages.

Sociologists now talk about the **new working class** when they describe those living in the prosperous south-east of England, with secure, well-paid jobs, and compare these to the poorer, more traditional working class who are increasingly concentrated in the north.

Another term that is becoming increasingly popular amongst sociologists is the **underclass**. It is argued that there is an increasing number of people, within the working class, who are missing out on the general prosperity and that their plight is worsening. This underclass consists of those groups in society who lack any power, and who receive the worst of everything, compared with the rest of society. Typical groups in the underclass are single-parent families, and many of the ethnic minorities.

Divisions in the working class

Once there was a pecking order within the working class which went from the respectable to the ordinary to the rough. But they all lived in the same areas. Some houses were nicer and better furnished, some families more feckless but it was the same world, with graduations between skills.

It's not that long ago that men learned trades as apprentices. And trades and skills meant unions and working class solidarity. There are still older working class people who belong mentally to this pre-war system. Look at any Sixties realist film and you'll see it – it's another world.

Then the Great Divide started between two new working class types – the people who moved into life's

Brooksides, lower middle class-type owner-occupied houses and those who went into the new council estates.

And the children of the former went to grammar school and were sucked up into the new middle class to do the new middle class jobs – teaching, planning and working with computers.

Skills counted for less with more automation. What mattered was whether you were *lucky* or not. Lucky was Southern, employed or self-employed, and owner-occupier. Unlucky was Northern, unemployed, on a council estate.

Imagine the rich 'working class' world of outer East London – taxi-drivers, print workers, self-employed double glazing installers, that kind of

job. It's where the husband plays golf and the wife gets the Hansel and Gretel German-style dark wood fitted kitchen costing several thousand, and 13-year-old Jason is asking for a Giorgio Armani sweater for his birthday. They were first in on video and now they have a video camera which they use on holiday in Miami.

The Luckies don't feel working class solidarity, even though there's nothing really planned for Jason's education or career, nothing to push him into the old middle class. They just keep giving him *things*. They think the computer, last year's big thing, will deal with his education.

The Unluckies are out of work in places where there's no moonlighting to be had.

There's not much work from Party Planners in Newcastle. Everyone can't clean windows. The unlucky working class lives in the North in decaying Sixties council estates. The estates are class ghettoes. They look it and they feel it. The ones who want to move up and buy their house, and wonder if it will hold its value.

The Unluckies buy in no-frills supermarkets where everything's basic. The Luckies eat from Marks. They have smoked salmon and prawns regularly. It's the difference between, say, Ilford and Kirkby, near Liverpool. There's always been a difference but now it's sharper with not much in between.

Source: The *Mail on Sunday*, 11 August 1985

1 According to the extract what was working-class life like before the 1960s?

2 What does the author mean when he talks about the 'Great Divide'?

3 'What mattered was whether you were *lucky* or not'? The author (a journalist) suggests that a person's lifestyle was mainly due to luck. As sociology students do you think luck is the only explanation? What other reasons may have caused this division?

4 Sociologists often talk about 'the new working class' and the 'traditional working class' when they analyse the differences between working class people in Britain today. Which names would apply
    a) to the Luckies?
    b) to the Unluckies?

The intermediate class

Have clerical workers fallen from the middle class to the working class?

The intermediate stratum, or the lower middle-class, has also changed considerably over the last 40 years. The most important change has been the sheer growth in numbers, as there has been a shift in the occupational structure towards service jobs which are usually white-collar.

Clerical work has seen a considerable decline in its status and levels of pay, such that it has been suggested that a process of **proletarianisation** (the move down from the middle to the working class) has taken place.

This argument has not been borne out by research as it has been found that the increase in the low-paid clerical workers is composed mainly of women workers (often employed part-time) and that male clerical workers have generally better prospects of promotion into supervisory positions. Also, clerical workers have better working conditions, receive better fringe benefits such as flexi-hours, sick pay provisions, and some of them have chances of promotion. Possibly most important of all, whereas most manual workers, when asked, describe themselves as working-class, clerical workers describe themselves as middle-class, even though their salaries are rarely higher.

The difference lies, then, in how they *see themselves*.

The service class

The last 40 years has seen a tremendous growth in the professions and to a lesser extent in management. There have been increases in the old established professions such as law, but far more important has been the growth in the new professions of social work, and teaching, which have drawn some of their recruits from the working class. This class now comprises almost 15 per cent of the workforce, compared to only about five per cent in the 1940s.

It has been argued that a managerial revolution has taken place, in which effective control of all industry has moved away from the owners of large companies to the managers. This is so, it is argued, because the ownership of firms is so widespread that no one person is in control, hence the power of the managers who effectively run the companies. Whatever the truth of this argument, the fact remains that the old idea of the boss owning a company and running it him/herself has become far more rare than in the past.

1 What is meant by the terms
   a) embourgeoisement?
   b) proletarianisation?

2 Has embourgeoisement taken place? Give three reasons why proletarianisation has not taken place.

3 Name three divisions which have occurred within the working class in the last 20 years.

4 Give two examples of jobs in:
     a) the working class;
     b) the intermediate class;
     c) the service class.

5 Which two classes have grown in size and which one declined?

Broad social class groupings		Groups within social classes	Divisions other than social class		
			Gender	**Ethnic group**	**Region**
The upper class	The rich	The 'establishment' or 'ruling class'	Women concentrated in the lowest-paid jobs in each class	Blacks concentrated in lowest-paid groups/unemployed	The worse-off found in the north and the inner cities
The middle class	Managers and professionals (mainly men); high pay	The 'service class'			
	Routine white-collar workers in offices, banks, shops and caring services (mainly women); low pay	The 'intermediate groups'			
The working class	Better-paid manual workers in secure employment in newer light industries	The 'new working class'			
	The self-employed				
	Less-skilled, less well-paid manual workers; job increasingly under threat as industry contracts	The 'traditional working class'			
	The poor; the unemployed	The 'underclass'			

Divisions in Britain today: A summary

The paradox of plenty

When we speak of 'decline,' we mean, of course, decline relative to other nations. While some countries like West Germany and Japan have grown very fast and others like France have grown fast enough to maintain their positions, Britain has only achieved a modest rate of growth – on average about 1 per cent a year this century – and has therefore slumped in the world league table.

But this also means that most people in Britain have never had it so good – a curious paradox. Most people are better off than their parents, who mostly are better off than their parents, who can remember the days when children ran around with no shoes on. As the latest (1984) edition of the government's statistical round-up, *Social Trends*, shows, Britons as a whole are healthier, better paid and are more comfortable in their homes.

In the past decade, there have been dramatic increases in the proportion of homes with telephones (up from 45 to 66 per cent), freezers (up from 32 to 51 per cent) and central heating (up from 39 to 60 per cent). Car ownership is up to 59 per cent and nearly everyone has a fridge, television and vacuum cleaner. Life expectancy has increased, we smoke less and play more sports. Spending on foreign package holidays breaks new records every year.

Another funny thing has happened on the way to the present: 60 years ago, nine out of ten households rented from private landlords. Now 60 per cent are owner-occupiers, 30 per cent are council tenants and only 10 per cent rent in the private sector. Home ownership has created a social revolution, but at a price. Housing takes an increasing proportion of national wealth: ten years ago, the total value of all private dwellings was about equal to the stock market value of all British companies. Now our houses are worth four times the productive sector of the British economy.

With three million unemployed, seven million below the poverty line and a growing gap between rich and poor, it may seem strange to talk of a 'paradox of plenty' amid decay and decline, but that in a sense is what we have in Britain.

Source: *New Society*, 24 May 1984

1   The author suggests that Britain has 'never had it so good'. Give four examples from the extract to illustrate this.

2   What does the author mean by a 'paradox of plenty'? Could you suggest any possible social and political problems that could occur as a result of this paradox? (A paradox is something that appears to be contrary to what is the truth, but may well be true itself.)

The wealthy

What is wealth?

One of the most obvious and taken-for-granted things about British society is the fact that some people have more possessions than others. Some people live in big houses, with smart cars and spend pleasant holidays in exotic places, while others scrape the barest existence from their work. What is not so obvious, however, is the scale of the inequalities in wealth and income, and the ways in which the rich obtain their money.

The meaning of 'wealth'

By wealth, we mean the ownership of goods not for use by a person, but kept for their value and which can be sold at any time. A house bought to live in is not wealth, but a second house bought by someone who already has one is. Wealth is most commonly held in stocks and shares (part-ownership of companies), land and property, though some people invest in works of art, or even rare wines!

The distribution of wealth

How is wealth distributed?

Official figures, released by the government show that the most wealthy 10 per cent of the population own 55 per cent of all the marketable wealth. At the other end of the scale, the poorer half of the population own four per cent of the wealth. Many sociologists are doubtful about these figures, arguing that they understate the proportion of the wealth held by the rich. Tax advisers help the rich to manipulate their wealth in such a way as to appear less wealthy than they really are and so they avoid paying quite as much tax. These critics claim that the richest 10 per cent own about 70 per cent of the wealth.

How did the rich get their wealth?

Who are the rich?

According to a recent study, the chances of becoming rich from a working-class or lower middle-class background are increasing. Today, 20 per cent of millionaires are from working-class or clerical backgrounds; this is double the proportion 30 years ago. However, it is important to remember that 40 per cent of millionaires come from very wealthy backgrounds, and a further 30 per cent inherited considerable sums of money (from £10 000 to £100 000).

Wealth and income

A Who has how much in Britain today?

Percentage of population	Number	Total share of wealth	Must have at least
Top 0.1%	43 500	7%	£740 000
Top 1%	435 000	21%	£189 000
Top 5%	2 175 000	41%	£73 600
Bottom 50%	21 750 000	4%	

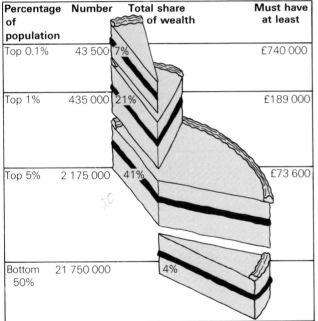

Source: Professor Shorrocks, Essex University and *New Society*, 22 August 1986

B Inequality of incomes

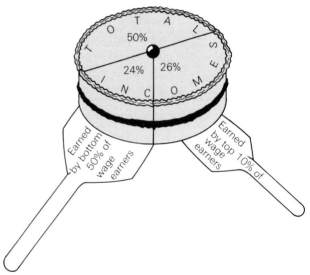

Source: Royal Commission of the Distribution of Income and Wealth, 1975

1 In diagram A, what proportion of the wealth is owned by
      a) the top 0.1 per cent?
      b) the top 1 per cent?
      c) the top 5 per cent?
      d) the bottom 50 per cent?

2 How many people are in these groups?

3 How much wealth must they have at the very least?

4 What conclusions can you draw about the distribution of wealth in Britain?

5 In diagram B, who takes a greater proportion of total earnings, the top 10 per cent or the bottom 50 per cent?

6 Draw a pie chart to illustrate the distribution of income.

The wealthy are composed of:

- the British aristocracy, who own vast tracts of land – the Duke of Westminster, for instance owns 300 acres of some of the richest parts of London in Belgravia, Mayfair and Westminster, amongst his total land ownership of 138 000 acres throughout Britain;

- the owners of industry and commerce – only a small proportion of the population, about 10 per cent own *significant* amounts of stocks and shares in companies;

- the 'struck lucky' – these are the people who through good fortune (and sometimes, talent) strike it rich. These include sports personalities, entertainers and those who had one good idea which was successful.

The distribution of income

How is income distributed?

Income is the flow of money people obtain for their work, from the State, or from their investments. The top 10 per cent of earners take about 27 per cent of all income, compared to the 2.5 per cent earned by the poorest 10 per cent. This is not the full story: the higher up the occupational ladder you climb, the greater the fringe benefits, or 'perks', that go with the job. A manager can expect to receive a company car and possibly free membership of private health schemes, assistance with the mortgage and private school fees for his/her children. The true distribution of income is therefore more favourable to the affluent than the official figures suggest.

Changes in distribution of income and wealth

Over this century there has been a very slow and small decline in the proportion of wealth owned by the rich. This has not gone to the poor, however, but to the better-off, who have become even better off.

In the last five years even this small redistribution has stopped.

In terms of income, a very similar process has taken place: a small shift of income from the top 10 per cent to the top 20 per cent and no improvement in the earnings of the bottom 50 per cent, who take exactly the same proportion of earnings as they did 35 years ago. This disguises a very real decline in the earnings of those at the very bottom of the earnings ladder, and the huge increase in the numbers of unemployed and aged, living on State benefits, which has taken place in the last ten years.

1 What is the difference between wealth and income?

2 Ought we to trust official statistics of income and wealth distribution? Explain your answer.

3 'Anybody can be rich if they work hard enough.' What comment do sociologists have to make on this statement?

4 What changes have taken place in the distribution of
  a) wealth?
  b) income?

5 What is your view on inherited wealth? Is it right that people should be able to leave all their wealth to their children or do you think that no one ought to be allowed to pass on their wealth, so that each generation could start off more or less equal?

Social mobility

Is Britain an open society where hard work leads to success?

Probably the major difference between social class and other forms of stratification, such as caste, is the ability to move up or down the ladder of social class. This movement is called social mobility. The amount of movement in society is the evidence to prove (or disprove) the claim that Britain is an 'open' society where people arrive in positions of social esteem depending upon their ability. High rates of mobility mean that the most able members of the working class can move up in the class system and the less able of the middle class move aside for them.

There are two measures of mobility: **integenerational** and **intragenerational**. Intergenerational mobility is the comparison of a person's occupation with that of his/her father. Intragenerational mobility is the comparison of a person's present occupation with his/her first occupation. We normally call this a person's 'career'.

The extent of mobility in Britain

The Oxford Mobility Study is a major investigation of patterns of inter-generational social mobility in Britain. It was based on a survey of 10 000 males aged 20–64, who were divided into seven social classes (see Goldthorpe's classification, page 36).

Overall, the authors concluded that 30 per cent of the men had moved up and 18 per cent had moved down the class stucture. However, most of the mobility was 'short-range' (that is, no more than two occupational groups up or down), and only seven per cent of those from social class 7 backgrounds (the lowest group) had reached class 1. On the other hand almost half of those in social class 1 occupations had come from social class 1 backgrounds.

We can say that is is possible for people to move up the class structure, but it is a lot easier for those from the top to stay there.

Women and social mobility

Women are split into two groups as regards the chances of upward mobility. Those women (the vast majority) who marry are concentrated in low-paid work and generally achieve little upward mobility, unless they marry 'above' themselves. Those women who remain single and pursue a career are likely to be slightly more successful than men in their chances of upward mobility.

Why is there movement up and down?

Sociologists have suggested five major reasons for social mobility.

Changes in the occupational structure

Over the last 30 years there has been a steady decline in the numbers of low-skilled jobs and a great increase in the numbers of professional and managerial positions. Quite simply there are many more high status jobs around. This allows more people to move up, with relatively few moving down.

Changes in fertility

The higher status groups in society have consistently had fewer children than the increase in the number of top jobs. This creates space at the top as the children of the highest group cannot fill all the vacancies.

Education

The education system has been expanded and improved to give intelligent working-class children greater chance of success. Combined with the expansion of the numbers of top jobs, this has allowed considerable numbers of working-class children into higher status jobs. Twenty-five per cent of men in the professions are from working-class backgrounds of one sort or another.

Environment

A person's background, parental encouragement and peer group support can create a determination to succeed, as well as giving the individual the 'correct' social attributes. The child from a privileged background may have the right manners and accent to pluck a plum job. However a determined, intelligent working-class child, given the right circumstances may well be equipped to succeed.

Marriage

Generally, people marry others from similar backgrounds to themselves. However, if women marry outside their class this usually means them taking the class position of the husband, as it is he who will generally be the main earner throughout their married lives.

1 A **meritocracy** is a society where people's jobs and incomes are a result of ability, not friendship or family connections. Is Britain a meritocracy?

2 Find out and compare your parents' occupations with those of your grandparents. What social mobility (if any) has taken place?

Social mobility and education

While direct discrimination against women, blacks and, probably, the working class still exists, such evidence that we have suggests that it may be on the wane, but at the same time indirect influence via the educational system has increased as family background has become more closely linked to educational success and failure.

As society tries to become fairer with equal pay legislation and so on, new 'unfairnesses' may arise as the better off try to find new ways of keeping their privileged position. It would not be surprising if the better off sections of society found that private schools could best defend their privileges, while within the State system, neighbourhood comprehensive schools develop to satisfy the ambitions of the middle class (who live in separate residential areas from the working class). Direct discrimination may decline, but new ways of ensuring that the middle and upper classes keep ahead in the education system and therefore in the race for the better jobs, will develop.

1 What is taking over from 'direct discrimination' as the most important influence on occupational attainment?

2 How does this work in practice?

3 What ways could you suggest that would ensure equal opportunities for all?

Social divisions in communist societies

Social differences have not disappeared in the communist societies of Eastern Europe, such as Hungary and Poland, nor in the Soviet Union. In these societies, the State is very important and controls virtually all aspects of life. For instance, most factories and shops are owned and controlled by the State. The output of factories is not determined by the demands of shoppers, but by the decisions of the government. In this sort of society, the idea that people can get ahead through being successful in business is clearly not possible. Also, as these are officially communist societies, the differences in income and wealth between people is supposed to be very limited.

In fact, studies of Eastern Europe have pointed to very great differences indeed between a few people who form 'the elite' and the vast bulk of the population. The elite own second houses in the countryside, have access to special shops where luxury goods are sold and generally enjoy many special privileges. The basis of the advantages of the elite is not success in business, but success within the bureaucracy of the Communist Party which controls the society, through the State.

Gender divisions remain, too, in these countries. Women have achieved equal legal and political rights with men and there are a far higher number of them in the top professions, amongst senior managers and important scientists, than in Britain. However, amongst the political leadership, the number of women is extremely low. Secondly, within the family, the Eastern European women appear to have exactly the same experience as their counterparts in Britain. They are expected to do the bulk of the housework, the child-rearing and the cooking.

1 Name two Eastern European communist societies, one from the text and one from your own knowledge.

2 How is the output of factories decided?

3 Can people become rich and powerful through economic success? Explain your answer.

4 What are 'the elite'. What sort of life do 'the elite' live?

5 Explain the difference in the basis of social divisions in these communist countries compared to Britain.

6 Is it true to say that women are 'liberated' in the Eastern European communist societies?

7 In your opinion, is it possible to have a society without any social divisions?

CHAPTER FOUR
GENDER

OBSTRU...

Men and women: Gender divisions in society

What is the difference between sex and gender?

Nowhere is the power of socialisation so clearly illustrated as in the creation of **gender roles**, that is in the different expectations we have of the proper behaviour for men and women. No one disputes that men and women are *physically* different (the division by sex) but sociologists argue that the differences in *behaviour* between men and women are not a result of these physical differences at all, they are learned (the division by gender).

Males and females: Occupations

On the right is a sample list of jobs. In each case over 75 per cent of the people involved are either male or female. Trace or copy out the list and indicate which sex you think dominates each job.

Occupation	Male	Female
Miners		
Butchers		
Nurses		
Typists		
Drivers		
Administrators and managers		
Postal workers		
Shop assistants		
Telephonists		
Cleaners		
Painters and decorators		

1 What reasons can you suggest for some jobs being done mainly by males and other jobs mainly by females?

2 Apart from physical differences, in what ways are females 'naturally' different from males?

3 Now leave your answers, without discussing them. Wait till the end of the chapter and then compare your views. Have they changed?

What influence do gender roles have on our lives?

Learning the gender roles begins as a baby in the family, and every experience that people have after that reinforces a few clear messages: that males and females ought to act differently; that these differences in behaviour are the result of biology and are therefore natural; that those who do not wish to fit in to the expected patterns of behaviour are 'deviants' (or freaks).

The roles themselves are fairly clear: women are weaker, more emotional, have motherly and homely instincts, and do not have strong sexual desires. On the other hand, men are stronger, less emotional, more aggressive and have powerful sexual drives. In order to understand how these roles are learned and how they influence the lives of women in particular, let us follow the lives of women through childhood, school, work, parenthood, leisure.

Are gender roles natural?

Sociologists argue that the expectations we have of males and females are not based on any natural, biological differences between them, but are the result of different up-bringing in different cultures. . . .

In *Sex and Temperament in Three Primitive Societies*, Margaret Mead describes three New Guinea tribes: the Arapesh, the Mundugumor and the Tchambuli. Among the Arapesh, the ideal adult has a gentle passive, cherishing nature and resembles the feminine type in our culture. In relationships between the sexes, including the sexual, the Arapesh recognise no temperament between men and women. The main work of both adult men and women is child bearing and child rearing – indeed they call sexual intercourse 'work' when the object is to make the woman pregnant! The verb 'to give birth' is used for both of the sexes. Mead observed that if one comments on a middle aged man as good looking the people answer 'Good-looking? Yes. But you should have seen him before he gave birth to all those children!'

Amongst the Mundugumor the opposite of the Arapesh holds true, where both sexes follow our idea of the 'masculine' pattern. The women are as forceful and vigorous as the men, they detest bearing and rearing children, and men in turn detest pregnancy in their wives. Both sexes are reared to be independent and hostile and boys and girls have similar personalities.

In the third tribe, the Tchambuli, there was a great difference between the sexes. However, the males showed what we would say are 'female' characteristics and the women showed 'masculine' characteristics. Women are self-assertive, practical and manage all the affairs of the household. Men are 'skittish, wary of each other, interested in art, in theatre, in a thousand petty bits of insult and gossip. Hurt feelings are rampant . . . the pettishness of those who feel themselves weak and isolated,' the men wear lovely ornaments (the women shave their heads and are unadorned), they do the shopping they carve and paint and dance.'

A similar pattern of sex differences occurs in a South-west Pacific society studied by William Davenport.

'Only men wear flowers in their hair and scented leaves tucked into their belts or arm bands. At formal dances it is the man who dresses in the most elegant finery and . . . when these young men are fully made up and costumed for the dance they are not allowed to be alone even for a moment, for fear some women will seduce them.'

Source: A Oakley, *Sex, Gender and Society* (M T Smith, 1972)

1 Describe the typical characteristics of males amongst:
  a) the Arapesh;
  b) the Mundugumor;
  c) the Tchambuli.

2 What does the information provided in the extract tell us about gender roles in our own society?

3 Can you provide three examples from your own experience when you have been treated differently solely on the basis of your sex?

Gender roles are learned in childhood

Childhood

How are gender roles first learned?

Gender socialisation begins as soon as the baby is born. Midwives ask 'Which do you prefer boy or girl?', indicating the different expectations we have. The adjectives used to describe children of different sexes indicate just what these expectations are. Boys are described as strong, tough, 'a little rascal'. Girls are described as sweet, pretty or angelic. Later on, as the child grows we have terms which are used to describe children who do not quite fit into the patterns of behaviour expected of their sex, for example 'tomboy' or 'cissy'.

Parents' expectations

Parents' expectations of children lead them to encourage different forms of behaviour. For instance, girls are expected to be neat and tidy, to appreciate wearing attractive dresses and so to be very aware of their appearance. The toys they are given and the games they are encouraged to play are very different from those of boys. Girls play at cooking, washing up, being mother with dolls. Boys play with balls, and building things, so that by an early age children have learned what behaviour, even in games, are expected of them.

Imitation

The children **imitate** adults, and are encouraged to do so. So the son imitates his father, and in so doing learns traditional views of what manliness is. The girl imitates her mother, so games might involve dressing up in mum's clothes, wearing her high-heeled shoes and putting on her make-up.

Identification

Identification also takes place, with children seeing themselves as their parents, or as heroes/heroines from comics and television. So as well as imitating parents' behaviour, they also play at being their parents/hero figures.

Group pressure

It is rare for the main characters of an action story to be female

This is applied to children by their friends (peer group) if they fail to act in the right way. Friendships develop along sex lines with separate groups of boys and groups of girls, both playing different sorts of games.

Are there differences in the ways that parents treat their sons and daughters concerning
  a) time to be in at night?
  b) places to go to?
  c) type of clothes?
Why do they say they do this?

Dominic's curls

Dominic hated going to the hairdresser's with Mummy. He had long brown curly hair and brown eyes and when his hair was properly cut, he looked very smart and manly. The trouble was he scarcely ever agreed to have his hair properly cut. He made such a fuss that his mummy usually didn't take him with her when she visited the hairdresser's.

One morning Daddy said, 'Get some of these curls cut off, Dominic. We're all having our photographs taken on Saturday. Then we can send a proper picture of the family to Aunt Judith in Australia.'

'No, no, no,' said Dominic, shaking his head. But his daddy winked at Mummy and went off into the garden.

The next day, Dominic and his mother went to the park. Dominic wore jeans and a pale sweater, and his curls were right down to his shoulders. As he began feeding the ducks, a little girl came up. She was pushing a pram.

'Hello,' she said

'Hello,' said Dominic.

'If you like you can play with me,' she said. 'I'm taking Amanda Jane for a walk. Have you got any dollies?'

'Of course not!' cried Dominic. 'Boys don't have dolls.'

The little girl looked surprised. And then she began to giggle.

'You can't be a boy!' she exclaimed. 'Not with all these long curls. You're a girl . . .'

'I'm not! I'm not!' shouted Dominic. And he ran home.

'When are you going to the hairdresser's?' he asked, on the way home.

'Tomorrow,' said his mummy.

'Then I'll come too,' said Dominic. 'I'll have my hair cut short this time – very short. Long curls are for girls anyway.'

Source: *50 Five Minute Tales* (Octopus Books, 1983)

School

Surely gender is not an important influence on what we learn at school?

In terms of academic attainment girls take and pass more examinations at the age of 16 than boys. However, the subjects they take them in are very different. They are less likely to take Maths, Computing and the natural sciences, more likely to study English, Human Biology and foreign languages. This is even more pronounced at A-level. Those girls who do go on to further education are most likely to be following vocational courses in clerical and caring skills.

There is some evidence that the intellectual abilities of girls and boys are slightly different, with girls being superior in the use of language, and in early adolescence boys develop greater ability in Maths. Even if these differences are natural, however, sociologists still argue that the more important influences on educational attainment of boys and girls are the social ones.

Teachers' expectations

In 1984 a survey of teachers showed that 40 per cent of them thought that a girl's career was less important than a boy's. This has led some sociologists to argue that teachers spend more time with boys and concentrate their efforts more on them. Indeed, one study found that teachers spend two-thirds of their time on the boys in class.

What is the 'hidden curriculum'?

It has also been found that teachers, like parents, have different expectations of behaviour for boys and girls. Boys are expected to be more boisterous, girls to be quieter and more obedient. As a result, teachers are likely to treat the children differently according to their sex.

The way that teachers act towards girls, and expect different behaviour and academic standards from them, has been called the **hidden curriculum** (a curriculum means the information taught at school). In effect boys and girls are taught different things at school, although it is not officially organised that way.

Subjects are often dominated by one sex

The hidden curriculum

In recent years most schools have made a big effort to teach boys and girls both domestic subjects and craft subjects. However, this has had no effect on the development of gender roles. The following extract from a study by Rosemary King illustrates the way that teachers unwittingly teach gender roles, even though they are trying to do just the opposite.

Teacher: 'Well, what must you do before you do any cooking?'
    Children: 'Roll up your sleeves and wash your hands.'
    Teacher: 'Right, girls go first.'

    The boys put on green striped aprons and the girls flowery ones. The teacher goes through the ingredients. 'We need four ounces of sugar.' She points to 4 on the scales. . . .
[The author then comments]

These practices were completely taken for granted by the teachers, who, when I talked with them, generally said they had 'never thought about it' and that to divide the class by sex was 'convenient' and 'natural'. They were

sometimes puzzled by what to them were my silly questions like 'Why do you line boys and girls up separately at the door?'

Source: R King, *All things bright and beautiful?* (J Wiley, 1978)

1 How does the extract illustrate the idea that boys and girls are treated differently?

2 Do the teachers intend to emphasise the differences between boys and girls?

3 The hidden curriculum means the values and ideas that teachers teach to pupils which are not meant to be part of the formal lesson. How does this extract illustrate the idea of the hidden curriculum as it applies to gender roles?

4 Do you think the teachers were right to regard the researcher's questions as 'silly'?

Pupils' expectations

Are girls 'forced' into particular career choices?

These are formed through the influence of teachers and the wider culture. Girls learn that they are not expected to look for a career – their main role is to be a wife and mother. The types of job regarded as suitable for them are either clerical (such as a bank clerk or a secretary) on the one hand or caring jobs (such as nursing) on the other. They are taught this through the advice and attitudes of teachers and through the attitudes of the wider society. Girls, therefore, actually *choose* to do these sorts of jobs and *choose* to see themselves as primarily wives and mothers-to-be. The result is that they regard school as relatively unimportant.

Work

Women's situation at work

What sort of job and conditions of work do women have?

Women form about 40 per cent of the workforce today, yet are seriously under-represented in management and in the professions (such as medicine and the law). They earn on average less than 70 per cent of men's wages

'There's no need for a woman to be stuck at home nowadays, George...there are plenty of opportunities for women to go out and get interesting jobs.'

and they are far more likely to be in part-time work than men. Finally, they are concentrated in a few areas of employment – clerical and caring, and service industries (such as shops).

Women's jobs in the USSR and Britain

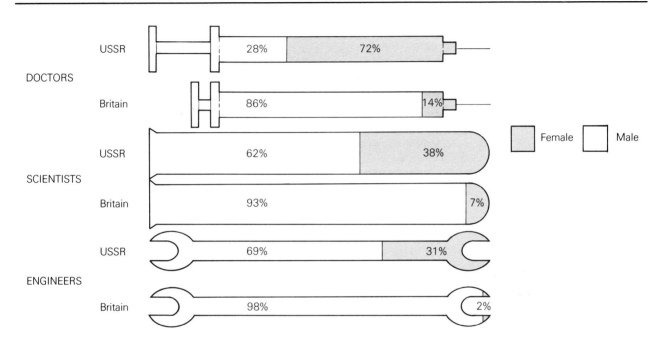

DOCTORS
- USSR: 28% | 72%
- Britain: 86% | 14%

Female / Male

SCIENTISTS
- USSR: 62% | 38%
- Britain: 93% | 7%

ENGINEERS
- USSR: 69% | 31%
- Britain: 98% | 2%

1 What proportion of doctors were female in
   a) the USSR?
   b) Britain?

2 What proportion of engineers were females in
   a) the USSR?
   b) in Britain?

3 What does this tell us about the range of jobs that women do in Britain? Are women 'naturally' less able or less interested in engineering and science, for example?

4 If Britain is to encourage more of its females to enter engineering and science, what must we do?

Source: A Jones, J Marsh and A G Watts, *Male and Female* (CRAC Learning Materials, Hobson's Publishing, Bateman Street, Cambridge)

What influences women's choice of employment?

The main reason is that women are still expected to be responsible for their children, unlike their husbands who must first have a career and second be a father. This means that women leave work in order to bear children and then care for them. They are then likely to return to work, but will have missed out on the chances of promotion. A second reason was given earlier: women learn at an early age that their main role is to be mothers. School and career choice are less important than marriage and a home. They may later regret this but they initially make this choice.

Male dominance and prejudice against women is also important. Some men like to believe that women are less intelligent, and that really their place is in the home. The result is that women are less likely to be promoted.

Women at work

The 1970 Equal Pay Act promised equal pay for equal work in 1975. . . . However, employers have devised a variety of techniques to avoid increasing their wages bills unduly. Strategies like the separation of male and female workers, the attachment of extra 'responsibilities' to male employees (such as heavy lifting), ensures that the differences are maintained.

If the employer does not want a life-long worker, he may choose a woman because it is 'well-known' that they have a higher labour turnover, and are less likely to join a trade union and therefore are easier to dismiss if the necessity arises. . . . Employers, along with many others, seem to believe that women do not mind doing boring, routine jobs, because that is where they have traditionally worked. Therefore they tend to choose women for routine fiddly jobs, because they have 'naturally nimble fingers'.

Source: E A Clarke and T Lawson, *Gender* (Bell and Hyman, 1985)

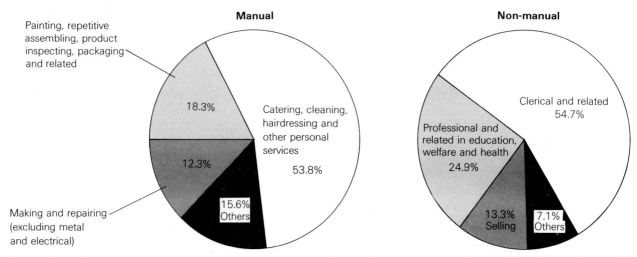

Women's work

Source: Department of Employment New Earning Survey 1979

1 Women on average receive about 70 per cent of the average male wage. How is this possible, if there is a law concerning equal pay?

2 Why are women easier to dismiss?

3 Why do you think women are more likely to accept boring work?

4 Are women more 'naturally nimble' than men?

5 According to the table, in which jobs are the majority of women employed
   a) in non-manual work?
   b) in manual work?

Women and the employment market

Two hundred years ago, women were regarded very much as the equal of men – they worked alongside them in all sorts of labouring work, for instance. However, as the industrial revolution began to require less workers, gradually women were pushed out of the industrial workforce and the belief grew that the proper place for a woman was in the home. Feminist sociologists have argued that what was happening here was really a battle of the sexes and the males won, banishing women to the home.

Why has the number of women working altered so much during this century?

At the turn of the century, less than 30 per cent of the workforce was female. However, the First World War (1914–18) took away the bulk of young men to fight. Women were recalled to the factories where they did all the work men had done. But, with the war over, the jobs were returned to the men. The same thing occurred in the Second World War.

In the 1960s, however, the numbers of women in the workforce began to increase quite noticeably. This reflected the changing attitudes of women themselves. They began to fight against the idea that once they had children they ought not to return to work, instead they began to seek work as soon as the youngest child attended school. Allied to the changing attitudes of women was the growth in 'service' industries (those which do not actually create anything but provide a service) and the growth in 'light' electronic industries (such as stereo or computer construction) which preferred women because they were cheaper to employ than men. They were also supposedly more nimble than men and because they were prepared to work part-time they were more flexible to employ. In short, female employees are attractive to employers.

Women, work and the family

These are some of the findings of a national survey on mothers with young children in the 1970s. It was conducted on behalf of *Woman's Own* magazine.

1 More than one in three working mothers of under-fives are working evenings or nights.

2 One quarter of mothers go out to work mainly because the family does not have enough money to survive unless the mother earns a wage. It has been calculated that three times as many families would be collecting supplementary benefit if the mothers did not go out to work. The problem is that being a mother seems to force women into a ghetto of poorly paid work.

3 Almost two-thirds of working mothers do semi-skilled or unskilled manual work compared with one-third of women workers generally and only one-fifth of men. The working mothers interviewed earned only about one-third of the average wage for male earners.

4 Much of the problem lies in employers' attitudes – they tend to allow only less skilled jobs to be done part-time. This results in women doing much lower grade jobs once they are mothers than their abilities and training equip them for.

5 One in six husbands has never looked after his child on his own. One-quarter have never put their children to bed. One in three never even read to their own children.
   Younger wives get slightly more help but, generally, wives are still left to shoulder the overwhelming majority of work involved in being a parent.

Even in families where the mother works full time three-quarters of fathers never take time off if their children are ill and never collect them from school.

Source: Based on the results of a national survey conducted by Gallup Poll Ltd, published in *Woman's Own*

1 Is it true that women only go out to work for 'pin money' (that is, a little extra money for luxuries)? Give evidence from the extract to support your answer.

2 What sorts of work do married women do?

3 Could you suggest from the extract any reasons why married women do this sort of work?

4 Does the extract suggest that husbands share the burden of being a parent equally with their wives? How do you think this might affect working wives (in such things as being absent from work for instance, or working over-time)?

Domestic labour

Is housework work?

Ask anybody what work is and they will probably reply with a description of paid employment, possibly giving the example of a clerk or manual worker. Few people would define housework as 'work'. Yet each day in Britain, millions of women spend a full day in the house, cooking, cleaning, washing and childminding. Each of these tasks by themselves if performed outside the home and paid would be considered a 'job'. In one famous study, *The Sociology of Housework*, Ann Oakley compared the work of housewives to that of car production line workers. She found the two 'jobs' very similar indeed. She concluded that the housewife worked as long as 72 hours each week, far longer than any worker in a factory; that housewives found their jobs very boring; that the amount of physical effort was certainly as great as the manual workers'; that the housewives felt very isolated, having no one to talk to very often, except for young children. The biggest difference, however, was that at the end of the week, the housewife received no wage and her work was not even rewarded by others with the *status* of work.

Parenthood

How are women expected to behave when they are married?

Once married, women find that they are expected to do the housework and to 'look after' their husband. His career becomes the important one and her role is to have children and be a good mother. Women who do not want children are regarded as 'odd' and if the house is untidy or dirty, then comments are made concerning her laziness.

When couples have children, then it is expected that the woman ought to give up her job and devote herself to the child. People refer to the **maternal instinct** which it is assumed that all women have. However, there is absolutely no evidence to prove that this exists.

Some sociologists have argued that there is increasing equality in the family and that today men and women are equal. But feminists reply that men are still in control and that the family is really a trap for women.

(For a more detailed discussion on relationships in the family, please turn to Chapter 7.)

Housework, image and reality

The media have created an image of what the perfect housewife ought to be like. In a study of magazine advertisements, Millum found that the picture of the ideal woman was of a hardworking housewife who was calm, satisfied with her life, attractive, enjoying doing the housework, with never a hair out of place. The problem is that if a woman did not feel this, then she feels guilty, as there has to be something wrong with her. Of course, this view of housework is also taken by all others not directly involved.

'I always say housework's harder work, but my husband doesn't say that at all. I think he's wrong, because I'm going all the time – when his job is finished, it's finished . . . Sunday he can lie in bed till twelve, get up, get dressed and go for a drink, but my job never changes.'

Source: A Oakley, *The Sociology of Housework* (Martin Robertson, 1974)

Source: *New Society*, 6 March 1987

1 Look at the cartoon above, what are the images of women portrayed?

2 Do you think that the cartoon presents an accurate picture of the housewife's life, according to your own experience?

3 According to the text, what happens when women do not achieve this ideal?

4 Is the work of women in the home appreciated as *work* according to the extract?

5 Do you think this would have any effect on the relationship between husband and wife?

6 Show the cartoon to your parents. What are their comments?

Leisure

How does gender influence leisure choices?

Virtually all leisure pursuits are related to gender roles. How many girls play football, for instance? And if they do, what sort of jokes are made about them? The gender roles of our society mean that men ought to be interested in 'tough' games (rugby) or those linked to pubs (snooker), and women ought to be interested in 'feminine' activities such as the caring ones of knitting or cooking, or the 'attractive' one of dancing.

Even in relationships, the girls are supposed to attract the boys to them, not to be the aggressive ones who introduce themselves to the boys and 'pick them up'. A girl who does this is seen as a bit pushy. When it comes to sexual relationships, girls have to be careful about their reputation. Those who have sexual relations with lots of boys are seen as 'scrubbers' or sluts, whereas boys who go with lots of girls are universally admired (or envied).

(Gender and the mass media is discussed on pages 264–5.)

'You can't kill attitudes by passing laws – I'll not go that easily'

RIP Male Chauvinism Died as a result of the Equal Opportunities Commission 1975

1 Choose any one of tonight's television programmes. Watch it carefully and write a brief description of the characters and roles of the main male and female characters. In class compare the types of parts females and males typically play.

2 Compare the contents and stories of comics/magazines for males and females. What happens to the stories if you change the sex of the main characters?

3 Find out the proportion of male to female teachers/lecturers in your school/college, who are in the senior posts, such as heads of department and principal/headteacher.

4 Conduct a survey of the careers that people in your school/college year would like to follow. Do clear sex differences emerge?

5 Find out the proportions of males to females doing science subjects, sociology and office skills. What differences, if any, are there by sex?

A summary

1 Draw a diagram summarising the experience of gender for women.

2 Write a paragraph, or sketch a diagram to show how you see your future.

3 Comparing them in class, can you tell which are written by males and which by females – without reading out the names?

CHAPTER FIVE
ETHNIC DIVISIONS

Ethnicity and race

Do racial groups really exist?

The whole topic of race and immigration is a minefield of passions and prejudices where even the language used is dangerous if not handled properly. The term 'race' has a long history of abuse. The idea that such a thing as a pure racial group exists is dangerous nonsense. There is a very general division of people into three broad and overlapping groups – negroid, mongoloid and caucasoid. However, in practice it is very hard to distinguish these groups from one another. The attempts of the Nazis to distinguish 'Aryan' people from other 'races' was a failure.

Sociologists tend to use the terms **ethnic groups** or **ethnic minorities** to distinguish people from each other. By these terms they mean groups of people who share distinctive cultures which are usually different from the culture of the majority of the people living in that society. If they use the term 'race', it has this meaning rather than any biological one.

In Britain there are very many ethnic groups, but some groups have drawn very little attention at all; the many thousands of Italians for instance, who settled in Bedfordshire during the 1950s. While other groups, particularly West Indians, Indians, Pakistanis and Bangladeshis, have been paid great attention. The common characteristic of those groups who have attracted much attention is their skin colour. So sociologists, following the lead of the leaders of these ethnic groups, commonly refer to all of them under the term 'Blacks' and/or 'Asians'. Clearly this glosses over the large differences between different ethnic groups, but it does allow us to talk about the common problems resulting from the prejudice that they all face.

Immigration to Britain

The historical background

When did Asian and West Indian people came to Britain?

Britain has always had a steady inflow and outflow of people. In the last century, Jews fled here from the persecution they faced in central Europe, while the Irish came in to escape from the terrible poverty there. Incidentally, the single largest immigrant group today remains the Irish.

The immigration which led to the presence of the West Indians, Indians and Pakistanis in Britain can be divided into three phases.

From the end of the Second World War until 1961

First West Indians came to Britain and then from the mid-1950s they were joined in ever-increasing numbers by Indians and Pakistanis.

Why? Britain experienced a period of great prosperity in the 1950s; in fact there were too many jobs for the workers available. West Indians and then Asians were encouraged to come here to take the jobs that the British did not want. The West Indians, in particular, thought of Britain as their 'motherland' where they would be very welcome.

From 1961 to 1972

There was a sharp decrease in the numbers of immigrants from the West Indies, but the numbers of Indian and Pakistani immigrants remained fairly high. However, to get the scale of immigration in proportion, by 1962 only 0.5 per cent of the population were non-white immigrants.

Why? In 1962 an Act of Parliament limited the numbers of immigrants allowed in. Effectively only those with jobs who had skills we wanted were allowed to enter Britain. Because Indians tended to be more educated, a greater number of them continued to come. Also, the wives and dependants of immigrants already settled here were allowed to join them.

From 1972 to the present

West Indian immigration was extremely low. Indian, Pakastani and Bangladeshi immigration fell overall.

Why? The relatives of Asian immigrants already here continued to come, though in small and decreasing numbers. Sudden rises in 1972 and 1976 were caused by African governments throwing Asians out; as they held British passports, the British government reluctantly accepted them.

Today, only about 4500 Asians are allowed to settle here each year, and only about five per cent of the population are black immigrants or their British children/grandchildren.

Why should immigrants want to come to Britain?

Why did Asians and West Indians come to Britain?

Apart from a short period of about seven years, there has always been a greater number of people leaving Britain to live abroad than entering. Those who came did so for a combination of the following reasons.

Push reasons

They may have experienced dreadful poverty in their original country and hoped to find a better life in Britain. This is the main reason for most West Indian and Pakistani immigration. They may have suffered persecution and been forced to leave, such as the Asians who were thrown out of Uganda.

Pull reasons

Because of labour shortages in the 1950s, immigrants from the Commonwealth were encouraged to come to Britain. The British textile industry, for example, has relied upon cheap immigrant labour to survive. The strong family ties amongst Asian immigrants meant that close relatives have been brought across to Britain wherever possible. Over two-thirds of Indian, Pakistani and Bangladeshi immigrants come to join relatives already settled here.

Citizens

Are Blacks and Asians who live here 'immigrants' or 'citizens'?

It may have been useful once to examine the problems faced by the ethnic minorities in terms of them being 'immigrants', but this is no longer so. Well over half of all Blacks and Asians living in Britain are British-born citizens; they are not immigrants.

- **Racial prejudice:** when people are disliked simply because they belong to a particular ethnic group

- **Racism:** the belief in the idea of the existence of distinctive 'races' and that some races are superior to others

- **Racial discrimination (racialism):** when people are treated unequally simply because they belong to a particular ethnic group

1 Are you racially prejudiced?

   Would you go out with an Indian boy/girl?
                    with a Pakistani boy/girl?
                    with a West Indian boy/girl?
                    with a White boy/girl?

   If the answer to the second question is No, give your reasons.

2 In a recent survey, 90 per cent of those questioned believed that there is prejudice against Asians and Blacks in Britain today. Thirty-five per cent of those questioned admitted to being prejudiced themselves.

   As an exercise, choose ten people outside you class and ask them the questions above. Then compare your results in class. Do any clear patterns emerge in the answers?

Ethnic ghettos?

Although Black and Asian people form only five per cent of the total British population, they are concentrated in a relatively few areas of a few major conurbations, in particular the Midlands, London and its surroundings, and West Yorkshire.

What influences the pattern of settlement of the ethnic minorities?

The formation of ghettos in British cities

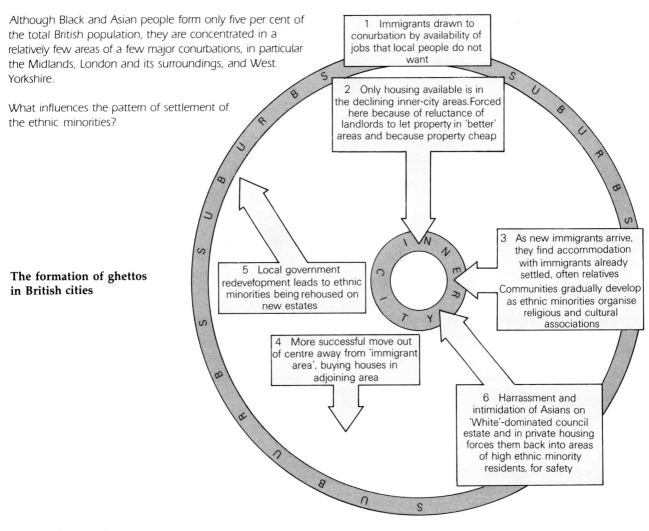

1 Immigrants drawn to conurbation by availability of jobs that local people do not want

2 Only housing available is in the declining inner-city areas. Forced here because of reluctance of landlords to let property in 'better' areas and because property cheap

3 As new immigrants arrive, they find accommodation with immigrants already settled, often relatives
Communities gradually develop as ethnic minorities organise religious and cultural associations

5 Local government redevelopment leads to ethnic minorities being rehoused on new estates

4 More successful move out of centre away from 'immigrant area', buying houses in adjoining area

6 Harrassment and intimidation of Asians on 'White'-dominated council estate and in private housing forces them back into areas of high ethnic minority residents, for safety

Racial attacks

Rarely do the newspapers mention the racist abuse and violence faced by many Blacks and Asians in their daily lives.

An alarming rise in racist attacks on school children has been blamed on the National Front and other right wing groups.

Teenage victims have been subjected to verbal abuse and physical violence – including stabbings. A few weeks before Christmas in Daneford School in London's East End a young boy, Minar Ali, was ambushed in a school corridor and stabbed with a razor blade. Four boys were later expelled. At Morpeth School, also in East London, more than 50 Bangladeshi children staged a two-day strike last month in protest against racial attacks. They said they had been abused and attacked by white boys. At Langdon School in Newham, a 16-year-old boy was stabbed with a screw-driver as he left school at the end of the day.

Source: Adapted from the *Observer*, 16 February 1986

This is a list of racial attacks in *one month* in the East London borough of Tower Hamlets.

Date of attack	Victim	Place	Incident
5.6.78	S.M. M.-child 10	Spitalfields	Threatened by thirty skinheads – shot airgun attack from car
6.6.78	M.A.	Old Montague Street	Windows smashed three times
6.6.78	M.U.	Canning Town	Robbed in own home at knife point
9.6.78	A.Z.	Whitechapel	White youths throw tins and bottles
10.6.78	A.Z.	Bethnal Green Road	Attacked by three youths, one with knife
10.6.78	Immigrants Advice Bureau	Hanbury Street	Nine fire attacks in three months
11.6.78	A.M.	Brick Lane	Two hundred white youths rampage in Brick Lane. Shops, car, windows smashed with bricks and rocks. A.M. lost three teeth, knocked unconscious, five stitches in London Hospital.
18.6.78	K.R.	Brick Land	Windows smashed
18.6.78	M.B.	Spitalfields	Flaming rags through letter box Child abused, stoned, attacked
18.6.78	M.A. M.U.	Pelham Buildings	Knocked to ground carrying shopping home
18.6.78	A.M.	Bethnal Green Road	Hit by stone, white youths throwing bottles. To hospital
6.78	A family	Edward Mann Close	Arson attempt with lighted petrol on flat door
21.6.78	A.	Approach Road	Kid attacked on way to school. Punch in face. Mother assaulted outside home by two white men
24.6.78	S.S.	Old Ford	One of eight victims of air gun attacks on estate in week; other reports elsewhere in Borough
24.6.78	CCTH		Report of twenty families asking them for transfers because of racist attacks in recent months
27.6.78	Ishaque Ali	Hackney	Murdered during street attack

These incidents have been documented for the month of June 1978 by the Bethnal Green and Stepney Trades Council which produced a report in September 1978 on racial violence in the East End of London.

In 1981, the Home Secretary set up an inquiry into racial attacks in Britain. His report found that what the black and ethnic minority communities had been saying was true. The research found that Asian people were 50 times and West Indians 36 times more likely to be the victims of racial attacks than white people.

Source: *Our People* (Thames Television, 1979)

1 Are there racist incidents in your school/college or neighbourhood?

2 Are they generally reported to the authorities or are these incidents hidden?

3 Can you suggest any way of stopping racist abuse and violence?

Race and life chances

In what way does membership of an ethnic group affect your life?

- **Life Chances:** refers to the possibilities a person has at birth of obtaining a high standard of living and general success in life

Being Black or Asian can powerfully influence the course and quality of a person's life in our society.

Work

Black and Asian workers are likely to be in semi-skilled and unskilled manual occupations. They are heavily under-represented in the professions (such as law and medicine) and in management posts. They are less likely to get promoted. They are more likely to have jobs involving shift work. They have higher unemployment rates than Whites. The most successful groups are those from African Asian backgrounds who are usually well-educated. Where Asians do break out of manual work, they tend to run small, family-based businesses requiring long hours of work, such as grocers' shops.

Why? A major reason is racial discrimination, but also because older immigrants with their poorer educational standards and lack of English were prepared to take the worst jobs. Also, certain industries, such as textiles deliberately recruited Pakistani and Bangladeshi workers because they accepted low wages and were prepared to work long shifts; these workers were then trapped in this industry. The younger generation of British-born Blacks and Asians are unlikely to accept this situation. Higher rates of unemployment exists amongst Blacks in particular because the type of semi-skilled jobs which they tend to do are the ones hardest hit by the recession.

Race and life chances

In most parts of the country, Black and Asian communities were unknown until the 1950s and 60s when West Indians, Indians, Pakistanis and others were encouraged to come here to work. Britain was then suffering from a shortage of labour.

London and Birmingham were favourite destinations, since that was where many of the unfilled vacancies were. The few areas of unemployment – the North East for example – attracted limited numbers. The textile towns of Lancashire, West Yorkshire and the East Midlands also drew in Black and Asian workers, because the local population seized the opportunity to opt out of the poorly paid shift work in the mills.

Also, cheap and dilapidated housing in industrial and inner city areas became available to immigrants as many whites moved out.

The Black and Asian population remains small in relation to the total. It continues to be concentrated in low status, low-paid work, in inner city areas and, increasingly, in the dole queues. This is partly because of widespread prejudice, and discrimination that is illegal but hard to prove.

The Black and Asian population is made up of a number of communities, fragmented along ethnic and linguistic lines. But this is changing: the majority of the younger generation were born in Britain.

Source: Adapted from S Fothergill and J Vincent, *The State of the Nation* (Pluto Press, 1985)

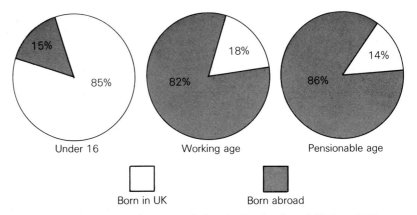

Place of birth of black and Asian population in England and Wales, 1981

Source: Census of Population

With the exception of racial discrimination, the disadvantages suffered by Britain's ethnic minorities are shared in varying degrees by the rest of the community. Bad housing, unemployment, educational underachievement, a deprived physical environment, social tensions – none of these are the exclusive preserve of ethnic minorities. . . . But the ethnic minorities suffer such disadvantages more than the rest of the population, and more than they would if they were white.

Source: Report on Racial Disadvantage, House of Commons Home Affairs Committee, 1980–1

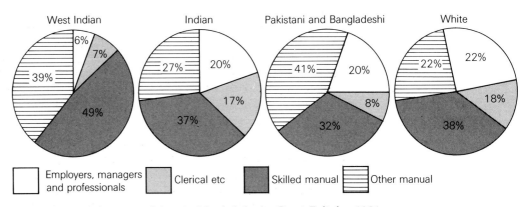

Worse jobs . . . and fewer: Men's jobs in Great Britain, 1981

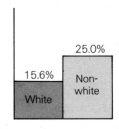

Unemployment 16–29-year-old men in Great Britain, 1981

Source: Labour Force Survey (1981)

1 In which areas did immigrants settle? Why?

2 Did they take work from the local people?

3 What sort of housing did the immigrants move into?

4 What proportion of Blacks and Asians under 16 years of age were born in Britain?

5 How much higher is the black and Asian unemployment rate than that of Whites?

6 What is the most common type of work for people of West Indian background?

7 What sorts of work are Pakistanis and Bangladeshis most likely to do?

8 Of the groups in the 'Worst Jobs . . . and Fewer' chart, which group has the highest proportion in higher level jobs?

9 Is it true or false to say that, overall, Blacks and Asians have worse 'life chances' than Whites?

Housing

There are clear differences in the types of housing in which different ethnic groups live. Asians have the highest levels of home ownership (more than Whites), but overall these are poorer quality homes in the 'less desirable' districts of the large cities, compared to the Whites who overall own homes in the suburbs. Blacks have similar levels of ownership to Whites, but are more likely to live in flats in overcrowded conditions.

Why? Because of prejudice again, with Whites reluctant to sell to Asian and black families, but also because of the different income levels of the various ethnic groups.

The police

Government research has shown that young Blacks get a particularly harsh deal from the police. It seems that young Blacks are more likely to be stopped, to be searched and to be arrested by the police. In court, they are more likely to receive a heavier sentence than white youths.

The main complaint from the Asian communities is that the police do very little to protect them from racist attacks. In the East End of London, Asians are regularly attacked by gangs of white youths, and Asian families have had petrol poured through their letter boxes, which was then set alight resulting in the deaths of a number of women and children. Generally the police argue that these are not racially motivated. Attempts at self-defence by Asian youths have been strongly opposed by the police who have prosecuted them. The result is a lack of confidence in the police and a feeling of bitterness, particularly amongst Asian and black youth.

Why? A study by the Policy Studies Institute, commissioned by the police themselves, indicated that many policemen were racially prejudiced (see the extract on page 70). They also believe that black youths offer a greater threat to law and order than whites and so are far stricter in their dealings with them.

To be fair to the police, by 1987 senior officers had introduced training programmes to combat racism and reports of racist attacks were being monitored in London.

Racism in the police force

In the early 1980s the Metropolitan Police asked a group of researchers to investigate policing practices 'on the beat'. The results were often rather shocking.

Similarly, racialist language is quite commonly used over the personal radio. For example JG (a researcher) heard the inspector of the relief with which he was working say over the personal radio 'Look, I've got a bunch of coons in sight'. The inspector was standing in a public place at the time and of course this message came up over the radios of all the police officers in the Division, many of whom would have been in public places at the time.

On one occasion DJS was with two officers who were dealing with a suspected bomb in a mailbag. Of the two postmen who noticed a sound coming from the bag in the back of their van, one was black and the other white. The black man was the driver, and the white man saw him as the boss; if for example he was asked a question, he often said 'I don't know about that, you'll have to ask my driver'. Later the police questioned the black man in a friendly manner and the answers were given with clarity, common sense and courtesy.

As they got back into the police car afterwards, one of the officers, checking through his notes, said to the other, 'Was it the coon who called us out?' The other replied 'Yes, believe it or not, it was the coon that was the driver.'

Source: D Smith and J Gray, *Police and People in London* (Gower, 1985)

1 What does the extract tell you about the taken-for-granted attitudes of the police officers about black people? Give an example to illustrate your answer.

2 Do you think the police officers were deliberately being racialist in the language they used referring to black people?

3 Some people have argued that passing laws against racial discrimination has little effect in combating racism. How does this extract illustrate this argument?

4 Some sociologists have argued that 'racism is deep in our culture' and that our language contains many words and phrases which we commonly use, which strengthen this racism.

   a) What does the phrase 'deep in our culture' mean?

   b) Can you suggest any commonly used words or phrases that we use, which, if we think about it, are racist?

Education

Overall, Blacks and Asians do badly in our education system, although there are considerable variations, with Indian girls doing particularly well and West Indian boys doing particularly badly.

Why? The main argument put forward by sociologists is that the education given to children in our schools is predominantly 'white' in its content, for instance the history of Africa or India is seen through the exploits of British explorers; the culture and civilisation of Africans and Asians is ignored. To combat this, programmes of education (multi-cultural education) have been developed which stress the positive contributions of Blacks and Asians.

Explanations for racial prejudice

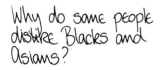

Why do some people dislike Blacks and Asians?

There are two basic types of explanation of why people are racially prejudiced. The first type stresses the **individual** and the second stresses **cultural** reasons.

The individual

Individuals who tend to 'bottle up' their frustrations and problems find an outlet for them in hostility against certain easily identifiable groups, such as immigrants. This is often linked to an 'authoritarian personality' which is very rigid and conventional.

Critics of this explanation argue that if 35 per cent of the population admit to being racially prejudiced, can so many people be unable to express their feelings, and suffer from an authoritarian personality?

The culture

This second approach, taken by most sociologists today, argues that prejudice against certain ethnic minorities is part and parcel of our culture. People are socialised into thinking in racial terms, through the history we learn at school, through the media and in some cases through the family. The reason why our culture contains so much prejudice is explained in two main ways.

Scapegoating

The real explanations for social problems such as unemployment or poor housing may be too complex for people to understand. A simple, easily understood explanation is that it is the fault of 'outsiders', such as the ethnic minorities; they are taking the jobs or the housing. The fact that this is not true is ignored.

More radical sociologists have gone a stage further and argued that blaming the Blacks and Asians for society's problems draws attention away from the root cause which is the great differences in wealth in our society. To them, both Blacks and Whites are being exploited, but they are blinded to this, preferring instead to blame the other group.

Stereotyping

This explanation goes hand in hand with scapegoating. When Britain was a colonial power, invading other countries (or 'tribes') and then exploiting them for its own good, it was necessary to *depersonalise* the people being oppressed, that is to make people believe that the conquered are somehow inferior to the conquerers. Africans were seen as 'children' who needed Whites to keep control over them, for example. Blacks and Asians, therefore, came to be seen as inferior and this view of them entered into our culture.

Racism in action

Source: *New Internationalist*, March 1985

1 The statements above are frequently heard. Do you agree, or disagree, with them?

2 What, do you think, are the real feelings of each speaker? (Explain each one separately.)

3 In each case, what would you do, or say, if you were the person being addressed?

4 The young man on the right says, '. . . they should be taught something about their own cultures.' What do schools teach about Africa or India? What attitudes does this create?

Immigration laws

- **1948 British Nationality Act:** encouraged Commonwealth citizens to settle in Britain and work here

- **1962 Commonwealth Immigrants Act:** entry restricted to those with special skills that were required. Controls were placed on the right of entry of family of those already living here. In 1969 a special certificate was introduced which family members had to have before they could enter Britain. These are very difficult to obtain

- **1971 Immigration Act:** entry further restricted. A special group of privileged immigrants was created called 'patrials', those with British grandparents. Many saw this as a way of allowing white immigrants but not Blacks

- **1981 British Nationality Act:** changed the basis of British citizenship to exclude certain groups, in effect Chinese from Hong Kong and African Asians holding British passports, from ever settling here

Racism and job opportunities

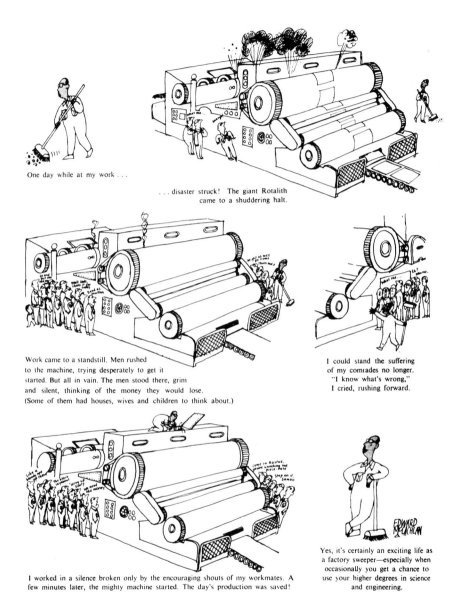

One day while at my work . . .

. . . disaster struck! The giant Rotalith
came to a shuddering halt.

Work came to a standstill. Men rushed
to the machine, trying desperately to get it
started. But all in vain. The men stood there, grim
and silent, thinking of the money they would lose.
(Some of them had houses, wives and children to think about.)

I could stand the suffering
of my comrades no longer.
"I know what's wrong,"
I cried, rushing forward.

I worked in a silence broken only by the encouraging shouts of my workmates. A
few minutes later, the mighty machine started. The day's production was saved!

Yes, it's certainly an exciting life as
a factory sweeper—especially when
occasionally you get a chance to
use your higher degrees in science
and engineering.

Source: *New Internationalist*

1 Why is the black worker sweeping the floor if he can repair the machine and has a degree?

2 How do the white workers respond to his help; are they grateful, for instance?

3 The black worker does not appear to be resentful of his treatment; how would you feel in his situation?

4 Trades unions' attitudes to black workers have been generally described as racist. What support for this point does the extract contain?

5 What suggestions could you make for combating racism in the workplace?

Combating discrimination

Are laws an adequate way of fighting racial prejudice?

Legal changes

1965 Race Relations Act

Racial discrimination was made illegal in employment, housing and the provision of goods and services to the public. It became an offence to 'incite racial hatred', for instance by publishing newspapers with racialist propaganda. Two Boards were set up to investigate accusations of racial discrimination and to promote racial harmony.

1976 The Commission for Racial Equality

This was set up, with stronger powers, to replace the two Boards formed by the 1965 Act.

Education

Programmes of multi-cultural education have been set up to show how to teach the history and cultures of the ethnic minorities.

How effective have these measures been?

Prejudice still exists, though it is more difficult to find out if discrimination does (because it is illegal, people will not admit to it). However, some changes have taken place; in 1984 whereas two-thirds of Whites over 55 objected to the idea of an Asian marrying into the family, only one-third of those aged 18–34 did. Indeed overall, the survey found young people to be less prejudiced than older people and more aware of discrimination against ethnic minorities.

Laws can prevent obvious discrimination but only a change in people's attitudes can really eradicate it.

CHAPTER SIX
AGE

Ageing as a social process

Surely ageing is a biological fact. Why are sociologists interested in it?

Ageing is, of course, a natural process that happens to us all and it can be seen in the physical changes that occur. For sociologists, the fascination with age comes from the fact that we *treat people differently* according to their age, and have very *different expectations* of what they ought to do. A 40-year-old man skipping down Southend High Street on a Saturday afternoon would be a ridiculous sight. He would be told to 'act his age', and onlookers would think he was either mad or drunk. But what if a four-year-old boy was skipping along? There would be absolutely no comment. Age has a social as well as a biological element.

The major age divisions which are recognised are **childhood, youth, adulthood** and **old age**. As most of the contents of this book are about the lives and experiences of adults, in this chapter we will concentrate on the significance of the other three divisions.

Certain forms of behaviour are related to age

Childhood

Have children always been treated as they are today?

We think of children as being 'precious', delicate creatures who are in need of protection, and we have special laws to protect them. It has not always been this way. It was only with the coming of industrialisation with its increase in wealth for the middle classes and the greater chances of children surviving at birth, that the idea of the 'precious' modern child was born. Before that (and amongst the working class, long after that) the child was seen as a miniature adult as soon as he/she emerged from infancy. So

children worked for long hours in agriculture and then in factories, until the reforms of the 1820s. In the last century children were divided into two groups: the children of the middle and upper classes who were regarded as delicate creatures in need of protection, and the children of the working class who were seen as far tougher and capable of looking after themselves. Both groups of children were strictly controlled by parents and, if they were disobedient, they were harshly punished.

Throughout this century, however, there has been a general acceptance that children of all kinds are in need of protection and guidance, but that blind obedience reinforced by violence is wrong. Normal 'beatings' by parents at the beginning of this century would now be regarded as a crime. In the modern family, the views of children are generally regarded as being worth taking into account and the relationship between the majority of parents and children is (ideally) one of partnership.

We ought to note though, that there is still much violence against children and the fact that social workers and the National Society for the Prevention of Cruelty to Children (NSPCC) still exist, indicate just how great the problem is.

Is childhood the same in all societies?

Childhood amongst the Ik

The Ik were a small tribe who lived in northern Uganda. The Ik regarded children as a great nusiance. So much so, that they were thrown out by their mothers at the age of three and expected to look after themselves.

In this environment, a child stands no chance of survival on his own until he is about 13 years old, so children form themselves into two age bands, the first from 3 to 7.

For the most part they ate figs that had been partially eaten by baboons, a few cherries, bark from trees, and when they were really hungry they swallowed earth or even pebbles.

Source: Adapted from C Turnbull, *The Mountain People* (Picador, 1974)

1 At what age does the mother regard the child as old enough to care for itself?

2 Would a child in Britain be capable of looking after itself at this age?

3 Some people argue that our abilities are completely controlled by our age and that our development is 'natural'. Does this extract tell us anything about our ideas of what children are capable of?

4 What does the extract tell us of the relationship between mother and child?

The changing attitudes towards childhood

	Up to the eighteenth century	1700	Industrialisation	1900	Twentieth century
ARISTOCRACY	**Boys** were treated as 'little men'; trained in the arts of war, and possibly learned some reading and writing **Girls** were educated to be mothers and wives; no formal schooling; household skills learnt	**RICH**	**Boys** were treated as little creatures who were to be strictly brought up to learn how to be 'gentlemen'; often attended public schools; children wore special clothes and were regarded as inferior to adults **Girls** were seen as being less important than boys; taught that they had to make perfect wives and run the household while men got on with business; rarely attended school; were treated strictly; special clothes for girls introduced	**MIDDLE CLASS**	**Boys** began to be treated with love and affection; encouraged to do well at school and in sports; children seen as in need of care and protection; if parents fail, State takes over; higher expectation of boys than girls **Girls** treated with love and affection; stress on being pretty and learning to be a successful wife and mother; as century progresses increasing stress on education and career For boys and girls: close family life
PEASANTS	**Boys** were expected to work in the fields as soon as able; no such thing as childhood; treated roughly **Girls** had no childhood; worked from earliest age; trained to be a farmworker first and a mother/wife second	**WORKING CLASS**	**Boys** worked from very early age in factories; treated with brutality by parents, very often; little time for childhood as we know it, as they never had time to play; strict discipline; no special clothes **Girls** treated as boys; worked from a very early age; no special clothes; not regarded as being very different from boys; treated strictly and punished with violence	**WORKING CLASS**	**Boys** By the middle of the century, the working class had adopted idea of the innocence of children and it was normal to treat children with love and affection Diminishing use of violence in discipline **Girls** As boys above, but less stress on educational achievement and career prospects; close family life

A rite of passage

The **bar mitzvah** is a ceremony (a rite of passage) which each boy goes through in the Jewish religion at the age of 13. It means that a boy has entered the adult Jewish community: has become a man, ready to fulfil the commandments gleaned from the Talmud, the book that codifies ancient Jewish laws and traditions. Many girls now participate in a parallel ceremony at the age of 12 called a **bat mitzvah** ('bat' means daughter).

Traditionally, the first public declaration of a child's new acceptance into adulthood takes place on the first Saturday after the boy's thirteenth birthday. This ceremony closes with the boy's father reciting the Hebrew blessing, 'Blessed are you who releases us from the responsibility of this child'. The blessing makes clear the boy's new responsibility to himself and the community's recognition of their altered responsibility to him.

So the social impact of the bar mitzvah is profound. It draws into consciousness a clear line between childhood and adulthood.

Source: *New Internationalist*, August 1984

But rites of passage are not just for youth

Everybody working in the offices came over to the Special Features Room as work finished that day. Even the Managing Director, a rarely-seen figure, turned up (late) especially for the ceremony. At exactly 4.30 p.m. one bitter February day, my father became the centre of interest. Speeches were made on his 35 years of service, broken only by time in the armed forces . . . 'Never missed a day's work in all that time.' . . . 'An example of hard work and commitment to the interests of Oakalls news- papers.' . . . 'a popular figure in the office'. My mum looked on proudly, her hair specially permed for the occasion, dressed in a brand new outfit. The office presents were given – a set of silver plated goblets and a copy of the front page of the paper on the day my dad first started work. For an hour the drink flowed and photographs were taken. Then my mum and dad caught the bus home, just like he had done for 35 years ('broken only by time in the armed forces'). And when he arrived home he was a pensioner.

1 What is a 'rite of passage'?

2 Give three examples of rites of passage which people go through in contemporary society.

3 In both extracts, the person had a new 'social status' after the rite of passage. What was this new status?

4 Compare the social status of the person in the second extract before and after the rite of passage.

5 What purpose does a rite of passage serve for the individual and society?

6 Is there a clear rite of passage in modern society to indicate the move from childhood to adulthood? Might this have any repercussions for young people?

The age of youth

What ages does youth cover?

We use the term 'youth' in normal conversation without a very precise notion of the age at which we enter and leave it. Does youth finish at 16 when you leave school? Or 17 when you can drive a car? Or maybe at 18 when you can vote and legally purchase alcohol. Perhaps youth is not directly restricted to any age but is over when you marry? Clearly the notion is confusing and perhaps that is the very core of the meaning of youth – it is a period of *transition* between childhood, when we are bossed

Sixteen – the magical number

around and regarded as having little to contribute to discussions on matters of importance, and adulthood, when we are weighed down with domestic concerns, the mortgage, and the rearing of children.

How do other societies distinguish between adults and children?

Many societies have very clear **social markers** which tell other people what a person's status is, either child or adult, as there is no 'in-between' stage. For example, in Jewish society there is the *bar mitzvah*, which is a ceremony that marks the break between boyhood and manhood. Today, it is largely ceremonial, but once signalled an important change in a person's life.

The ceremonies which act as social markers of status are known as **rites of passage** and although less common than they were we still have some left. Soon after birth, for instance, we celebrate with baptism, and our countdown to death begins with our retirement.

There is no form of rite of passage into adulthood in British society, where entry into adulthood is rather confused and unclear. Although we are 'of age' officially at 18, a large proportion of young people continue to be economically dependent on their parents and continue to live in their parents' house. It is this 'age of transition' that we call youth.

- **Culture:** a whole way of life that guides our way of thinking and acting. People within a culture regard it as somehow natural, for example, the difference between British values and Italian values

- **Subculture:** exists within a culture and is a distinctive set of values that marks off the members of the subculture from the rest of society, for example, youth (sub)culture

- **Contraculture:** a form of subculture which actively opposes the dominant culture of society; for example, terrorist groups

The origins of youth culture

When did youth culture first start?

Youth and youth culture are relatively new. It was not until the 1950s that the distinct identity of a (sub) culture of youth was recognised. Although British youth culture has always been very different from US youth culture, its origins come from there and it has always been strongly influenced musically and artistically by it. This can be seen in the popularity of American films and records here.

Three closely related facts are crucially important in understanding the birth of British youth culture. The first is the growth in affluence of young people in the 1950s. The second is the development of new means of recording and transmitting music and entertainment, which led to mass culture. The third is the speed of social change.

Why did youth culture start when it did?

Affluence

The 1950s was a period when there was an unlimited number of jobs and wages were increasing rapidly. The result was more money in people's pockets. Most importantly, young people shared in this prosperity but were not bogged down with mortgages and heavy household bills. What they earned, they were able to spend.

Mass culture

The 1930s had seen the development of the record industry, the film industry and the rise of radio. The 1950s added television to this and technical advances in record players. The adult market had reached saturation, so the commercial companies turned their sights on the newly affluent youth.

Social change

The increasing speed of technological change (think of the advances in computing for instance in the last 10 years) has influenced patterns of behaviour and meant that the expectations and behaviour of one generation is not relevant to the next. This has meant that youth has had to develop its own ways of acting.

The spread of youth culture

At first the main consumers of the clothes and music were the working class; after all they left school first and had money of their own to spend. Gradually, however, the youth culture of music and distinctive clothes spread to the middle class. The form it took was different though, as the middle-class youth were (and still are) more likely to be in full-time education until 18 or even 21.

Time to wake up from the youth dream

The very idea that acned people represent some kind of unique and unified culture divided from the real world by the single fact of age is ridiculous. The whole generation gap game died a final death a decade ago. The cult of us against them teendom was a historical freak which was a result of all the social disruption caused by World War II. It brought in a new set of values and vices in the mid-1950s. But 20 years on everybody knew how to spend money and how to disco dance and the youth thing was no longer a rebellion but a tradition. Punk rock and all that was the theatrical death rite of the beast of teenage. Now there's just people again.

But yesterday's teen producers turned today's media product producers have simply moved from acned to hackneyed in their desire to cater for this supposed golden age group. So, instead of producing good movies, people try to make young ones, saddled with awful rock tracks. They also make young people's television where discos, gender bending and unemployment are substituted for character, plot and intelligence. . . . And all this is based on the one ridiculous assumption that all young people want the same things – they want young things.

The current obsession with youth is actually a sign of a culture come of age. Before the teen explosion, young people were simply old people in smaller sizes. Now it is the other way around, nobody is a teenager anymore because everybody is.

Source: Adapted from the *Observer*, 1985)

The writer thinks that there is no longer a youth culture.

1 When does he see youth culture beginning and ending?

2 Is the music and entertainment for youth today created by them, according to the writer?

3 Who are teenagers now?

4 What is your opinion of the writer's argument? Give reasons for your conclusions.

5 One way to test the author's argument would be to contrast the style of clothes worn by youth and that worn by the over 23s. Are there significant differences? Now, suggest two other ways and then check to see if they confirm or reject the writer's opinion.

The purpose of youth culture

Why should young people develop values different from older people?

We know why youth culture developed in the 1950s in Britain. But sociologists have asked what, if anything, does youth culture actually do for youth? The answer seems to be that youth culture helps solve the specific problems faced by young people. The trouble is, however, that sociologists disagree over exactly what these specific problems are.

The first approach, that all young people face similar problems, claims that young people are unsure of themselves in the difficult period of transition from childhood, when a person has no responsibilities, to adulthood, when a person is absolutely loaded down with them. In order to cope with this period of uncertainty, youth develop a culture which provides them with a clear way of behaving and looking. The **peer group** becomes all important and young people can feel safe in the security of their group. The differences between young people are not seen as being very important.

The second approach, that young people face very different problems according to class, gender and colour, argues that the different problems faced by different sections of youth are so great that they develop their own 'responses'. For instance the black working-class youth in the inner city grows up in very different circumstances from the white middle-class youth in the suburb. The results are reggae/Rasta culture as opposed to mainstream music.

The peer group

How important are our friends in influencing our behaviour?

Before we go on to look at the different sorts of youth styles, we must briefly glance at a key group for young people, the peer group. As children, most of us are brought up in families which, ideally, provide us with protection, emotional security and a sense of belonging. As we grow up the constraining bonds of the family prove too tight, we need more freedom but without losing that sense of security. Is seems that the role of the peer group is to do just that; it gives independence and security. The peer group consists of other people of the same age who are seen as the correct people to judge our behaviour against.

The peer group can be a decisive influence on a young person's lifestyle. We have all heard of someone in trouble with the law having 'got in with the wrong crowd', and it is true that status within the peer group partially comes to replace loyalties outside.

The influence of the peer group

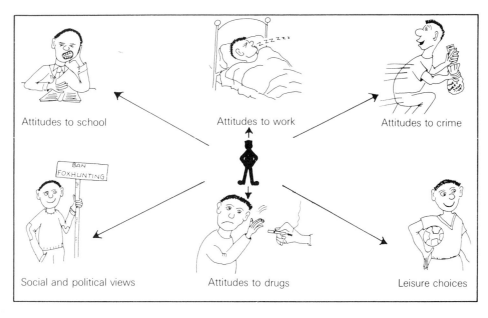

Attitudes to school

Attitudes to work

Attitudes to crime

Social and political views

Attitudes to drugs

Leisure choices

1 Give an example of the importance of the peer group in attitudes to school.

2 How important do you think the peer group is in attitudes to drug use?

The varieties of youth culture

There is a wide variety of youth cultures which reflect the range of problems faced by youth. As mentioned earlier, black inner-city youths have very different experiences of life than do white, suburban youth. These differences are reflected in the styles of clothes, the choice of music and the forms of expression of the different groups.

Before we examine these different forms of youth culture, it is important to remember that all young people seek as much enjoyment as possible from life and they are not too concerned with long-term planning. This, combined with the fact that most adolescents are free from major worries over household bills and family responsibilities, means that they are more able to plunge themselves into wholehearted enjoyment than most adults.

● **Style:** a term to summarise a way of dressing, appreciation of a certain type of music, use of particular speech expressions and a whole set of likes and dislikes which mark off a particular group as different.

Middle-class youth culture

As middle-class youth are more likely to stay in the education system to take A-levels or a degree, their form of youth culture is likely to be based on student life and often linked to some form of protest politics. Isolation from the 'real world' in tolerant university surroundings lets them explore new lifestyles and attitudes without the possibility of being disciplined, unlike the working-class youth living at home and coming in conflict with parents.

Working-class youth culture

Working-class youth has developed a number of quite distinct 'styles', which reflect the splintering of the working class in the 1970s and 1980s into the more- and less-affluent (we looked at this on pages 38–9).

At one extreme, the least well-off developed the youth cultural style known as 'the skinheads'. Here, the emphasis was on 'manliness' and racism. These two values lie deeply embedded in traditional working-class culture, and it has been suggested that skinheads have taken these working-class values and exaggerated them into a form of subcultural style. Manliness is shown by wearing the traditional working men's clothes of braces and boots, wearing their hair short and stressing tough aggressive behaviour. Racism is shown by the targets of skinhead attack – usually Asians and Blacks.

A different response to the changes in the working class has come from those who are considered as the 'new working class'; those people who have a relatively high standard of living. The youth here have developed a youth culture based upon ownership of fashionable 'named' clothes, which give their owner status. The 'casuals' wear Benetton or Pringle sweaters which prove to others that they have taste and money.

The future of youth cultural styles amongst the working class will depend vary largely upon the chances of getting work. Clearly, if there are no jobs, then buying expensive clothes, stereo equipment and cars will have to stop. Yet against this there are now very firmly established expectations that youth have concerning possessions; they think it is only fair that they have decent clothes and stereo equipment. With less money to spend, but the same amount of advertising and commercial pressures to buy goods, plus high expectations, the future looks gloomy for youth.

1 Why are there different styles amongst youth?

2 There are two examples of working-class styles mentioned in the main text. Name three other examples of youth styles that exist today.

3 Do you think you associate yourself with any particular style? If so, what is it? Briefly describe it.

4 Now construct a chart of all the current youth styles, with a description of each. You may want to use a number of headings, such as clothes, music, etc.

5 Write a brief description of how you see the future of youth. Alternatively, you could draw a sketch of the future fashions as you imagine them.

Black youth culture

Any survey of job opportunities and living conditions finds black youths of West Indian descent at the bottom of the pile. On top of this black youth faces racist attitudes amongst large sections of the white community. Sociologists have suggested that in order to cope with their problems and low status in British society, black youth have 'turned to their roots', adopting a culture which is based on some imagined version of black or West Indian culture. By adopting 'reggae' music and 'Rasta' styles, the black youth escapes the white society and gives itself status.

Rastafarianism: An example of youth culture as a 'solution'

Rastafarianism is originally a religious cult movement which believes that the promised land for blacks is Ethiopia and their prophet was Ras Tafari, crowned Emperor of Ethiopa in 1930. Blacks are the 'lost tribe' who are held in captivity in Babylon (the white-dominated West) who will one day return to the promised land.

The dreadlocks and the smoking of marihuana are related to the Rastafarians' rejection of this world and material things including their own bodies. The 'locks' are the result of not washing (to show contempt for the body) and the smoking of marihuana helps induce a state which brings the Rastafarian nearer to Jah (God).

The adoption of elements of Rastafarians by second generation blacks in Britain was less religious than symbolic. They are able to find a distinct culture which celebrates being black, giving them prestige and a very different style of clothes (the national colours of Ethopia have been adopted by the Rastas) and music.

Rastafarianism does not solve the problems black youth faces of racism, and unemployment, but it gives them a decent self-image.

Source: Adapted from M O'Donnell, *Age and Generation* (Tavistock, 1985)

1 From which group in society does Rastafarianism draw its recruits?

2 What solution does Rastafarianism provide for British black youth?

3 Using the idea that youth culture is a type of solution for the problems of various groups, take any one youth culture and suggest how it could be related to the problems faced by these young people.

Asian youth culture

One group who rarely receive any publicity are the youth of Asian origin. It seems that the family remains centrally important in their lives and they are far more conformist than most other youth. Girls are particularly sheltered, and traditional Asian views on the role of the female mean that they are strictly controlled. There is recent evidence that the influence of British culture is starting to weaken the control of Asian parents and that some sections of Asian youth are attracted to British youth cultural styles. So it is now common to see Asian girls dressed in fashionable western-style clothes.

On the margins

Two feminist sociologists, McRobbie and Garber have used the term *structured secondariness* to describe girls in youth culture. By this, they mean that girls are expected to hang around boys, to watch them playing football, to be by their side in pubs as the boys talk and to look good.

Most youth cultures . . . were male focused, with females occupying only marginal positions. McRobbie in her analysis of the magazine *Jackie*, illustrates the way in which girls orient their lives around fantasising over pop stars, listening to records and striving to keep their boyfriends.

Source: E Ellis Cashmore, *No Future* (Heinemann, 1984)

1 Is this your experience of female youth culture?

2 If not, how do you view it?

3 If you go out to a club (or pub?) this weekend, closely observe the way girls and boys act, bearing in mind the information above. Report back to the class at your next meeting on what you have observed.

Girls in youth culture

Studies of girls' youth culture show that they tend to focus on being attractive and getting boyfriends. Fashion, music and going out may well be an important concern for male youth, but they are absolutely central to female youth culture. It is claimed that these concerns reflect the aim of girls to get themselves a regular boyfriend as a step to marriage and children; supposedly a female's main aim. However, in the 1980s the changing attitudes towards women mean girls are far less likely to think so much in the long-term and are simply interested, like boys, in getting a partner.

The position of girls in youth cultures very much reflects their position in society. The boy is expected to be the boss and the girl is expected to abandon her group of friends in order to join his, when he wants her. She is expected to be attractive and to boost his image by her good loooks. She is not expected to be domineering and to contradict him in public.

What causes the differences in subcultural styles?

Youth

Youth culture occurs in the period of relative freedom from childhood constraint and adult responsibilities.

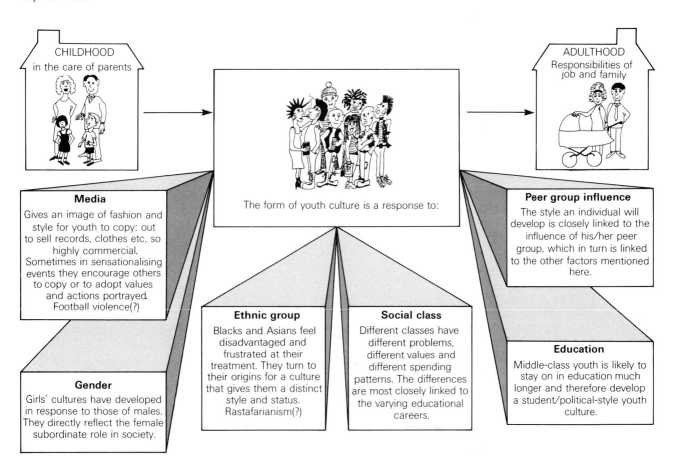

CHILDHOOD
in the care of parents

ADULTHOOD
Responsibilities of
job and family

The form of youth culture is a response to:

Media
Gives an image of fashion and style for youth to copy; out to sell records, clothes etc. so highly commercial. Sometimes in sensationalising events they encourage others to copy or to adopt values and actions portrayed. Football violence(?)

Peer group influence
The style an individual will develop is closely linked to the influence of his/her peer group, which in turn is linked to the other factors mentioned here.

Ethnic group
Blacks and Asians feel disadvantaged and frustrated at their treatment. They turn to their origins for a culture that gives them a distinct style and status. Rastafarianism(?)

Social class
Different classes have different problems, different values and different spending patterns. The differences are most closely linked to the varying educational careers.

Education
Middle-class youth is likely to stay on in education much longer and therefore develop a student/political-style youth culture.

Gender
Girls' cultures have developed in response to those of males. They directly reflect the female subordinate role in society.

Take a selection of the current youth styles plus some older ones such as teddy boys, skinheads, Rastafarians, hippies etc. and analyse them using the headings of the boxes above.

Commercialism and youth culture

Who creates youth style and music?

Youth culture developed in Britain first amongst the working class. It was not entirely accidental; working-class youth had money to spend. Recording and clothing companies saw this, as did the advertisers. Soon a whole industry developed to cater for (or perhaps create) the changing fashions of youth. As soon as a new style emerges it is taken, cleaned up, standardised and marketed. Punk, for instance, which started as a protest against 'good taste' and commercialised music, soon fell victim itself. There were punk shops selling standard punk clothes. It moved from protest to product. As the amount of money available to some youth declined, so the 'Oxfam' fashion, of second-hand clothes bought in charity shops developed. Within a year specialist (and, therefore, expensive) second-hand clothes shops emerged to cater for this fashion.

Music too undergoes this cleaning up and mass marketing. The original Sex Pistols music was just that, too strong in language for the record companies, but later cleaned-up punk groups provided the right balance between novelty and mass appeal – the recipe for fat profits. Few original bands escape this process of commercialisation.

The whole of youth culture is soaked through with exploitation by the mass media, recording companies, film makers and fashion houses, so that when we examine any particular youth style we need to ask ourselves just how much of it derives from youth itself and how much from manipulation by the media.

Commercialisation of youth culture

Teenagers didn't really exist before the Fifties. Before that decade young people consumed what older people did – just less of it. They danced to the same bands as their parents, kissed to the music of the same singers, didn't even dress very differently. But suddenly someone realised that although teenagers have less money, almost all the money they have is spent on leisure. So they supplied a leisure culture based on fashion – and made a fortune. It's a commercial dream. Records and clothes go out of date within a matter of weeks and you buy more not because you need it, but just because you want to 'keep up'. You can take this point further, 'youth culture', critics like Charlie Parker believe, 'is a form of social control'. In other words, one by-product of youth culture is that young people spend their energy on it as well as their money – energy that might have been dangerous to the establishment.

Source: C Brazier, 'Cashing in on the youth revolution' in *New Internationalist*, August 1984

1   What happened to make youth culture as we know it now, according to the writer?

2   Why is youth culture the perfect dream?

3   What is the 'by-product' of youth culture?

4   The author seems to be arguing that youth have no say in the creation of their own culture. Do you agree with him?

The generation gap

Is there really such a great gap between parents and their adolescent children?

So far, I have stressed the differences between youth and adults. Some sociologists have gone so far as to say that the division of people into age groups is actually more important than the division into social classes. Is this so?

Probably the differences between the generations have been overstressed and the similarities remain unappreciated. This is probably no comfort to those students reading this book in the middle of a dispute with their parents on just how much freedom they ought to have! However the fact remains that all surveys indicate that youth is only marginally rebellious and soon 'returns to the fold' of conformity.

The results of a *New Society* survey of young people's attitudes in 1986, revealed them to be very conformist indeed. Attitudes towards drugs, and even sex, were quite conservative. Most were politically apathetic rather than radical. Most wanted jobs and the spending power that went with them. Most believed in marriage and disapproved of adultery. Unfortunately, like the older generation, many of the younger generation shared feelings of racial prejudice.

The elderly

How have attitudes towards the elderly changed?

Old people feel trapped by the attitudes of young people

Today, 20 per cent of the population is above retirement age and that figure is going to continue increasing until the end of this century. Improvements in hygiene, in standards of living and, to a lesser extent, in medical care have caused this rapid expansion in life expectation. A full discussion on the causes of the growth in the elderly and the consequences for society can be found in Chapter 8. Here we will concentrate on changing attitudes to the elderly and the problems they face.

Never before in history have there been so many elderly people. A time traveller from the seventeenth century would be just as shocked to see all the old faces around as by the changes in technology. Indeed he would be shocked by the numbers of people over the age of 40, never mind 60! In most societies, old people would be of enough rarity to guarantee them some degree of status. Furthermore, in societies based on agriculture there is little change, each generation learns from the previous one. It was true to say that old people may well have had relevant advice to give to younger generations. The pace of change in advanced technological societies like our own means that the experience of one generation is not really useful to the next. The result is that the old in our society have low status. For many, old age is a time to be feared, a time of decline preceding death.

But it is not all bad. First of all, people do not just live longer, they remain active and healthy longer. It is claimed that the most affluent and relaxed period of people's lives now is the first eight years after retirement. Secondly, there is no real evidence that the elderly were treated with any great respect in the past. The elderly of today remember being respectful to the elderly when they were young, but they would say that, wouldn't they!

The supercentenarians of Abkhazi

In a few parts of the world, remote from the hustle and bustle of Western life, there are people today who are living extraordinarily long lives. One such place is Abkhazi in the Southern USSR.

In Britain the number of supercentenarians (people over 100) is estimated at 1 in 4000 of the population. In this area of Russia, the number is 204 in 4000. Perhaps the most inportant reason for long life is the attitude of these people to growing old and in the way their society is organised. At an age when most people in this country are thinking of drawing their pension, Abkhazians think of them- selves as in their prime. They are not obsessed by age as we are. No one is forced to retire at 60 or 65 and older people go on working in the fields, caring for the flocks of sheep, doing housework and looking after their grand- children and are involved in everything that goes on in the community.

Source: *People not Pensioners* (Help the Aged, 1978)

1 What is the main reason for the long life span?

2 What are the main differences between the way old people in Abkhazi act and the way old people act in our society?

3 Give three examples of how you treat old people differently from people your own age. Could you imagine treating old people in the same way as those of your age?

Family life and the changing life styles of the elderly

A big house used to be a good idea with a family.

But now that you are alone again it may seem more of a burden than an asset.

The upkeep of a large, near empty home can be an expensive liability, as well as a quiet and lonely place. The rooms you rarely use, repairs that are never done, and a garden which seems to grow bigger by the year. Isn't it time you took a closer look at *Countryside's* exciting range of luxurious apartments.

Created with you in mind, the care and dedication applied to the design and construction of these exclusive apartments is the hallmark of *Countryside's* reputation for building quality homes of character and elegance.

Any essential repair and maintenance jobs are taken care of, and with a residential housekeeper, it's nice to know someone is there to cope with any emergencies.

Strolling in the beautifully landscaped garden, relaxing in the

friendly atmosphere of the residents lounge, or the comfort of your own apartment. Whichever you choose, you can be sure that *Countryside's* unique blend of complete privacy when you want it, or a shared environment when you don't, allows you the privilege of enjoying the retirement you deserve.

If you live in Essex or East Anglia and would like to visit one of our luxury retirement apartments but find it difficult to do so, we will be happy to collect you, show you round and take you home again.

For further details please complete the coupon or telephone **Eve Bayley** on **(0277) 234136.**

Advertisements like this are becoming increasingly common.

1   Which group are they aimed at?

2   Why are builders finding this group a worthwhile target for advertising?

3   What is the 'family life cycle' (see pages 118–19)? Why is it relevant to the advert?

4   What does the advert tell us about old age in Britain?

CHAPTER SEVEN

FAMILY AND MARRIAGE

Families and households in Britain today

What changes are taking place in family patterns today?

- **Family:** a group of related people living together, such as a married couple, with or without children, or a single parent plus children

- **Household:** a person living alone, a family or a group of people who live and eat together (for example, three students sharing a flat)

Watching adverts and situation comedies on television, you would get the impression that the typical household today is mother, father and two children. In fact, only one-third of households in Britain are of this kind. Indeed the household where the father goes out to work, while the mother stays at home to look after the chidren, is quite rare, accounting for only 15 per cent of households. Over a half of children under 15 now have mothers who go out to work, and so the term **dual worker family** is used to describe these families.

There has been a large growth in recent years in **single-** or **lone-parent** households where there is one parent living with her/his young children. These now make up 13 per cent of all families with young children.

Two other types of households have been on the increase in recent years. First, there are households where people live alone, without any family, which now form 25 per cent of all households. Secondly, there are married couples living together with no children, either because they do not want children or because they are unable to have them. These now form about 27 per cent of British households.

Is the family as we know it in decline?

Some writers in recent years have argued that traditional family life is rapidly disappearing in Britain, and point to the statistics quoted above as evidence. However, these statistics present only a 'snapshot' of households at any one time. They do not show the continuous change in the **family cycle** as couples marry, then have children and then these children leave home, possibly to live alone, then in turn to marry (or cohabit) and have children. The married couple plus dependent children is only one stage of this cycle. Also, the statistics refer to the numbers of *households* in Britain, not the number of *people*. Although couples with children may only form a third of households, two-thirds of people live together in families of parents and children.

Varieties of families in Britain – 1

In the table on the next page, the type of household, such as a married couple, is measured in the first column as a percentage of *households*, and in the second column as a percentage of all *people* in Britain. The results are quite different. Those people who argue that the family is no longer of the stereotype of parents plus dependent children use the statistics from the first column, and those who argue that the family is alive and well use the second column for their information. It is an excellent example of how the interpretation of statistics can lead to different conclusions.

Type of household	Percentage of households	Percentage of people
One person	22	8
Married couple	26	20
Married couple with dependent children	32	49
Married couple with independent children	8	10
Single parent with dependent children	4	5
Other	9	8

Households and people in households, 1981

The first column of the table shows that only 40 per cent of households consist of married couples living with children. Figures like this lead to the claim that it is wrong to describe the typical family as a unit of parents plus children. . . .

The second column of the table shows that you get a very different picture if you consider people rather than the units they live in. . . . In fact six out of ten people (59 per cent) are currently in parents-plus-children households. Eighty-three per cent of children are brought up in households headed by married couples.

The point is that snapshots of household types are misleading about families, and they ignore the life cycle. People pass through various stages of family life and the period of parents plus young independent children is just one phase, most go through the earlier phase of marriage without children and the later phases when children leave home and set up on their own. Many of the single person households are formed by the widowed late in life and represents the final phase of the family life cycle.

Source: Adapted from R Chester, 'The Rise of the Neo-conventional Family' in *New Society*, 9 May 1985

1 According to the table, what proportion of *households* are married couples with independent children?

2 What proportion of *people* are formed by married couples with dependent children?

3 Give the figures for one person living alone as a percentage:
   a) of households;
   b) of people.

4 The author, Chester, states that 59 per cent of people live in households which consist of parents with children. By examining the table, can you explain how he arrived at this figure?

5 Briefly summarise what this table tells us about:
   a) interpreting and using statistics;
   b) the family in Britain today.

Marriage

The collapse of marriage

Are people avoiding marriage?

There is a common belief that the institution of marriage is crumbling in Britain. People who support this argument point to the numbers of single-parent families, usually headed by a woman, which we have seen compose 13 per cent of all families with dependent children. Others indicate the increasing numbers of people preferring to live together (known as **cohabitation**). Then there is the decline in the numbers of people marrying. The final and most damning piece of evidence is the explosion in divorce which took place in the early 1970s.

Single-parent families

Although 13 per cent of families with dependent children are headed by a single parent, they form only five per cent of all families. Furthermore, it is not necessarily true that the parents are rejecting marriage as such. Eighty per cent of single-parent families are the result of death, divorce or separation, and it is often a transitional stage to a second marriage. Only 20 per cent are actually single parents who never married.

Single-parent families

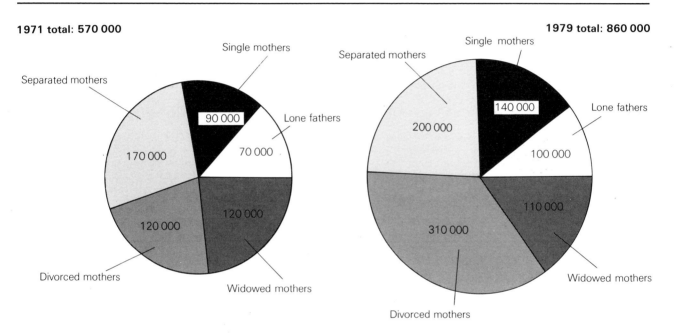

1971 total: 570 000

Single mothers — 90 000
Separated mothers — 170 000
Lone fathers — 70 000
Divorced mothers — 120 000
Widowed mothers — 120 000

1979 total: 860 000

Single mothers — 140 000
Separated mothers — 200 000
Lone fathers — 100 000
Divorced mothers — 310 000
Widowed mothers — 110 000

Source: Office of Population Censuses and Surveys

Oh dear!
Who pays the bills?
Where do I live?
I can't work and look after the children?
Who will give me help and support?
Do children need a father figure?

Never mind!
Perhaps I can get supplementary benefit – though it's not much to live on.
Maybe it's better to be poor than have the children hearing us arguing all the time!

Reasons for growth in the number of single-parent families:
- *Divorce, separation, death of partner;*
- *Women not wishing to marry when pregnant.*

1 Are single-parent families more often headed by men or women?

2 Name four types of people who are likely to head single-parent families.

3 What sorts of problems are single-parent families likely to face? Can you suggest any ways of coping with these problems?

Single-parent families – a problem?

Boyson condemns 'evil' single parents

People who choose to live as single parents were condemned yesterday by Dr Rhodes Boyson, the local government Minister, for creating 'probably the most evil product of our time'.

He launched his attack at a fringe meeting organised by the Church Society at the Conservative party conference in Bournemouth.

He blamed the one-parent family for many of the problems facing Britain, and said that such families would be increased by 'the rise of artificial insemination and casual sex relations'.

'Single parents have made their case so well that they have expanded their subsidies from the public purse from some £15 million in 1960 to £1 billion in 1983,' he said.

'Low paid members of normal families are taxed at standard rate to subsidise not only those forced to be one-parent families by misfortune but also to subsidise those who have specifically chosen to be one-parent families.'

Dr Boyson said that one in seven children lived in one-parent families, with one in three in the inner cities. He blamed 'the wildness of the uncontrolled male young' on a lack of fathers.

'Boys can generally only be civilised by firm and caring fathers. The banishment of the father means that boys take their values from their aggressive and often brutal peer groups and are prepared for a life of violent crime, of football hooliganism, mugging and inner city revolt.'

The family was under attack from extreme feminists, the youth cults, and homosexual lobbies, he said.

Dr Boyson criticised what he called 'the fashion of the flaunting and propagation of homosexuality and lesbianism, as anti-family and anti-life'. Holding up a book produced by the Inner London Education Authority, . . . he asked how many of his audience felt that heterosexism was a disease.

He accused Ilea and other education authorities of producing material aimed at 'the corruption of normal and traditional values going on in our schools'.

At another meeting Mr Geoffrey Pattie, a Defence Minister, attacked leftwingers for undermining civil rights in schools, universities, public libraries and hospitals.

'There are pressures to conform to anti-racism which means ignoring God-given differences between the sexes, and to anti-heterosexism which means encouraging young people to experiment with homosexuality at an impressionable age.'

Ms Sue Slipman, director of the National Council for One Parent Families, criticised Dr Boyson and said that 84 per cent of the one million one-parent families had been caused by divorce, separation or loss of a partner.

Source: The *Guardian*, 10 October 1986

Do you agree with Dr Boyson's views on single-parent families?

Cohabitation

In the late 1960s only about three per cent of women marrying had previously lived with their husbands, today the figure is nearer 25 per cent and increasing. About 10 per cent of women between the ages of 20–29 cohabit. So, it is true that a very great change is taking place in the numbers of young people who cohabit, where previously they may have been expected to marry.

However, what we can definitely say is that cohabitation is still a stage before marriage and that the majority of people who cohabit eventually marry. People tend to live together and if their relationship lasts they marry, particularly if they have children.

Numbers marrying

The numbers of people marrying have declined considerably since the 1960s and the rates have now fallen to the levels of the 1920s. Marriage at the moment is less popular than ever before in this century.

But this is not the whole story, part of the explanation is that people are now delaying their marriage until later in life, so that men are likely to marry at 26 and women at 23½. This has the effect of lowering the marriage rates and making it look as if fewer people are deciding to marry, when in fact they are just delaying marriage (possibly cohabiting first). It is still true to say that nine out of ten people get married.

Divorce

Divorce is examined in detail on pages 121–3.

The growth in divorce has been rapid in Britain in the last 20 years. Indeed it is claimed that 1 in 3 of new marriages are likely to end in divorce.

However, of those who divorce about 70 per cent remarry, which indicates not so much a rejection of the institution of marriage, but simply a dissatisfaction with their partner and the desire for another one. Many of those who are cohabiting are simply transferring from one marriage to another.

In terms of family life, however, the growth in divorce and re-marriage has created a new type of family structure in Britain. This is the **reconstituted family**, where two parents both with children, marry and so the resulting family consists of children with different parents.

Can you suggest any possible problems that occur in 'reconstituted' families?

Conclusions

Marriage and the family are not under such great threat as has been suggested. However, changes are taking place in such things as cohabitation, increasing divorce, reconstituted families and single-parent families, which are altering the traditional view of marriage and the family in Britain.

Finally, the different nature of the family patterns of the ethnic minorities add yet more varieties of family life to those already existing in Britain. Arranged marriages, extended families and no divorce are characteristic of Asian families, for instance.

Varieties of families in Britain – 2

Ethnic minorities and the family

Immigration has brought a number of family forms to Britain that are clearly different from traditional patterns. Such families put a much greater emphasis on the demands and duties of kinship.

Asian families are a clear example of this. Ballard argues that the basic pattern of a south Asian family consists of a man, his son and grandsons, together with their wives and unmarried daughters. This family has been transferred into a British setting. The man is clearly the head of the household, controlling the family finances and negotiating the major family decisions.

The male dominated nature of family life creates a very different experience for women within the ethnic minorities. In the early years of immigration, many women found themselves cut off from outside society. Social and language barriers kept them trapped in the home. Some Asian families created a state of Purdah [the woman must keep herself covered and is allowed no contact with men outside the family].

The reason for the attempt by ethnic minorities to control the lives of women is the need to maintain family honour. Every member should be seen to behave properly.

Serious problems have been created with the second generation, the immigrants' children who were born and have been brought up in the United Kingdom. School teaches these children to want more independence, as opposed to the family stress on loyalty and obedience. It must also be remembered that many of the first generation immigrants grew up in societies where there was no such thing as adolescence or youth culture, so conflict is inevitable when their children act like British teenagers.

West Indian families in Britain present a further distinct family pattern, that reflects their culture of origin. The colonial system based on slavery weakened the bonds between men and women. The lack of stable employment later left the man unable to support a family by his own efforts. The mother-child relationship became the central structure of the family.

Driver suggests that there are two types of black family structure in Britain. There is the nuclear family, where both partners share the full range of domestic tasks. But there is also the mother-centred family. The black mother is left to bring up the children, run the home and provide income. She must do this in England without the range of support that she could have obtained from female relatives in the West Indies. This is caused by the lack of stable employment for men.

Source: A Wilson, *The Family* (Tavistock, 1985)

1 From the description of the South Asian family, would you call it 'nuclear' or 'extended'?

2 Who is the clear head of the South Asian family? Give two reasons for your answer.

3 Describe the situation of women in the more traditional South Asian family.

4 Why should there be 'serious problems' for the Asian family 'created with the second generation'?

5 There are two patterns of West Indian family in Britain. What are they?

6 What reasons can you suggest for the growth of the two different types of West Indian family?

A comparison of marriage types

In Britain, we regard marriage as the 'union of a man and a woman'. However, this is not the only type of marriage in the world. Opposite are some of the varieties of marriage that exist.

General types	Name	Description		Where?	Why?
Monogamy	Monogamy		One man married to one woman	Europe today	A balance between males and females, with a cultural stress on the relative equality of male and female; Christian culture
	Serial monogamy		Couples marry, divorce, then re-marry different partners	USA Britain	Decline in the sanctity of marriage; not seen as lasting a lifetime; associated with increase in divorce; secular culture
Polygamy	Polyandry	or more	One woman married to a number of men	Parts of Tibet	Restricts numbers of children so keeps population low; useful in agricultural societies with limited amount of land
	Polygyny	or more	One man married to a number of women	Mormons of Utah, USA Muslim states of Middle East	Maximises possible number of children; important in societies with a high death-rate; possibly linked to imbalance of sexes (too many females); Muslim and Mormon cultures

Polygyny

It is widely believed that polygyny (having more than one wife) originated in response to the social and economic needs of rural African societies. It provided as many hands as possible to cultivate the land, and fight against high infant mortality. Children in Africa are believed to increase the prestige, wealth and social status of the family, and are thus always welcome. Yet polygyny was transferred almost intact to the cities among rich and poor, workers and intellectuals alike. . . . In Senegal 32 per cent of men had two or more wives. However, urban polygyny is difficult to justify in terms of salaries and costs. Salaries are low, families are large and few individuals within families are breadwinners (because of unemployment).

Marianne Diop is 56; she works as a secretary in a hospital. Her husband is a retired postman. Mr Diop has married four wives in all, sired 22 children and divorced twice. He now shares his life with his second and third wives, Marianne and Animata. They live in different houses but within walking distance.

Mr Diop only involves himself in crises, like the birth of an illegitimate child to his daughter. The everyday needs of the children are the mother's concern.

It would be unfair to portray Mr Diop as a selfish indifferent man. But with two wives, two households and 22 children, it is not difficult to understand why he does not find enough time for all. Some children are neglected while others are favoured; some receive enough support and guidance, others very little. It is the institution of polygyny which creates these conditions.

One evening when I was there, Marianne's husband – who always took turns in spending two nights with every wife – failed to show up when he was expected. That night Marianne said to me, 'How can one man love four wives equally?' She also confessed her husband's companionship had become less and less important to her, and she lived mainly for her children.

Source: Adapted from D Topouzis, 'The men with many wives' in *New Society*, 4 October 1985

1 What does polygyny mean?

2 What reasons does the author suggest for its origins?

3 Have people in cities abandoned polygyny?

4 Who appears to benefit most from polygynous marriage?

5 What is the relationship between Mr Diop and his children?

6 What is the relationship between Mr Diop and his second wife Marianne?

7 Can you explain why the relationships are like this?

8 Briefly, what comparisons can you make between the typical British family and the polygynous one of Senegal?

9 How does the extract tell us that culture does not change as quickly as technology and economic situations?

Polygamy has certain disadvantages

Types of family

A family is best described as a group of people living with or near each other, who are closely related by marriage or blood. (Unrelated people who live together and give each other help are usually known as a 'commune'.) 'Kin' means a wider circle of people who are related to one another and who generally give each other help. However, the contact is not as close as between the family.

There are four main types of family organisation: the **extended family**, the **nuclear family**, the **single-parent family** and the **reconstituted family**.

The extended family

This generally consists of three generations of people, that is grandparents, parents and children, who all live very close to each other and maintain close contact.

The extended family is usually found in societies where a large group of people living together can be of real use. For example, in an agricultural society where people live off the produce of the land, a large group of people can sow, reap and care for the animals most efficiently. Or in an industrial society, where there is great poverty, the mutual aid provided by a large group of workers is most useful in surviving in periods of crisis. There is clear evidence for it amongst the working class in Britain until the 1950s and it exists today amongst Asian immigrants in Britain.

The nuclear family

This is much smaller than the extended family and generally consists only of parents and their children, of which there is usually a maximum of three. Contact with the wider kin is much weaker and less frequent than amongst members of the extended family.

The nuclear family is usually found where a large group would be more of a hindrance than a help. In some simple societies based on hunting, food is in short supply and a small, fast moving group is more likely to survive. Nuclear families are also found in advanced industrial societies, such as our own, where there is less need to rely upon the family for help. This appears to be the most common form of family in Britain today.

The single-parent family

This consists of a single parent plus his/her dependent children. It is *usually* headed by a female. In Britain, the single parent reflects the rise in the divorce rate and, to a lesser degree, pregnancy outside marriage or death of a partner.

Reconstituted families

As the number of divorces and remarriages increases, so do the numbers of families which are headed by step-mothers or step-fathers. Indeed, the children of the family may be a combination of two previous marriages. About 1 in 14 children are currently living with step-parents, and this figure can only go on increasing.

Copy out the diagram below, so that it is large enough to write on. Using information in the text, complete the boxes.

Family type	Description	Circumstances in which found
Extended		
Nuclear		
Single-parent		
Reconstituted		

Changing form of the family

Before industrialisation, when most people obtained their living from the land, people lived for a relatively short time (a typical person in seventeenth-century England would expect to die in their early 40s). They apparently married and had children fairly late in their lives. The result was that it was unusual for a family of three generations to live together, simply because the chances of people surviving to the age of being grandparents were slim.

What was common was that families of parents, children and their spouses often lived close to one another and had frequent contact. Households were often large, not because there were extended families living together, but because it was common practice in pre-industrial Britain for the better-off to take the children of the poor as servants, or helpers. When they grew up, they left their adopted 'home' to look for better employment.

So for most people, the nuclear family was normal, but people lived nearer to one another and had greater contact than today.

The better-off were more likely to live in extended families because they had longer life expectancies, caused by better diets and less work, and also because family members were more likely to stay at home as their parents could provide for them, with land and jobs.

The pre-industrial family

In the 1970s, two books over-turned the theory that most families in Britain were of the extended type before indus-trialisation, as was normal throughout most of Europe.

Laslett, in *The World we have lost*, studied the parish records of births, marriages and deaths of 100 English villages from the sixteenth century to the nineteenth century. He concluded that most households throughout this period had an average size of 4.75 persons; in other words, the normal family type was the nuclear family throughout this period.

Anderson, in *Family Structure in nineteenth-century Lancashire*, studied the census material for Preston, Lancashire in 1851. He concluded that there was an increase in the size of the family at about this time. He explains this by saying that the increase in jobs provided by industrialisation meant that more distant relatives were attracted to the town and these came to live with the families already living there. Some stayed at home to look after the children and some worked in factories. The result was a type of community and family structure similar to that found in East London in the early 1950s, which has now died out.

1 What was the most common family type in pre-industrial England: extended or nuclear?

2 What happened with the growth of industrialisation?

3 Why did these books change sociologists' ideas about the family before industrialisation?

4 What type of family was most common in Europe before industrialisation?

In what ways did industrialisation influence the form of family in Britain?

For the poor, the effects of industrialisation on the family structure were considerable. Jobs in agriculture declined and those in factories expanded rapidly, so that people were forced to move into towns. Long hours of work, in dreadful conditions, with low pay and no form of welfare state meant that the extended family became a very useful way of pooling resources in times of need or illness. Also, after the early stages of industrialisation were over, life expectancy increased. So, by the middle of the nineteenth century, the extended family had become common amongst the working class and this form of 'self-help' continued well into this century.

Gradually, better conditions of life and the activities of the Welfare State eroded the mutual need that had created the industrial extended family and there has been a move towards the nuclear family. Contact with wider kin is maintained though, through the use of telephones and cars. This means that a family does not have to live together to keep in contact.

For the middle class, the extended family was normal throughout the nineteenth century. The main reason for this was **nepotism**, that is jobs and income were obtained through the father. The younger generation stayed at home because it was in their financial interests to do so, and middle-class women were trapped at home because it was not considered right for them to work.

Early in this century there was a move towards the nuclear family, as the younger generation were able to find their own jobs, and there grew the cultural stress on the close relationship between husband, wife and children to the exclusion of the wider kin. So small nuclear families developed.

An influence on both the middle and working classes, leading to nuclear-style families, has been the increase in **geographical mobility**. In order to find work in modern societies, it is necessary to move. The smaller, nuclear family with its looser ties to kin, allows people to move more easily.

Geographical mobility and technology have altered family life

The role of the family in society

It would not be unrealistic to argue that the family forms the cornerstone of our society. A world without the family would seem strange to us. However, there is some disagreement between sociologists on whether the family is a good thing for society, or not. We can understand this better if we examine the role of the family under two headings: the beneficial view (the family is useful) and the critical view (the family is harmful).

The beneficial view

How do families benefit their members and society?

The role of the family in small-scale agricultural or hunting societies was absolutely central. Indeed, in many cases the tribe was really a few extended families joined together. Individuals were taught the skills necessary to survive, were given work and received status and authority in the wider tribe according to their position in the family.

Industrialisation, urbanisation (the growth of cities) and the sheer numbers of people in society have altered the position of the family in modern society. But it still remains an extremely important social institution which fundamentally influences the course of our lives. The family acts as the link between the individual and society and, according to the beneficial view, it benefits both.

Socialisation

The individual

In order for a person to become truly 'human', that is to act in socially acceptable ways, an individual must be socialised (see Chapter 1). This is the basic role a family performs for individuals, moulding them to the expectations of society. Only through this can a person play a full part in social life.

Society

Society cannot exist without rules and expectations of behaviour. A society full of unpredictable individuals would simply collapse in chaos. The family socialises children into correct forms of behaviour. If children (or adults) fall out of step with society in some way, the family is usually the first place where punishment takes place, so the family not only socialises, but also acts as an agent of social control (see pages 203–5).

Emotion

The individual

Young children need to be shown care and affection to become stable adults. The family is ideally the place where this affection is freely given. Even for adults, there is a need for people to discuss their problems and to feel needed. At its best, the family can keep a person emotionally fulfilled and stable.

Society

If society is to continue, then people must be motivated to carry on and not to drop out. By giving people a reason to work, to uphold the rules of society and to conform, the family effectively ensures the continuation of society.

Economic provision

The individual

Young children need to be supported until they reach the age of self-sufficiency. The family provides for them and for adults who are not working through incapacity or unemployment. All aid from the State is channelled through the family to individuals.

Society

The modern family does not work together producing goods as in pre-industrial times, but today families do *consume* as a unit. Clothing, food and household items all make the family a major agency of spending in our society and, therefore, it is still very important economically.

Reproduction and sexual activity

The individual

Although sexual activity is common outside marriage, for most people regular sexual activity is limited to their husband/wife, or the person they intend to marry. As a result of this pattern of sexual activity, most of us are born into families.

Society

A society can only exist if there are people. Quite simply families produce the people who compose each generation. If unregulated, sexual activity causes problems of jealousy and conflict. By having a culture which stresses that the correct place for sex is within permanent relationships, much conflict is eliminated.

Social status

The individual

Being born into a family gives an individual identity – a name, background and a social class position.

Society

Families promote social order by locating people along class and status lines. Individuals know where they belong, where others are in the class structure and their own position with regard to them.

The importance of marriage and the family in pre-industrial societies

Isaac Shapera studied the life of the Kgatla tribe in South Africa in the early 1930s.

The household usually consists of a man with his wife, or wives, and dependent children, but often includes other people as well. . . . They live eat work and play together, consult and help one another in all personal difficulties and share in one another's good fortune. They produce most of their own food and material needs; . . . they are the group within which children are born, reared and trained in conduct and methods of work and they perform the ceremonies connected with birth, marriage, death and other ritual occasions. . . .

The family gets its food by growing corn, breeding animals and collecting wild plants which can be eaten . . . [and] it builds its own huts. In all these activities every-body except the infants take part, men, women and children having special jobs according to sex and age. The women and girls till the fields, build and repair the walls of the huts, prepare food and beer, look after the chickens and fetch water, wood (for fires) and collect wild plants. The men and boys herd the cattle, hunt and do all the building.

Source: Adapted from I Shapera, *Married Life in an African Tribe* (Penguin, 1971)

1 Who lives in the household?

2 Name four examples of things that the family does together.

3 Amongst the Kgatla, being invited to certain ceremonies indicates who is regarded as most important to the person involved in the ceremony. What does this tell us about the family?

4 Some people have described the pre-industrial family as an 'economic unit'. What do you think they mean by this? Use the extract to illustrate your answer.

5 Write a brief description, or draw a diagram, to indicate the tasks of the family in Britain today. Would you say it is as important today, as in the past?

The anthropologist, Levi-Strauss, met, among the Bororo of Central Brazil,

. . . a man about thirty years old: unclean, ill-fed, sad and lonesome. When asked if the man was seriously ill the natives' answer came as a shock: What was wrong with him? – nothing at all, he was just a bachelor, and true enough, in a society where labour is . . . shared between men and women and where only the married status permits the man to benefit from the fruits of woman's work, including delousing, body painting, and hair plucking as well as vegetable food and cooked food (since the Bororo woman tills the soil and makes pots), a bachelor is really only half a human being.

Source: G Hurd *et al, Human Societies: An Introduction to Sociology* (Routledge and Kegan Paul, 1986)

1 Describe the man Levi-Strauss met amongst the Bororo.

2 What was 'wrong' with him?

3 What is the advantage of 'married status'?

4 What are our attitudes to unmarried middle-aged men? Could you give reasons for your reply?

5 What does your reply to question 4 tell you about the importance of marriage in our society?

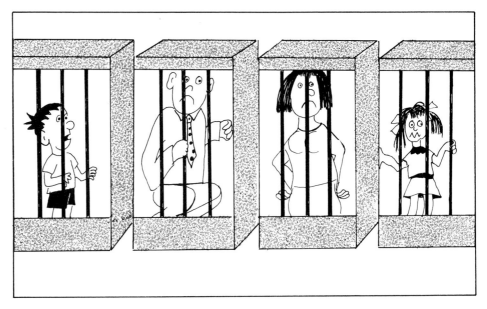

The critical view

Haw do families harm their members?

The analysis of the role of the family which we have just examined is generally associated with the *functionalist* school of thought in sociology. This approach usually examines any social institution, such as the family, or education system by asking the question: What function does this social institution perform for society?

Asking this sort of question, usually leads these sociologists to stress the beneficial aspects of the institution under question, and to underplay the harmful aspects, so the family is seen as giving such things as love and affection.

Other sociologists are critical of the functionalists' account of the family and point out the various harmful aspects of family life. These critics point out that violence against children and wives is commonplace and each year in Britain some children are actually beaten to death by their parents.

Violence against wives

In the last ten years there has been the growth of 'refuges' for women who are repeatedly attacked by their husbands. (These are usually large houses where the women can stay to escape from their husbands.)

Incest

Another disturbing aspect of family life is the sexual molesting of children, generally by their fathers. Nobody knows the full extent of this problem, as it is rarely reported. Nevertheless, according to social workers, it is far more common then generally believed.

Love and marriage, love and marriage

Emotion

The intense emotional ties of the modern nuclear family can lead to forms of psychological damage and emotional hurt. Constant conflict between parents can lead to divorce, broken homes and great emotional suffering. In some cases this is associated with crime. Some psychologists have gone even further and have suggested that emotional conflict within the family can actually cause mental illness.

Women repressed

Finally, feminist writers have constantly pointed out the unfairness of family life to women. They usually give up their jobs to have children, then are isolated at home in the role of housewife, and are expected to look after everyone else in the family, unpaid.

The family, therefore, must be seen as having many drawbacks as well as benefits.

Go together like a wife and carriage

Negative views of the family

In the past, kinsfolk and neighbours gave the individual continuous moral support throughout his life. Today the domestic household is isolated. The family looks inward upon itself; there is an intensification of emotional stress between husband and wife, and parents and children. The strain is greater than most of us can bear. Far from being the basis of the good society, the family, with its narrow privacy and tawdry secrets, is the source of all our discontents.

Source: E R Leach, *A Runaway World?* (BBC Publications, 1967)

At the present time, at least, if not in the future, there is no better guarantee of long life, health, and happiness for men than a wife well socialised to perform the 'duties of a wife', willing to devote her life to taking care of him, providing, even enforcing, the regularity and security of a well-ordered home.

Source: J Bernard, *The Future of Marriage* (Souvenir Press, 1973)

1   According to Leach, in the past who, apart from family members, gave aid and support to individuals throughout their lives?

2   How has this changed and with what results?

3   Does Leach see the family as a good thing?

4   According to Bernard, who benefits from marriage?

5   Draw up a list of benefits and disadvantages of marriage for:
     a) males;
     b) females.
     In your opinion who benefits?

The negative side of the family

Child sex abuse reports rise by 90%

Reported cases of child sexual abuse have risen by an estimated 90 per cent in the past year, the National Society of the Prevention of Cruelty to Children said yesterday. The charity estimates that more than 2850 children were placed on local authority registers last year compared with 1500 in 1984.

The society believes the increase, the largest recorded, shows a growing awareness of the problem rather than a great increase in the number of children being abused. The proportion of under-fours being sexually assaulted was 14 per cent last year . . .

Twenty-nine per cent of young boys reported assaulted were under the age of four, compared with 11 per cent of girls. The majority of reported sexual assaults are of young girls aged 10 to 14.

Most of the people who sexually assault children are fathers, close male relatives or stepfathers. However reported assaults on under-fours contain suggestions – still to be analysed in depth – that neighbours and other child carers may be to blame.

There are more reports of sexual assaults on children among those on low incomes and living in bad conditions but this may be because middle class people tend not to be monitored as closely by social workers or health visitors.

Dr Alan Gilmour, director of the NSPCC, said: 'It is far more likely that the case of sexual abuse will be reported in a tenement rather than a stately home.' . . .

Dr Gilmour renewed his criticism of the Government for failing to keep national figures of the incidence of child abuse or to ask local authorities to compile standard figures. . . . However, there are no moves to order authorities to keep special child sexual abuse registers.

The initial analysis of the first 200 who sought refuge in Britain's first 'safe house' for runaway adolescents, run by the Church of England Children's Society, shows that one in six who have run away from their parents has been sexually abused.

One in seven of the children – nearly all under the age of 16 – has been referred to the centre by the police after being caught soliciting in London.

Each case has been confirmed by staff at the centre, who found that many complaints to teachers or social workers had been dismissed earlier as fantasy.

Source: The *Guardian* 19 June 1986

1 What was the percentage rise in child sex abuse cases?

2 Which groups are most at risk?

3 Who is most likely to make the assaults?

4 Do you think the statistics reflect an accurate picture of what is happening? Explain your answer.

Alternatives to the family

Is it possible to eliminate or replace the family?

Critics of the family have long sought an alternative that would provide the beneficial aspects of economic and emotional security, without the restrictions on freedom that the family normally imposes.

Abolition of the family

The first, and obvious solution is to abolish the family completely. The two best known attempts to abolish family life were in the USSR after the communist revolution, and the activities of the revolutionary Khmer Rouge which took over in Cambodia in the 1970s.

In both cases the family was seen as the link that perpetuated the values of the old society. If the new communist society was to succeed the younger generation had to be brought up with a new set of values. Family life and marriage were weakened and children encouraged to see the State as their 'family' rather than their own kin.

In the USSR (and, as far as we know, in Cambodia) the result was chaos with an increase in crime, in deserted children and social problems in general. The State simply could not cope with people as individuals, it needed the organisational unit of the family. Soon, in the USSR the family was re-introduced and even promoted as the ideal way to live. The Khmer Rouge regime collapsed and has been replaced by a society which stresses family life.

Communes

The second alternative to the family is the commune, that is a group of people living together who generally share their possessions and treat children as 'belonging' to the whole commune, not just to their parents. A number of communes exist in Britain today usually based on religious ideals. However, probably the most famous form of commune is the kibbutz of Israel, although only two per cent of the population actually live in these communes. Kibbutzim are generally agricultural based, with some element of industry. Jobs are allocated on a rota (so everybody does 'good' and 'bad' work), and rather than wages, each kibbutz provides for all the wants of its members. Marriage is not regarded as important; couples can simply share rooms if they desire. Children themselves do not usually live with their parents but with others of their own age group in dormitories, simply sharing the evening meal with their parents if they so desire. According to the kibbutz philosophy, children should not see themselves as possessions of their parents but as independent members of the kibbutz.

1 What do you think about the idea of a commune?

2 Would you live in one with your friends?

3 What would your attitudes be to sexual relationships?

4 Who would look after the children?

5 What would happen if you had a difference of opinion? How would you sort it out?

6 How would you organise the finances?

7 Do you see any problems?

Family relationships

Have husbands and wives always had the relationship they have today?

In essence, the family is no more than a special relationship between a group of people. These relationships are never static; they are changing over time. The relationships between husbands and wives, and between parents and children are vastly different today from a hundred years ago. In order to fully understand the changes, we need to divide them into three categories – relationships between: husbands and wives; children and parents; the older generation and the family.

Husbands and wives

Sociologists have divided the changing relationships between husbands and wives into three phases.

Phase 1 Pre-industrial societies

Before Britain became a society almost totally based on industry, about 150 years ago, most people lived in the country and worked in agriculture. At this time, husband and wife were generally equal in their dealings with one another. Both of them worked to earn income and they relied heavily upon each other. However, most sociologists agree that the relationship between them was not very close.

Phase 2 Industrial family

In the second phase of the development of the modern family, during the last century, women lost their independence and equality. The result of laws restricting the working hours for women, and the Victorian beliefs concerning the purity and fragility of women meant that they withdrew from the workplace and increasingly the role of housewife and mother became the norm. Men became the breadwinners and, as they were the ones with the money, they also took charge inside the family.

It is important here to distinguish between the working class and the middle class, as there were considerable differences between them. The wife in the middle-class family was not expected to work either in or out of the home. Instead, she supervised the work of the cleaning lady and the nanny. The husband's role was to go out to business and to provide for the family.

Life in the working-class family was different in that the household chores and childrearing were seen as exclusively the wife's tasks. Husbands spent long hours at work and they preferred to pass their leisure in the pub, in the company of male companions. In these circumstances, women turned to each other for assistance, in particular to mothers and daughters. Help was freely given and very powerful bonds developed, which were much stronger than those between husband and wife. The father, although the head of the household, was also a bit of an outsider because of his long absences. Violence against wives and children was quite common.

Phase 3   The symmetrical family

Between the 1930s and the 1950s, a change took place in the relationships between husbands and wives in middle class families. A warmer, closer relationship began to be accepted as normal. A slow move towards equality began too, with joint decision making and an increase in shared leisure activities. The wife remained responsible for the home and the children (now with no nanny to help her), but increasingly the husband would see it as his duty to help her. Because of this move towards equality in husband/ wife roles, the sociologists Young and Willmott used the term **symmetrical family** to describe the new form of family relationship.

Gradually, these ideas spread to the working class, so that by the 1960s many younger working-class couples shared their household chores and their leisure activities, with the husband replacing the mother as the main helper to the wife.

When a husband and wife share housework and their leisure, sociologists call this a **joint conjugal role relationship**. However, when they perform separate tasks and have different leisure pursuits, sociologists describe their relationship as a **segregated role relationship**.

Using these terms, how would you describe the relationship in
   a) the phase 2 family?
   b) the phase 3 family?

Reasons for the move towards the symmetrical family

Why has there been a move towards a symmetrical family?

Women began to reject the housewife role. They demanded a greater say in decision-making in the home and to be considered equal to their husbands. Further, they insisted that men ought to become involved in tasks about the home. Contraception allowed them to limit the number of children and gave them the freedom to obtain paid employment. Financial independence from husbands in turn strengthened their position of equality in the family.

The resettlement of many working-class people from the inner cities in the 1950s into overspill estates and the increasing affluence of others who bought their own homes led to a much greater interest in home improvements and home life generally. Men preferred to stay in, improving their homes, watching television or playing with the children than going to the pub. This new form of leisure pattern amongst working-class men, led to the term **privatised worker** being used (indicating that the worker was interested in his private family life).

Changing relationships between husbands and wives

Traditional relationships

This extract comes from a 1950 study of a working-class mining community in north-east England.

The comedian who defined home as the place where you fill the pools in on a Wednesday night was something of a sociologist. With the exception of a small minority of men . . . the husbands of Ashton for preference come home for a meal after finishing work and, as soon as they can feel clean and rested, they look for the companionship of their mates.

The wife's position is very different. In a very consciously accepted division of labour, she must keep in good order the household provided for by the money handed to her each Friday by her husband. While he is at work, she should complete her day's work – washing, ironing, cleaning or whatever it may be – and she must have ready for him a good meal.

The wife's confinement to the household, together with the acceptance of the idea that the house and the children are primarily her responsibilty, emphasise the absence of any joint activities and interests for husband and wife.

Source: N Dennis, F Henriques and C Slaughter, *Coal is our Life* (Eyre and Spottiswoode, 1956)

Symmetrical family

In a study of middle-class households in the late 1950s it appeared that a change was taking place in relationships between husbands and wives. Young and Willmott later decided on this evidence and further research that the family in Britain today is best described as 'symmetrical', meaning that husbands and wives regarded each other as equal and shared domestic tasks.

Most Woodford men are emphatically not absentee husbands. It is their work, especially if rather tedious which takes second place in their thoughts . . . 'In the old days,' as one wife said, 'the husband was the husband and the wife was the wife and they each had their own way of going on. Her job was to look after him. The wife wouldn't stand for it nowadays. Husbands help with the children now. They stay more in the home and have more interest in the home.'

The couple share the work, worry and pleasure of the children. 'We have the same routine every night,' said Mrs. Foster, 'I'd put one child to bed and my husband puts the other. We take it in turns to tell them stories too'.

Husbands usually have their own specific tasks within the family economy, particularly in decorating and repairing the home.

Source: P Willmott and M Young, *Family and Class in a London Suburb* (Routledge and Kegan Paul, 1960)

1 How would you describe the husband/wife relationship in Ashton: segregated or conjugal? Why?

2 Do you think the husbands and wives in Ashton spent much leisure time in each other's company?

3 In what way had the middle-class relationship changed between husband and wife?

4 By the 1970s Young and Willmott described most families in Britain as 'symmetrical'. What did they mean by this?

Is the form 'symmetrical' a true description of the husband-wife relationship today?

Feminists have bitterly criticised this symmetrical family/privatised worker description of modern family life. They argue that husbands benefit far more from marriage than wives. It is still regarded as the woman's task to look after the children, to cook and to do the housework. Husbands 'help' their wives and are regarded as being good husbands if they occasionally relieve their wives from childminding, or wash the dishes. Women, too, give up their careers far more often than men in order to look after the children. Staying at home with young children is often lonely and frustrating, as well as being exhausting.

The changing relationships within the family

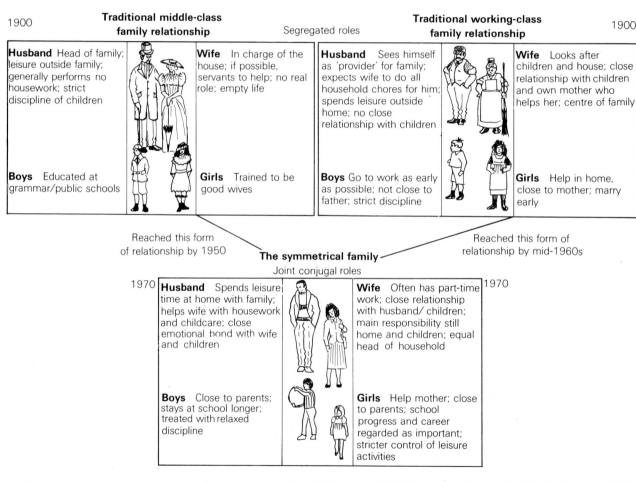

1900

Traditional middle-class family relationship

Segregated roles

Traditional working-class family relationship

1900

Husband Head of family; leisure outside family; generally performs no housework; strict discipline of children

Wife In charge of the house; if possible, servants to help; no real role; empty life

Boys Educated at grammar/public schools

Girls Trained to be good wives

Husband Sees himself as 'provider' for family; expects wife to do all household chores for him; spends leisure outside home; no close relationship with children

Wife Looks after children and house; close relationship with children and own mother who helps her; centre of family

Boys Go to work as early as possible; not close to father; strict discipline

Girls Help in home, close to mother; marry early

Reached this form of relationship by 1950

The symmetrical family

Joint conjugal roles

Reached this form of relationship by mid-1960s

1970

Husband Spends leisure time at home with family; helps wife with housework and childcare; close emotional bond with wife and children

Wife Often has part-time work; close relationship with husband/children; main responsibility still home and children; equal head of household

1970

Boys Close to parents; stays at school longer; treated with relaxed discipline

Girls Help mother; close to parents; school progress and career regarded as important; stricter control of leisure activities

Source: Adapted from M Young and P Willmott, *The Symmetrical Family* (Penguin, 1975)

The view that there has been a move towards greater equality in marriage between husband and wife has been challenged by feminists.

Draw a simple chart to show which activities/tasks are done

in your household in one week by:
a) the husband;
b) the wife.

Do you agree with the last part of the diagram above?

The other side of the picture: Inequality at home

In the early 1970s, Ann Oakley studied a small number of housewives in London.

Wives were asked: 'Do you agree with men doing housework and looking after children?'

They replied: 'I don't agree with men doing housework'; 'I don't think it's a man's job ... I certainly wouldn't like to see my husband cleaning a room up'; 'I don't think it's mannish for a man to stay at home. I like a man to be a man.'

'Unmanly', 'unnatural', 'unmasculine' and 'henpecked' were words which constantly appeared in these replies.

	Number of respondents	Housework			Childcare		
		High	Medium	Low	High	Medium	Low
Working class	20	2	1	17	2	8	10
Middle class	20	4	9	7	8	4	8

Husbands' help with housework and childcare by social class

Source: Adapted from A Oakley, *The Sociology of Housework* (Martin Robertson, 1974)

1 Examine the table. Overall, do husbands help with
   a) housework?
   b) childcare?

2 Are there any differences between the working and middle class?

3 Looking at the comments of the wives, do you think that they expected their husbands to take equal responsibility for housework and childcare?

4 Bearing in mind this information and your own experience in your home, would you definitely argue that the typical relationship is symmetrical?

Children and parents

How has the relationship between children and parents changed?

This century, and particularly the last 40 years, has seen a revolution in the way that children have been treated by parents. Before this the father was the undisputed head of the family, with children expected to accept his orders without question. There were no benefits from the State, little protection against the violence in the home, and it was generally agreed that children were inferior creatures whose opinions were not worth listening to.

There were, however, social class differences. The sons of the *middle class* were likely to attend a grammar or public school and be groomed for a career in the professions. The girls were not educated for a career, but to be good wives. Because the children were often sent away from home for their schooling, the relationship between parents and children would often be rather cool.

Parents and children in a simple society

But the pygmies have learned from the animals around them to doze with one eye open and a sleepy midday camp can become filled in a minute with shouts and yells and tearful protestations as some baby, crawling around this warm friendly world, crawls into a bed of hot ashes or over a column of army ants. In a moment he will be surrounded by angry adults and given a sound slapping, then carried unceremoniously back to the safety of a hut. It does not matter much which hut because as far as the child is concerned all adults are his parents or grand-parents, they are all equally likely to slap him for doing wrong, or fondle and feed him with delicacies if he is quiet and gives them no trouble. He knows his real father and mother of course and has a special affection for them and they for him, but from an early age he learns he is the child of them all. . . .

The pygmies have no special words to indicate their own parents, like 'mum' and 'dad'. For them all adults in the group are given the same name.

Source: C Turnbull, *The Forest People* (Picador, 1976)

In Britain, children are extremely close to their parents, rather than any other people, Parents' love is focused almost exclusively on their own children, not on other people's.

1 Who has the 'right' to discipline children in pygmy society?

2 From your own experience, who has this right in Britain today?

3 What does the passage mean when it says 'he learns he is the child of them all'?

4 Why do you think the pygmies have no special word for 'mum' and 'dad'?

5 What does the extract show us about the belief in our society that the only 'proper' way to bring up a child is to have an extremely close relationship between parents and children to the exclusion of everybody else? (In your answer you might find it helpful to think about the idea of 'culture'.)

Amongst the *working class*, children were expected to contribute financially to the family at the earliest possible opportunity, leaving school and assuming adult responsibilities at a very early age. Although the relationship between father and children was cool, that between mother and daughter was usually strong.

In the last 40 years, attitudes towards children in first the middle, and later the working class have shifted towards a stress on emotional warmth, greater freedom, a decline in the father's authority and an increasing acceptance of the need to listen to the views of children.

The reasons for the changes in child/parent relationships are connected with the smaller size of families, so that children are treated more as individuals; with higher educational standards and maturity of children, and with a change in views on the correct way to bring up children. Psychologists and other experts now tell us to bring up children with love and affection in order to create an emotionally stable adult.

However, it would be wrong to say that *all* parents now bring up children with love and affection. Cruelty to children is still widespread, and the National Society for the Prevention of Cruelty to Children (NSPCC) estimate that about 6000 children are deliberately injured by their parents each year.

An "outsider's" view of parent-child relationships

In 1985 Stopes-Roe and Cochrane studied 120 Sikh, Hindu and Muslim families living in Britain about their views of the British.

Our Asian respondents gave us their views of English family life. Their opinions on family life pursued a similar theme; the apparent separateness and independence of family members. The Asian parents in particular seized upon the differences in family ties in Asian and English families. Some saw the English emphasis on the marriage relationship and the weaker ties with parents, brothers or sisters and children as a difference. But it could also be seen as destroying family life altogether. 'Their family life – what is it?' asked a Muslim father. 'They live separately and they split up soon. There is little co-operation and unity.' A Hindu mother put it down to selfishness. 'They are not willing to invest their whole lives in family and children.'

Both parents and young children commented on the expectation of early independence for children of English families – at 18 or even 16 years old. But the parents had stronger things to say about it. As two Sikh fathers put it 'Children are neglected – and their children pay rent – it's not right'. 'They're very individual – they kick their children out at 18.'

Source: Adapted from M Stopes-Roe and R Cochrane, 'As others see us . . .' in *New Society*, 1 November 1985

1 From the comments the Asian respondents made, find *four* differences between Asian family life and (their view of) English family life.

2 Which style of family life do you prefer? Give reasons for your answers.

3 Imagine a situation in which you find that you need help. Which family do you think would be more likely to give it, the British or the Asian?

4 What is your view on the comments about being 'kicked out' at 18?

5 The Asian family stresses obedience, especially by girls, to the wishes of the parents. If parents disapprove of an activity then the children cannot do it. What are your views?

Describe in your own words what has happened here

Now describe what has happened here.
Are there any differences? What do you think the two stories can tell us concerning our expectations of male and female roles?

Gender differences emerge too in the way children are socialised (see pages 51–4). Girls are expected to help their mothers with housework, such as cleaning and washing up; while only a very small proportion of boys help their mothers. The children are given different toys, with girls receiving dolls, which they wash and dress, and boys receiving racing cars which they pull apart. We expect different behaviour too. Girls are supposed to be gentle, and boys tough and boisterous. If they do not conform to this, comments are made. Even our language is different, if boys are handsome, then girls are pretty. Clearly the family is passing on the appropriate patterns of behaviour expected of boys and girls in our society; ultimately for the girl the stress is on motherhood, for the boy on a successful career.

The older generation and the family

For the first time in history, a person can now reasonably expect to live into his/her 70s. This means that there has been a huge growth in the number of three generation families (grandparents, parents, children).

It is often claimed that old people were held in high esteem in pre-industrial societies, though it is difficult to prove this. It is likely that, since so few people lived to any great age, there was a degree of status in simply having survived. As the oldest male in each family usually owned the land (in agricultural societies land equals wealth), he clearly remained powerful until his death.

Are old people isolated?

In modern society old age is normal and, as the older generation have little economic power over the young, the status of old people generally is low. This affects relationships within the family. Some writers have gone so far as to claim that old people are often abandoned in our society and are not wanted by their children when they become a burden. To support this argument they point to the growth of 'nursing homes' for the elderly. However, the evidence does not seem to support this extreme argument. It is true that over half of those aged 75+ live alone, but this seems to be because they *choose* to do so.

Children or, more accurately, daughters still look after their parents, and maintain close contact by telephone and visits. One useful way of under- standing the importance of older people in the family, is to look at the **family life cycle**. By this, sociologists mean that as people move through the various stages of life, from young married couple with dependent children through to old age, help, both physical (baby-sitting) and financial (loans), flows from one age group to the other. Where grandparents are healthy and possibly financially sound, they give help to their children who are in the phase of setting up home and family and therefore in need of help. As the older generation become infirm, it is their turn to be helped.

A family cycle?

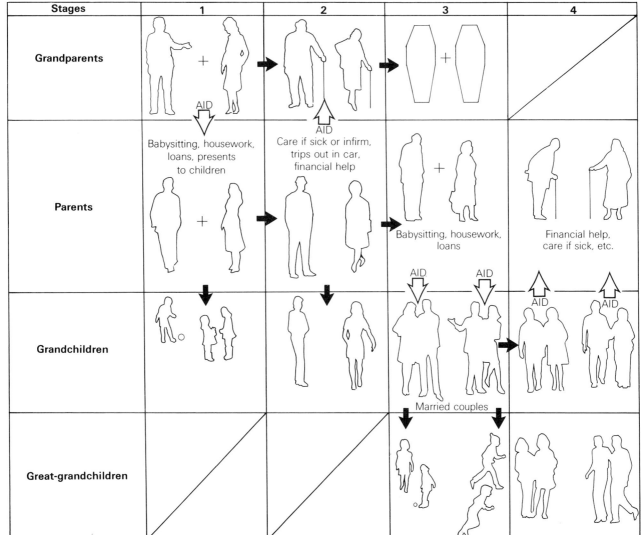

The family life cycle

The family and industrialisation: A summary

	The pre-industrial family	Industrialisation and the family	The family today
Structure	Mainly nuclear families, but the better-off had larger households, as people came to stay with them; late marriage; small families because of the high death-rate of children	Working-class families – became extended as numbers of children increased because of higher child survival rates (results of medical improvements) and people crowded into limited housing available in towns Middle-class families – became extended, as younger generation remained at home until they were economically free to leave and set up own house	Nuclear families, with connections by telephone/car to wider kin (although Asian families are extended)
Relationships	Not very close or warm; marriage and child-rearing mainly for economic reasons; idea of 'love' is unusual	Working-class – children close to mother; father and mother not close at all; women oppressed by men Middle-class – children not close to parent; father-mother, cold relationship; women oppressed by men	Close family relationships, the 'privatised' family; husband and wife fairly equal. 'symmetrical'; women still expected to be responsible for domestic matters; children are seen as extremely important
Functions	Family very important as all worked together in the home or on the farm; family looked after its members if they survived to old age	Working-class – family very important for survival; pooling of economic resources; helped each other where possible in all matters; older generation looked after by younger generation	Mainly emotional, but still practical and financial help (loans etc.) when needed; State and voluntary services assist or replace the family in many of its functions
Wider setting	Agricultural society, people living in the countryside in small villages	Industrialised society, people living in large towns	A mobile family moving for promotion and to take job opportunities; people living in suburbs; light industry and offices are places of work

Divorce

It is commonly argued that marriages are increasingly likely to end in divorce and therefore marriage for life, as we have traditionally known it, is disappearing. It is true that the number of divorces has increased rapidly: since 1960 the increase each year has been about 10 per cent, from 26 000 then to over 170 000 today and if we go back to the 1930s, the annual divorce figures were less than 5000 per year. The rise in divorce in Britain reflects the trend in most European countries. There was a massive upsurge after the Second World War, caused by the disruption of the war to family life and relationships. In the 1950s there was a slight decline, but divorce continued at a higher level than before the war. Then, in the 1960s, there was another sharp rise to today's high level.

Patterns of marriage and divorce

Changes in the law and the divorce rate

Year	Number of divorces	Major changes in the law
1857		Divorce available through the court for the first time. This law allowed men to obtain divorces if their wives were unfaithful. However, this reason was not sufficient for women to obtain divorces; they had to prove cruelty against them, as well. The law reflected the Victorian attitudes towards women. No divorce available for the working class, only a 'legal separation'.
1921	3000	
1923		Women received equality with men under the law, regarding grounds for divorce. They began to get custody of the children.
1931	4200	
1937		The law extended grounds for divorce to include adultery, cruelty (mental and physical) and desertion. Divorce became easier to obtain.
1941	7500	
1945		End of the Second World War – great social disruption
1949		People could apply for legal aid to obtain divorces. This was particularly helpful for housewives who had no income of their own.
1951	39 000	
1961	32 000	
1969		The irretrievable breakdown of marriage became the only grounds for divorce, no proof of 'misconduct' was necessary. Two years' mutually agreed separation, or five years' if only one partner wanted divorce, was all that was necessary.
1971	111 000	
1981	145 000	
1984	145 000	

Source for divorce figures: *Social Trends* (HMSO, 1986)

Using the information above, draw a graph to show the changes in the divorce rate.

Today one in three marriages are likely to end in divorce

But the institution of marriage is not dead. It is important to remember that today in Great Britain, 78 per cent of people in private households still live in families headed by a married couple – a proportion which has fallen only slightly from 1961 (82 per cent).

Source: *New Society*, 3 January 1985

A comparison of marriage rates

Persons marrying	1974	1984
Bachelors	302 000	255 000
Divorced men	64 000	81 000
Widowers	18 000	12 000
Spinsters	305 000	260 000
Divorced women	62 000	77 000
Widows	18 000	12 000

Source: Adapted from *Social Trends* (HMSO, 1986)

1 What is the clear trend in divorce statistics?

2 What do the changes in the law tell you about attitudes to marriage?

3 Do the legal changes tell us anything about the position of women in society?

4 Give three *legal* reasons why there has been an increase in the divorce rate.

5 If a person marries today, what chance is there of them remaining married, according to the information above?

6 What proportion of people live in households headed by a married couple?

7 The information given above seems contradictory, if you compare the likelihood of divorce with the percentage of married people.
Can you offer any explanation to resolve this apparent contradiction? (An examination of the table of marriage rates might help.)

Reasons for the rise in divorce rates

Legal changes

Why have divorce rates increased so greatly this century?

Quite simply, it is much easier to obtain a divorce today than ever before. Since 1969 the only reason needed to obtain a divorce has been the 'irretrievable breakdown of the marriage'. So, if two people feel they cannot stay together any longer, they can divorce. This contrasts very strongly with the previous situation where one partner had to prove that the other partner had done something wrong, such as being unfaithful or using violence against them.

It would be wrong however to see changes in the law as causes of increases in the divorce rate. The law changed as a response to changes in the attitudes of people towards marriage and the family.

Decline of religion

The importance and influence of the churches have been in decline throughout this century. Marriage has traditionally been viewed as a holy institution and the 'bonds of matrimony' as sacred. The decline of the churches' influence has meant that people do not regard their marriage vows as tying them for life to their partners. In line with this, the stigma (disgrace) attached to divorce which prevented many people from divorcing has been considerably weakened.

The attitudes of women

There is general agreement that it is women who are the 'losers' in many marriages. They give up their work, their financial independence, in return for the role of housewife and mother. The rising status of women in society and their increasing refusal to accept the traditional 'inferior' roles of housewife and mother, with the man in charge of the household, has meant that 70 per cent of divorces are now started by wives.

A housewife talking

I think a lot of women now, they all want to work because they all feel like me, feel they are chained in and life's passing them by, without going out and doing something and talking. I find this, talking I sort of want to talk and when Nick [her husband] comes home and is tired, he'll come in and he just switches off mentally and he just laughs at me and says, 'Well, I'm just neutral, coasting'. He sits back and I'm saying, 'Talk, talk to me, for God's sake talk to me.' I've got nobody to talk to all day and I do think now women need to get out, because staying in the house in the company of just little ones does drive you mad, especially when the husband comes home and can't be bothered to talk to you because he is tired out. I know when someone comes in I usually talk them to death.

Source: S Sharpe, *Double Identity* (Pelican, 1984)

1 Why do many women want to work, according to the speaker?

2 What is the main problem in her life? How could her husband help her to overcome this problem?

3 In your opinion, who benefits more from marriage, men or women? What reasons can you give for your answer?

The clash of backgrounds

The sheer size and complexity of modern urban society (large towns and cities) means that it is likely that couples from very different social and ethnic backgrounds will meet and marry. Clearly the potential for trouble between the couple will be increased by their different expectations and attitudes. Alongside this problem of 'cultural diversity' is the fact that the community in most cities has been weakened with the growth of suburbs, where everyone minds their own business. The traditional pressures imposed on a couple with a faltering marriage, by the local community and by the extended family, no longer exist.

The romantic marriage

Traditionally, and even in Asian arranged marriages in Britain today, love was not the most important element of marriage. It was more important that there was a stable union between two well-matched people, linking two families. By contrast, the cultural stress in contemporary Britain is on 'falling in love'. Indeed, a recent survey of people under 25 found that romance was regarded as the most important quality in a good marriage. But if the couple 'fall out of love', there is little to hold them together. By contrast, where love is not so important but the maintenance of the family is, the bonds holding the family together are far tougher.

Three views of marriage

Divorce is one kind of mechanism for dealing with the pressures and problems caused by marriage. However, there have traditionally been other ways of reducing marital conflict.

In pre-1948 China, the roles of husband and wife were clearly defined. Respect and not romantic love was demanded between husband and wife. There was an extended family system, so that intimate emotional contact between husband and wife was less intense than in our own system. Incorrect marital behaviour was prevented in part by supervision by older relatives. If the wife built up a reservoir of hatred and fear, it was more likely to be aimed at the mother-in-law, rather than the husband.

Source: Adapted from W J Goode, *World Revolution and Family Patterns* (Free Press, 1970)

For many girls, in particular working-class girls, marriage and motherhood are attractive and seemingly realistic goals. Marriage stands out against the starkness and drabness of work, it provides acceptable evidence of maturity and adulthood, and it is an important investment for the future.

It is only after marriage that women realise its isolation and emptiness.

Source: M Brake, *The Sociology of Youth Cultures and Youth Subcultures* (Routledge and Kegan Paul, 1980)

Hardnev Jassar has been looking for a husband for her daughter, who is 19 for two years now. 'He must be a decent working man, but he need not be rich or educated,' she says.

Source: P Harrison, 'The Patience of Southall' in *New Society*, 4 April 1974

1 The first two extracts compare traditional attitudes to love with girls' attitudes today. Write a paragraph comparing the two views on marriage.

2 Which in your opinion would lead to a lower divorce rate? Explain the reasons for your answer.

3 Looking at the third extract, would you like your mother to find a husband/wife for you? Suggest two advantages of arranged marriages.

4 Rank the qualities listed below in order of importance to you in choosing a partner. Then ask your parents to rank them if they were choosing a partner for you. How different are they, if at all? Why are they different?

attractive	well-educated
good job	fun-loving
pleasant personality	sexy
honest and truthful	

The continuing strength of marriage: Conclusions

Is the institution of marriage on the verge of collapse?

The points made so far on the increase in divorce do seem to support the argument that marriage is less firmly rooted in our society than in the past. This assertion is supported by the fact that on present trends one in three of contemporary marriages will end in divorce.

However, it is important to remember that the liberalisation of divorce (which has made divorcing easier), the weakening of pressures in the outside community, and the freedom from fear of stigma, have all encouraged people who were unhappily married to take the option of divorce instead of being trapped. More unhappiness would have been caused by two people continuing to live together when they did not really want to.

A second important point is that divorcees are very likely to marry again; indeed about 70 per cent find another partner, the majority within five years. So divorcees are not rejecting marriage, but their particular relationships. This is clearly linked to the high expectations mentioned earlier. This pattern of divorce and remarriage has been called **serial monogamy**.

Finally, surveys indicate that the majority of people firmly believe in the family and marriage, and almost 90 per cent of adults do still marry.

Children and divorce

How does divorce affect the children?

Each year about 160 000 children are caught up in divorces, almost a third of these under the age of five. The first result of this is that many of these children will live, for some time at least, in single-parent families. At the moment, 1.5 million children live in these circumstances.

The effects of divorce on children

It is generally agreed that unhappy marriages with all the bitterness and tension involved may be more harmful for children than a straightforward separation.

Younger children seem to adapt less well than older children. This is particularly serious when one sees the rise in the number of children under five years old who become involved in divorces. A major problem is the use of children by parents as weapons to get at each other. This, and battles over custody, may cause greater emotional disturbances than the actual divorce. Re-marriage creates step-families which do have special problems coping with the arrival of 'new' mothers and fathers. Friction is common in these situations.

CHAPTER EIGHT
POPULATION

Demography

The study of population concentrates on the changing *size* of the population; the changes in the *age* structure of the population; the changing patterns of *where* in the country people live; and finally the proportions of one *sex* compared to the other. The correct term for the study of the population is **demography**.

Where do we get the information from?

The government does most of the fact finding. Every birth, marriage, divorce and death has to be notified to the local government registrar. The information is then sent on to the government statistical office. A second crucial source of information is the **census**, which is the national survey of every household in Britain taken every ten years by the government.

What use is the information that is collected?

If a government wants to plan ahead sensibly for the welfare of the population then it needs to know how many people there are, where they live and how old they are. They can then make decisions on such things as:

- the health services – if they are going to be more elderly people then more geriatric wards have to be built, nurses trained in handling old people etc. If more babies are going to be born, then greater investment must take place in maternity services. Also, knowing where the majority of people live allows the government to put more resources in these areas;
- the welfare services – if there are more old people, for example, then more money needs to be allocated to pensions and to home helps and specialist social workers;
- education – knowing the numbers and ages of children allows the government to plan the numbers, types and locations of schools.

At any one time the size of the country's population is the result of:

- the number of births;
- the number of deaths;
- the number of people entering or leaving the country.

Births

When discussing the changes in the number of births each year, sociologists often talk about the **birth-rate**, which is the number of babies born in a year for every 1000 people in the population. The higher the birth-rate, the more babies are born. Sometimes the term the **fertility rate** is used. This means the number of children born for every 1000 women of child-bearing age (approximately 15–40 years of age).

Changes in the birth-rate this century

How has the birth-rate changed this century?

Generally this century the birth rate has fallen. In 1901, for example, the birth-rate was 28.6, by 1951 it had fallen to 15.7, and in 1984 it was 12.8, under half that at the beginning of the century.

The decline in the birth-rate was not regular though, and in certain periods the birth-rate has actually increased. The increases occurred in the period immediately after the Second World War, then again from the middle of the 1950s to 1964, and finally since 1978 there has been a slight recovery in the numbers of births from the lowest point in 1977.

There was an old woman who lived in a shoe. She had so many children 'cos she didn't know what to do

There was a young women who lived in a shoe. She had only two children, 'cos she knew exactly what to do

Reasons for the fall in the birth-rate over this century

Why has the birth-rate fallen this century?

The most obvious reason is that methods of birth control have become increasingly available over the century and more widely used. However, to know that something exists does not mean that it will be used. People chose to use birth control methods to limit their family size. The following reasons have been suggested.

The costs of children

In the past when there was no State pension, then the best investment for old age was a large family to look after you. Today, the costs of keeping children until they leave full-time education at 16 (or increasingly 18) are high and the need for them in old age has declined.

Standards of living

Closely linked to the first point is the fact that people prefer to have a higher standard of living than spend their lives and their money rearing children.

Declining influence of religion

Churches have generally looked with disapproval on the use of birth control. The decline in the influence of the churches has meant that people no longer regard birth control as wrong.

Changing attitudes of women

This is probably the most important influence on the declining birth-rate. Over this century, women have changed their views on their role. Traditionally women were expected to stay at home most of their adult lives, to be housewives and mothers. Today, women want careers of their own and see being a mother as just one part of their lives. The result has been the fact that fewer children are wanted, so that women can return to work. Childbearing now occurs much later in life, commonly around 30 years of age and women return to work on average only 3½ years after the birth of their last child.

Cultural expectations

All the explanations above combine together to lower the birth-rate and, as a result, it has become regarded as *normal* to have only two children. People are now coming to expect this from marriage and to regard larger families as slightly abnormal.

Reasons for the periodic rises in the birth-rate this century

The reasons for the rise in births in the late 1940s was that the Second World War (1939–45) had separated many couples, and on being reunited they wished to start, or complete, their families. Six years of births were compressed into only a few post-war years.

The rise in the birth-rate in the late 1950s and early 1960s was due to a period of low unemployment and high wages. Young couples were particularly well-off and married young. Early marriages plus affluence led to large families.

The latest rise in the birth-rate, in the 1980s (although it is still very low compared to the 1950s) was caused by two things. First, those women who had delayed having children, as we saw earlier, now began to have them. Secondly, those people born in the 1950s expansion were now old enough to have their own children.

Family size

Do all classes and ethnic groups have the same family size?

Family size and social class

The result of the decline in the birth-rate has been smaller families. In 1900, for example, an average family had 3.4 children. Today, the size of family is almost halved, with the average number of children down to less than two per family.

However, the decline in family size has not proceeded at the same pace across the social classes. The middle class has always been ahead of the working class by about twenty years in reducing average family size. This seems to be because they first saw the advantages of smaller families and were more likely to know about, and want to use, contraceptives. Today, the differences in family size is very small; the most popular number of children in all social classes is two.

Family size and ethnic groups

The average family size for the ethnic groups in Britain varies considerably. There are two main factors which influence the size of families to Asians and Blacks. The first is the culture of the country from which they come, and the second is the age and sex distribution.

Culture

The culture of most ethnic minorities stresses the importance of having many children, in much the same way as the British culture did before the Welfare State was introduced. The reasons are the same: children look after their parents in old age. Secondly, the religion of most of the immigrant groups frowns upon forms of birth control, particularly amongst the Muslims from Pakistan and Bangladesh. However, it does appear that over time the influence of British culture and the stress upon family limitation has an effect and the children of immigrants gradually drop their birth-rates nearer to those of the white population.

Age and sex distribution

This is also important. There are more people in the ethnic minorities of child-bearing age and the result is a relatively high number of births. Amongst Pakistani and Bangladeshi groups, in particular, the wives were left in the country of origin while the husbands tried to build up a new life in Britain. Only relatively recently have the wives rejoined their husbands, so that the birth-rate is affected by this rather like the situation in Britain after the Second World War.

The present situation is that there has been a large drop in the number of children born to those of Caribbean and Indian origins, and a large increase in the numbers of children born to those of Pakistani and Bangladeshi origins.

The age and sex of the population

Below are three 'population pyramids'; pyramid A represents the typical sort of distribution of age and sex. The bottom of the pyramid is wide, because the numbers of people being born each year is gradually increasing. The pyramid gradually narrows as people die and so the numbers of older people gradually diminishes until there is hardly anybody over the age of 90.

The two sides of the pyramids represent the numbers of males and females in the population. They ought to be roughly equal.

The pyramid B represents Britain in 1981. The pyramid C is an estimate of the situation in 2021.

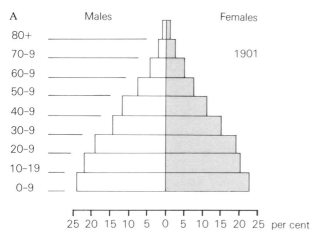

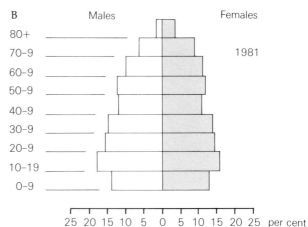

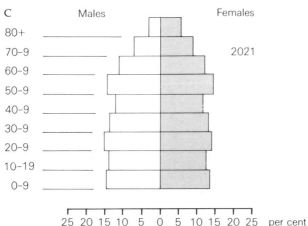

Source: *Social Trends* (HMSO, 1986)

1 What is happening to the numbers of people over the age of 60 in the three pyramids?

2 Describe the changes in the 0–9-years-old group.

3 Can you suggest any reasons for these changes?

4 In the pyramid for 1981 what is noticeable for the 10–19 group? Can you suggest any explanation for this?

5 Comparing males with females, is there any age group in which the number of women is noticeably greater than the number of men?

6 It has been suggested that Britain has an 'ageing' population. Using the information given above, can you explain what this means?

Deaths

What has happened to the death-rate in the last 100 years?

The usual measure of changes in the numbers of deaths is the **death-** or **mortality rate**, which is the number of deaths each year for every 1000 people in the population.

The death-rate declined very rapidly in the last century and in the very early part of this century. But since the 1920s there has only been a very slight fall. At present, the death-rate is 11.7 for males and 11.2 for females.

Reasons for the decline in the death-rate

In the last century there was a massive programme of public health improvements – decent drainage and guaranteed supplies of pure water, for example. This eliminated many of the killer diseases, such as cholera and typhoid. In this century, programmes of immunisation began to combat other diseases, such as polio and diphtheria, and the introduction of the National Health Service improved health care standards.

However, it has been argued that the improvements in the standards of living this century are more important than medical advances. Improved diets, better quality housing and shorter working hours have all led to a much stronger resistance to illness than ever before.

Infant mortality

A very important element of the declining death-rate has been the fall in the number of infants dying, generally measured by the **infant mortality rate**, which is the number of children under one year of age dying for every 1000 children born.

The fall in infant mortality has been very marked this century, with big reductions even in the last 30 years. In 1961, for example, the death-rate was still about 22, whereas by 1984 it had fallen to less then ten. Compare this with a figure of 72 per thousand in 1921! The reasons for the decline in the infant mortality rate are much the same as for the death-rate in general, but also reflect the much improved midwife and maternity services of the State. It ought to be noted however, that the death-rate for infants of working-class families is much higher than that of the middle class. This is partly a reflection of the better standards of housing and diet of the middle class.

Life expectancy

Is it true that people live longer nowadays?

The number of people aged over 65 is nearly five times greater now than in 1901. Today, 15 per cent of the population are in this age group. At the age of 20 a young man can expect to live to his early 70s and a young women to her late 70s. In short, people live longer lives than they have ever done

before, and an increasingly larger number of people can *expect* to have longer lives.

Long life is caused by the very reasons that lowered the death-rate; that is, higher standards of living, better housing conditions, better diets, better working conditions and shorter hours, and medical advances.

Sex differences in life expectancy

Women are more likely than men to survive into old age. The reasons are that they are less likely to smoke or drink as heavily as men. They are less likely to be killed in motor vehicle accidents; and they are less likely to work in dangerous occupations. Of course, in the past the two World Wars led to many more men dying than women. By the age of 75 women out-number men by two to one.

Problems associated with an ageing population

For society as a whole, the **burden of dependency** increases. By this we mean that the costs of supporting the elderly, for example in pensions and extra hospital places, must be paid for by extra taxation. For families, the problem will be the need to care for an increasing number of elderly people at home. This burden falls mainly on the wife or daughter. For the old people themselves, there will be some cases of loneliness, of poverty and of a long period of physical decline before death.

Migration

International migration

Is immigration an important influence on the size of our population?

In 1984 201 000 people came to live in Britain and 164 000 left the country to live abroad. When people come into a country to live, it is termed **immigration**. When people leave the country to live abroad, it is called **emigration**.

Since the 1950s the numbers emigrating from Britain have been slightly higher than those coming here to live, although unusually in 1983 and 1984 more people came into Britain than left. The difference between immigration totals and emigration totals is known as **net migration**.

Britain attracts people from the Indian subcontinent (Indians, Pakistanis and Bangladeshis), from Australia, the EEC and the United States. British people generally emigrate to Australia and Canada.

Consequences of the growing numbers of the elderly

FOR INDIVIDUALS
Positive consequences:
Escape from the drudgery of work; more time for leisure interests, education, learning new skills, involvement with family
Negative consequences: Loss of income, status and sense of purpose with loss of jobs (especially if it is professional/managerial); loss of social contacts and deterioration in health

FOR THE FAMILY
Positive consequences:
The elderly can provide help and companionship for the younger generations, babysitting, childcare, etc. (depends on their stage in the 'family life cycle').
Negative consequences:
Infirm, elderly people place a great burden in terms of care on the younger generation. It is usually women who have to look after them, some having to give up their jobs and social lives.

FOR SOCIETY
Health and social services demands are very heavy and costly, with over 35 per cent of welfare costs for older people and pensions for the retired, involve heavy insurance burden on those working – known as the 'burden of dependency'.

The rapidly changing nature of society means that the experience of the old is no longer valued by the young. This leads to a loss of status of the elderly in society.

But
much of the so-called burden of dependency is really a reflection of *political* decisions to make people retire at 60/65, causing poverty and loss of status. Retirement creates jobs for the young.

To find out more about the elderly, take a tape recorder and ask them about their lives and their family. Compare your information with what is here.

You might want to question your own grandparents (if over 60) and some people in special homes for the elderly.

More information can be obtained from the charity 'Help the Aged'.

In the 1950s immigrants began to arrive first from the West Indies and then from the Indian sub-continent. They came because of poverty at home and because there were not enough workers in Britain to fill all the job vacancies. From 1962 onward there was a series of laws restricting the numbers of new immigrants. Since then, those arriving have been the *dependent* relatives (such as children and wives) of those already here. (There is a full discussion on immigration on pages 62–3).

Internal migration

The move to the south-east

The distribution of Britain's population is increasingly becoming unbalanced. More people are emigrating to the south-east (excluding London, which is actually losing population) from other parts of Britain. The greatest decline in population has been in Scotland, Wales, the West Midlands and the north of England. In these areas, in particular, the birth-rate cannot match the numbers leaving. Some of the greatest areas of growth have been Suffolk, Norfolk, Essex and Cambridgeshire.

Why? The main force driving people to move is the lack of jobs in the north, Scotland and Wales. As most of the jobs are now in the south-east, that is where people have to go.

What changes in population are taking place within Britain?

Would a sight like this have been likely in 1890? Explain your answer.
Go to a local graveyard, check the dates and ages of the deceased. What does this information tell you?

Births, deaths and migration this century

The graph below shows a) the numbers of births and deaths in the United Kingdom over the century and b) the changes in migration. The difference between the numbers of births and the numbers of deaths is known as the **natural increase** (or **decrease**).

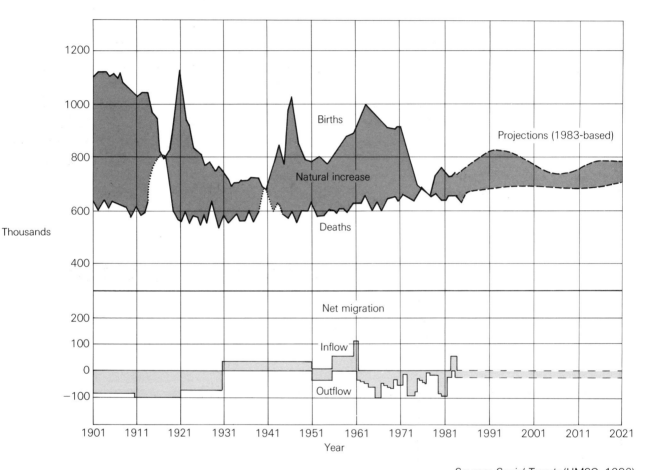

Source: *Social Trends* (HMSO, 1986)

You must also read the main text to answer these questions.

1 In what three years were the numbers of births at their highest after 1915?

2 Can you suggest reasons for these peaks in the numbers of births?

3 What change occurred in the numbers of births after 1964?

4 What reasons can you suggest for this change?

5 What happened to the numbers of births between 1948 and 1955?

6 Can you explain these changes?

7 In what year was there the highest inflow of immigrants? Can you suggest a reason for this (see pages 62–3)?

Factors influencing population size

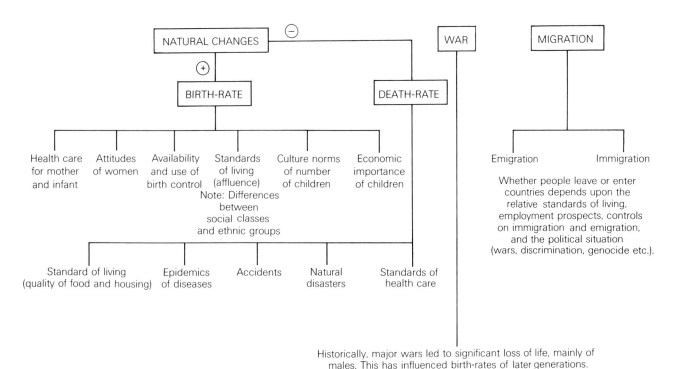

NATURAL CHANGES (−)   WAR   MIGRATION

(+)

BIRTH-RATE   DEATH-RATE

Health care | Attitudes | Availability | Standards | Culture norms | Economic
for mother | of women | and use of | of living | of number | importance
and infant | | birth control | (affluence) | of children | of children

Note: Differences
between
social classes
and ethnic groups

Standard of living | Epidemics | Accidents | Natural | Standards of
(quality of food and housing) | of diseases | | disasters | health care

Emigration   Immigration

Whether people leave or enter
countries depends upon the
relative standards of living,
employment prospects, controls
on immigration and emigration,
and the political situation
(wars, discrimination, genocide etc.).

Historically, major wars led to significant loss of life, mainly of
males. This has influenced birth-rates of later generations.

Look at the things affecting:
    a) the birth-rate;
    b) the death-rate;
    c) migration.

Make brief comments on each of these, using the information provided in this chapter.

World population

An increasing proportion of people live in the under-developed nations of the world. This is because in most developed nations the birth-rates are so low that deaths equal births.

By contrast there are high birth-rates in the under-developed countries and more infants are surviving than in the past. High birth-rates and increasing life expectancy are the two

ingredients of a population explosion, and 90 per cent of the increase in population of the world in the next 25 years will be in the under-developed nations.

The now affluent industrial-ised countries experienced population explosions them-selves in the nineteenth century. Before that time, births and deaths were in a rough balance, with very slight population growth. As

industrialisation progressed, medical advances and higher standard of living meant a steep decline in the death-rate, particularly in infant mortality. The population increased rapidly. Then, in the early part of this century, people began to limit their families, as they no longer needed large numbers of children. This led to the current situation of a balance between births and deaths.

This process from pre-industrial slight growth of population to the present ageing population is known as 'demographic transition'.

The continuing large families in under-developed nations make perfect sense. In societies with virtually no welfare system or pensions, and high risk of unemploy-ment and sickness, large families are a hedge against disaster. The larger the family, the more likely it is that some member will be making an income.

In such countries it is the elderly with fewest children whose poverty is most acute. The World Fertility Survey, conducted in 60 countries in 1980 showed that for Third World countries one of the main reasons for wanting a large family was to provide for the parents in their old age.

When it was thought that the demographic transition would occur automatically, when the industrial development of a country reached a certain state, it now seems that the distribution of income and welfare within a country is crucial. Poorer countries with fairer distribution of income and with social security systems show more rapidly falling birth-rates than richer countries where industrialisation has mainly enriched the better-off.

When the European countries experienced their population explosions they coped by importing large quantities of food and materials from abroad and by exporting population (to the empire). This solution is not possible for Third World countries today, too poor to import food (indeed having to export it) and with the richer countries imposing strict immigration control.

Source: Adapted from 'World Population' in *New Society*, 31 January 1986

1 Where is the bulk of world population growth taking place?

2 What three stages of population change are there in the 'demographic transition'?

3 If all the poor people in the Third World (under-developed nations) were given free contraceptives and advice, would this limit population growth?

4 Why does the theory of demographic transition not apply to the Third World?

5 What does the article suggest is the best method to ensure a decline in population growth?

6 Look at the diagram on page 137 and make brief comments on each of the factors influencing population as they apply to the Third World.

7 What differences emerge between the Third World and Britain?

CHAPTER NINE
URBAN LIFE

Urbanisation . . .

De-urbanisation . . .

Community . . .

Inner-city problems . . .

The changing countryside . . .

Urbanisation

What caused the growth in cities?

- **Urbanisation:** the process whereby the majority of the population gradually move from the countryside to live in towns and cities

The growth of cities in Britain really begins with industrialisation, around the end of the eighteenth century. Before 1800 only about 15 per cent of the population lived in towns and cities; 100 years later 75 per cent of the population lived in them.

The original growth of the cities was because people moved there from the countryside. As these were generally young people they then caused a rapid increase in the population by having children of their own – the process that is happening in Third World cities today.

The reasons for the move to the cities were of two types.

The nineteenth century saw the rapid expansion of the cities in Britain

Pull reasons

There was work in the cities in the new factories and although the wages and conditions of employment were dreadful, they were better than those in agriculture.

Push reasons

The enclosure of land by large farmers meant that small tenant farmers were evicted (made homeless) and that their land was combined into larger units by the owners. The introduction of machinery and modern mass farming techniques meant that there were fewer jobs available in the countryside. At that time there were no welfare provisions and it was a case of starve or move.

De-urbanisation

What caused the decline in cities?

The large towns and cities have come to be places where the bulk of the population live. At present 90 per cent of the population live in urban areas. However, certain important changes have been taking place.

The move out of the cities

There has been a move away from the cities, towards the outer suburbs, New Towns and the countryside over the last ten years. At the extreme, London has lost 10 per cent of its population and actually declined by two million people from its peak. On the other hand, New Towns such as Milton Keynes and Basildon have increased their populations by 15 per cent.

Why? People prefer the better standard of housing available and the cleaner, less polluted environment of the suburbs and countryside. Cars and trains make travel into the big cities for work fairly quick and easy. However, firms are also moving out of the big cities, preferring the low costs of the New Towns to the advantages of being in the city centres.

Since the 1960s there has been considerable movement out of the cities to the New Towns and the countryside

Flight from the cities

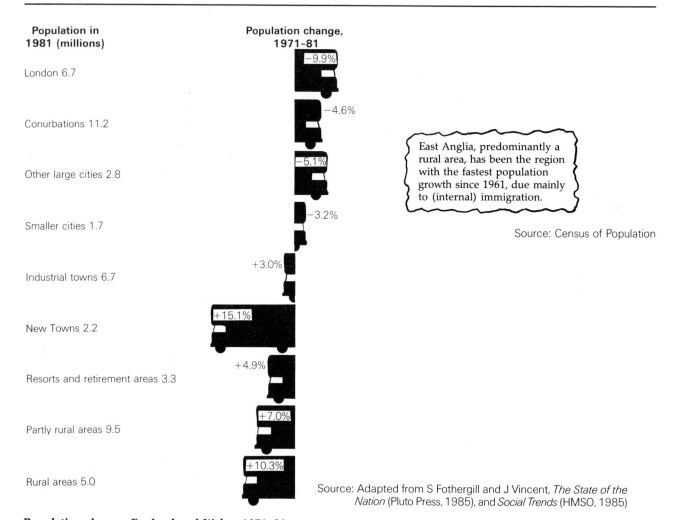

Population in 1981 (millions)

London 6.7

Conurbations 11.2

Other large cities 2.8

Smaller cities 1.7

Industrial towns 6.7

New Towns 2.2

Resorts and retirement areas 3.3

Partly rural areas 9.5

Rural areas 5.0

Population change, 1971–81

−9.9%

−4.6%

−5.1%

−3.2%

+3.0%

+15.1%

+4.9%

+7.0%

+10.3%

East Anglia, predominantly a rural area, has been the region with the fastest population growth since 1961, due mainly to (internal) immigration.

Source: Census of Population

Source: Adapted from S Fothergill and J Vincent, *The State of the Nation* (Pluto Press, 1985), and *Social Trends* (HMSO, 1985)

Population change, England and Wales, 1971–81

The current prosperity of the east is largely:
a) an accident of geography, with the discovery of North Sea oil and gas;
b) due to the fact that the east of Britain is now facing the right way for trade. The rise of the east coast ports reflect the growing importance of links with Europe and Scandinavia. For example, Felixstowe was almost derelict after the last war, today it is Britain's largest container port;
c) East Anglia in general has a good standard of industrial behaviour. It has the lowest rate of industrial stoppages of any region in Britain. The eastward trend in the move of British industry does seem to be a move away from old premises and old working practices;
d) Communication networks are starting to benefit the east and the rural areas with the creation of new motorways, such as the M11 and the M25 orbital around outer London. The new roads network mean new patterns of employment, the new technologies can choose pleasant greenfield sites to settle in. They are not bound to go to old industrial areas like Liverpool and Manchester.

Source: Adapted from D White, 'Tilting Britain onto its Side' in *New Society*, 14 June 1985

1 According to the diagram, which area had the greatest loss of population between 1971–81?

2 According to the diagram, which two areas had the greatest gains?

3 Find the meaning of the term 'conurbation'.

4 What reasons could you suggest for people moving to the New Towns and rural (country) areas (see page 141)?

5 What sorts of towns are considered as 'retirement areas'?

6 According to the extract, which area in Britain has the fastest growth rate, overall?

7 Why should Europe influence the growth rate of an area in England?

8 Your local authority ought to have a 'development plan' for your area. Obtain a copy from your civic centre or central library and find out what is happening to business and population in your area.

Community

The loss of community

What changes took place in peoples lives as cities grew?

As societies moved from being predominantly rural and agricultural, to being urban and industrial, the changes that took place were not just physical, such as the growth of roads, houses and factories, they were also changes in the way people behaved and thought.

Tonnies, a sociologist writing at the end of the last century, said that it was possible to distinguish quite clearly between the social life of the traditional rural society, which he called **Gemeinschaft**, and the social life of the fast moving cities, which he called **Gesellschaft**.

Gemeinschaft

This type of society is one where people have close contact with others, forming a tight social network, and where there is a sense of 'belonging'. People hold very similar values, and in general are very similar to one another. Individuals know each other not just in one role but in many, for instance as brother-in-law/employer/next-door neighbour/regular at the pub. This form of society has also been called **community**.

Was life so idyllic then? Wages were low and healthcare was non-existent. Houses were owned by farmers who were also the only employers. People chose to move to the cities.

Interview your history teacher – ask her/him what a typical farmworker's week was like in the last century.

Gesellschaft

This is the type of society where people have only a superficial relationship with other people, seeing them only at work for instance, but never outside (having a **single-role** relationship). There is little sense of belonging to any community and people are prepared to move away with little regret.

Emile Durkheim, writing at about the same time as Tonnies, suggested that the only thing holding modern industrial (he called it **organic**) society together was the fact that people needed each other in order to survive. In the traditional, rural society (he called it **mechanical**), people were so close because there were so alike.

These sociologists supported the general belief that life is far more anonymous in the cities, with people having few close friends and what contacts they have are short-lived and very narrow.

Community in the city

Are people living in the cities more isolated from each other than those living in the countryside?

However, the research by Willmott and Young in the 1950s in Bethnal Green, London, and of Rosser and Harris in Swansea, showed that at that time there were very close-knit working-class communities within the inner cities. Although these areas have now been demolished, there is still evidence that cities may be just as much communities as are small villages. This is mainly because people break up the large towns into neighbourhoods with which they associate. Furthermore, groups of people join together into clubs based on interests and sport. All this pulls people together.

Increasingly there has been a move into city centres by affluent young people who restore dilapidated houses and create 'new' expensive upper middle-class neighbouthoods. This is known as 'gentrification'.

The community and urban life

The common view is that urbanisation has broken up traditional social bonds, replacing them with anomie (a breakdown in law and order) and alienation (people feel they do not belong); the past represents human warmth and solidarity, the present anonymity and isolation. But a recent study challenges this view. Most people do still have social relationships with people who live nearby. A sizeable minority have relatives living close at hand, have friends within ten minutes' walk and the overwhelming majority have friendly dealings with their neighbours.

It is therefore wrong to suggest that urban communities no longer exist. But there are pressures on it. The growth in mobility is one. More people own and move house, thus dispersing family and friends. One clear finding from research to date is that the sense of community is not more common in small towns than in cities. The scale of the place or the density of the population has nothing to do with it. What does count is people's length of residence. The longer they live in a place, the stronger and more extensive their links.

So newer places are likely to have weaker social networks. But physical layout is important too. The post-war programme of clearance not only broke up local networks but also redeveloped the old districts in forms that made it more difficult for people to get to know their neighbours – people in high rise flats, for instance, are more likely to say there is 'no community' in their area. . . .

The upshot is that whereas in the past community attachment was particularly strong amongst the working-class residents, it may now be stronger amongst the middle class. The traditional community, a densely-woven world of kin, neighbours and friends, is being replaced by the new neighbourhoodism in which people set out to join local organisations and make new friends. Middle-class people are more enthusiastic joiners, everything from the local tennis club to the 'Stop the Bypass' campaign. In this sense they are more involved and active in the community than the working class.

Source: Adapted from J Lawrence, 'The Unknown Neighbourhood' in *New Society*, 6 June 1986

1 What is the traditional view of city life?

2 Does recent research bear this out?

3 Name three factors which influence the creation of a sense of community.

4 In the past it has been the working class who have had the stronger community life. What is happening now?

5 Ask your family/neighbours if they feel there is a 'sense of community' in your area. Do they know the names of most of the people in your street? Does it fit the evidence in the extract above?

Exploding cities

Source: P Cohen and C Gardner, *It ain't half racist Mum* (Comedia, 1982)

Inner city problems

What special problems are faced by people living in the inner cities?

In 1980, 1981 and 1985, there were serious riots in inner London, Birmingham and Liverpool. The causes are described in the diagram opposite. The riots drew attention to the severe problems of youth in the inner cities, but we should be aware that other groups suffer tremendous deprivation too, in particular parents with young children and the elderly.

The modern housing estates of tower blocks developed in the 1960s have no play facilities for children, and women who are at home all day feel imprisoned in their apartments. Depression is common. The elderly are often trapped in areas where they no longer want to be, with neighbourhoods having changed character drastically in the period since they went to live there. They are particularly frightened of crime.

British cities in the 1980s
Take your own photographs of city scenes

All residents of the inner cities face similar problems of noise and pollution from traffic, and a decay in the environment as local authority spending programmes have been cut back. There are fewer doctors than in the suburbs and welfare facilities are poor. Increasingly as firms move out of the cities, employment prospects decline and when this is coupled with the very high costs of housing, this means that poverty is on the increase.

Inner-city disorder

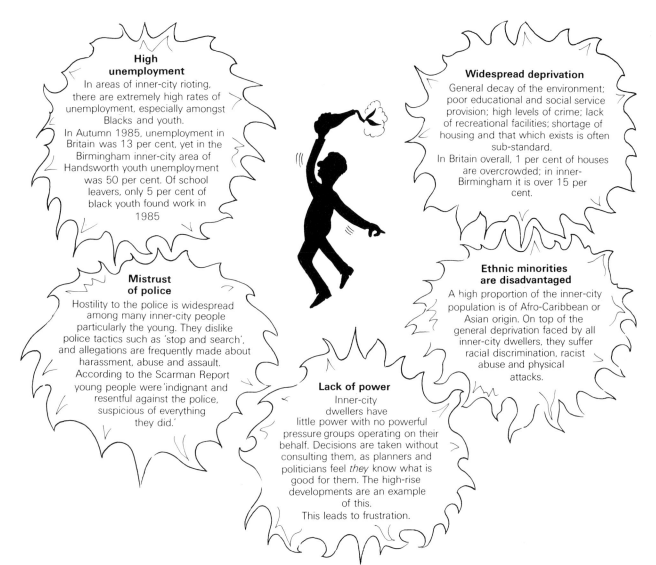

High unemployment

In areas of inner-city rioting, there are extremely high rates of unemployment, especially amongst Blacks and youth.
In Autumn 1985, unemployment in Britain was 13 per cent, yet in the Birmingham inner-city area of Handsworth youth unemployment was 50 per cent. Of school leavers, only 5 per cent of black youth found work in 1985

Widespread deprivation

General decay of the environment; poor educational and social service provision; high levels of crime; lack of recreational facilities; shortage of housing and that which exists is often sub-standard.
In Britain overall, 1 per cent of houses are overcrowded; in inner-Birmingham it is over 15 per cent.

Mistrust of police

Hostility to the police is widespread among many inner-city people particularly the young. They dislike police tactics such as 'stop and search', and allegations are frequently made about harassment, abuse and assault. According to the Scarman Report young people were 'indignant and resentful against the police, suspicious of everything they did.'

Ethnic minorities are disadvantaged

A high proportion of the inner-city population is of Afro-Caribbean or Asian origin. On top of the general deprivation faced by all inner-city dwellers, they suffer racial discrimination, racist abuse and physical attacks.

Lack of power

Inner-city dwellers have little power with no powerful pressure groups operating on their behalf. Decisions are taken without consulting them, as planners and politicians feel *they* know what is good for them. The high-rise developments are an example of this.
This leads to frustration.

In your local library ask to see the newspapers for October 1985, particularly the Sunday papers. Find out all you can about the inner city riots.

Third World cities

The fastest growing cities are in the Third World. Migration from the countryside to the towns has more to do with social changes in the countryside than with population growth as such; changes such as the growing of crops for sale rather than for use, and the introduction of agricultural machinery which replaces workers. This leads to poverty and unemployment, forcing people to seek work in the cities.

The problem with urbanisation in the Third World is that urban populations are growing faster than employment prospects and this leads to tremendous poverty and crime.

Mexico city: The city of the future

It took London 130 years to grow from 1 million people to 8 million. Mexico City did it in 30 years from 1940 to 1970.

Mexico City is a place of shanty towns sprouting TV aerials, of traffic jams and shops full of parts from wrecked cars, of huge armies of police and street vendors, of graft, political godfathers and the world's second largest national debt.

Above ground is pandemonium.

Altogether 20 million mechanised journeys are made in the city every day. Four million are taken by private car, 10 million on a fleet of 7000 battered and belching buses and the rest by metro and taxi.

City workers spend on average 2½ hours every day travelling to and from work, even though few live outside the city limits. Average vehicle speed on the clogged roads is said to be 12 kilometres per hour, falling to 4 km/h at peak periods.

Vehicles are responsible for two-thirds of the pollution, which sends a thick smog across the city, reducing visibility to a couple of kilometres on most days. (It is not helped by the high altitude which results in greater carbon monoxide in exhausts.)

Lack of adequate sewers and drains make widespread disease inevitable. The rats run and the rivers stink. Each day up to a thousand new migrants arrive at the main bus stations on the north and east side of Mexico City, for whatever horrors there may be in Mexico City, the migrants go there because they believe life will be better than in the villages. One in 10 dwellings in the city lack a water supply, but in rural areas the figure is 5 in 10. Three in 10 homes in the city are not connected to a sewer against five in 10 in the country. One in 10 lack electricity compared with almost 7 in 10 in the villages. People are wealthier here and, despite the over-crowding and pol-

lution, they live longer. Ten per cent of city dwellers are under-nourished, against 90 per cent in rural areas.

Most migrants will be joining relatives who have already made their home in one of the city's great slum suburbs – perhaps Netzahualcoyotl, near the airport, which has grown from nothing to home for about 2.5 million people in 25 years.

Most of the women will work as maids in middle-class homes. The men may work in factories or, as members of the army of shoe-shiners, and street vendors who line the streets of the city centre. But women and children (there are an estimated 100 000 children in the city) make up a large proportion of the workforce – especially among the lowest paid.

In a detailed study of one poor community in the 1960s, Oscar Lewis, author of *The Children of Sanchez*, found that women and children made up 76 per cent of the workforce.

Source: Adapted from F Pearce 'Mexico, the City Unlimited' in *New Scientist,* 18 October 1984

1 How long did it take London and Mexico to grow from 1 million people to 8 million?

2 Was the main cause of the growth of Mexico City immigration, or a high birth-rate?

3 Is Mexico City a clean, unpolluted, quiet city?

4 Why do people want to live in Mexico City?

5 Looking at the information provided on the changing patterns of where people live in Britain, can we say that London and Birmingham are going to be like Mexico City in the future? Briefly explain the reasons for your answer.

The changing countryside

The view that life was pleasant in the countryside in the nineteenth century compared to the squalid life of the cities is a myth. Life was just as hard and poverty was just as common. Unemployment, homelessness and disease were facts of life.

In the twentieth century, there are still large amounts of poverty in the countryside; one of the lowest paid occupations is that of farm labourer, and there is a lack of hospitals, local public transport and social services. Nevertheless for those people who are able to commute to relatively well-paid jobs in the towns and cities, there are considerable attractions to life in the countryside. Since the 1950s, there has been a move away from the city, to life in the small towns and villages in the countryside. The main reasons for the move have been the development of transport links (railways and motorways) to the large conurbations, which have attracted both companies and workers out of the city centres.

The effects on the countryside have been quite dramatic. There has been a decline in agricultural land as more housing developments are created. House prices in general in the countryside have risen to the point where local people cannot afford to buy, leaving the way clear for the commuters to buy up the properties. The small, local communities have been altered by an influx of new people, bringing new attitudes and ideas. Some small communities have been completely swamped by huge new developments and New Towns, such as Milton Keynes.

CHAPTER TEN

EDUCATION

An outline of the education system

What is the structure of the present education system?

The British education system is divided into three levels:

- primary, from age 5 to 11;
- secondary, from age 11 to a maximum of 18;
- tertiary, from a minimum age of 16 onward.

All schools and colleges, but not universities, are run by local education authorities (LEAs), the educational arm of local government. There are 105 LEAs in total.

Primary education

This consists of infant and junior schools. Usually these schools take any child from a particular area and are co-educational, that is they take both sexes.

Secondary education

This consists of all schools taking pupils between the ages of 11 and 16 (minimum school leaving age), plus sixth-formers up to the age of 18. Up to the late 1970s, there was a wide range of secondary schools, including grammar and secondary modern schools, but today the majority of schools are comprehensive. Ninety per cent of all secondary pupils attend comprehensive schools, which take the whole ability range. Choice of school is through a mixture of choice and geographical closeness.

Tertiary education

Education beyond secondary school is divided into further education and higher education. Further education colleges generally cater for technical qualifications below degree standard, as well as GCSE and A-level courses. Higher education includes colleges of higher education, polytechnics and universities, all of which offer mainly degree courses and above.

Do public schools help to give the children of the affluent a better chance of success?

Independent education

- **Private schools:** all schools which charge fees
- **Public schools:** those higher status schools which belong to an organisation called The Headmasters' Conference.

The independent sector includes all schools, colleges, and the University of Buckingham, that charge fees. Public schools are the best-known and controversial part of the independent sector. About seven per cent of school children attend private schools. Since 1980, the Conservative Government has run an 'assisted places scheme' through which the fees of 'gifted children' are paid at public schools, if the parents could not otherwise afford to send them there. (Gifted children are supposedly those of high intelligence.) Opponents of private education claim that these schools allow the children of the rich to receive a separate and special education.

The shared experiences of attending the most exclusive schools creates a sense of superiority and comradeship among the children of the rich. This sense of 'being special' is maintained throughout life, and as adults the ex-public school boys tend to help each other into positions of power, thus 'reproducing' another generation of rich and powerful people. Naturally they send their children to public schools and so the cycle is repeated.

When they leave school, they are more likely than students from State schools to go to Oxford and Cambridge and from there into the top positions of our society, where they wield great power.

Public schools

Backing the old school tie

Most Cabinet ministers eventually go for private secondary education.

The overwhelming majority of the Cabinet, . . . have opted to go private for their children.

The new Transport Secretary, Mr John Moore, has gone private for his three teenagers; so too did the long-serving Welsh Secretary, Mr Nicholas Edwards, for his son.

In a Cabinet packed with public school old boys, led by a quartet of Old Etonians, it was predictable that many would send their own children down the Tory establishment path.

The Foreign Secretary Sir Geoffrey Howe, who went to Winchester, gave his three children a private education. His counterpart at the Home Office, the Old Etonian, Mr Douglas Hurd, sent the three, now grown-up, children from his first marriage to private schools. The two young ones from his second will almost certainly follow.

But even those Conservative ministers who wear their own grammar school educations as political virility symbols have not been able to resist private education for their children. The Thatcher twins went private: Mark to Harrow and Carol to Queenswood until 16 and then to St Paul's for A levels. The young Tebbits attended independent schools in London.

Ministers are strikingly coy about their children's education partly, no doubt from a desire not to expose their children to security risks and inordinate publicity. But the sensitivity on the issue appears to go deeper.

Mr Jack Straw, a Labour shadow spokesman and MP for Blackburn, wrote to each Cabinet minister about their children's education two weeks ago and has had three replies. One minister affirmed that his children were privately educated, two very senior figures told Mr Straw that it was none of his business.

Mr Straw is confident that the inevitable question about Labour Shadow Cabinet members' personal commitment to state education will not produce embarrassing answers.

The Labour leader, Mr Neil Kinnock, has sent his children to local state schools in Ealing. The children of the shadow education spokesman, Mr Giles Radice also attended state schools, according to his private office.

Mr Straw said: 'All the rest of the shadow cabinet who had the opportunity to send their children to a comprehensive did so.'

Source: The *Guardian*, 27 May 1986

1 What does the term 'Old Etonians' mean?

2 How many public schools are mentioned in the extract? Which are they?

3 Does the extract tell us anything about attendance at public school and the 'top jobs'?

The history of schooling in Britain

How did the present
education system develop?

Before 1870

There was no organised education system. Children could possibly attend charity schools run by the various churches. The rich paid for private tutors or sent their sons to private schools.

1870 The Forster Education Act

This Act introduced a basic network of state-supported primary schools. Attendance was voluntary.

Why? Britain was falling behind its competitors (principally Germany) in industrial development. One problem was a lack of educated workers needed for the new technology of the time. This is similar to the situation today regarding computer literacy and Britain's need to compete with Japan and the USA.

The situation before 1944

The education system was clearly based on class divisions. All children received a basic elementary education up to 14, but education beyond that age was restricted to the middle and upper classes. Middle-class children went to fee-charging grammar schools, with a few scholarships available to working-class boys. The upper class sent their children to expensive public schools.

1944 The Butler Act

This introduced the concept of **meritocracy**, that is each child was to receive an education based upon his/her ability rather than his/her parents' ability to pay, as had occurred up to 1944.

Three types of schools were introduced: grammar; secondary technical; secondary modern. Children were to be sent to the type of school most appropriate to their educational needs, based upon assessment in an examination at 11 (the '11+'). Because there were three types of schools, the system was known as the 'tripartite system', though in practice only grammar and secondary modern schools were built in the main. The minimum leaving age was raised to 15.

Why? Introduced in the last year of the Second World War, the Act was partly a response to the obvious unfairness of the pre-war period to which people were not prepared to return. Educational reform was part of a wider package of reforms including the National Health Service and the Social Security system. A second reason was that industry needed an increasingly high standard of education amongst the workforce.

1944–64

In practice, the tripartite system became a means by which the middle class passed the 11+ and went to grammar schools, while the majority of the working class failed and went to secondary modern schools. The upper class continued to attend public schools. The 11+ examination was not a reliable or accurate test of a child's ability. Many bright children, who failed the 11+, were sent to secondary modern schools where they were not *expected* to achieve much. They were not encouraged, therefore, to take examinations, such as GCEs (General Certificate of Education).

1965 onward: The comprehensive school reforms

Since 1965, against considerable opposition, there has been a shift towards comprehensive schools, which take all children of a given locality regardless of their ability.

Why? Those in favour of comprehensives argued that there were three broad areas of advantage: economic, social and educational.

Economic

One large school, it was argued, would be cheaper than a number of smaller ones and better facilities, such as swimming pools or craft workshops, could be provided.

Social

There would be a breakdown of the class divisions which had been strengthened by the tripartite system where middle-class children attended grammar schools and working-class children, on the whole, attended secondary moderns. By mixing the social classes in one school it was hoped to weaken the class barriers.

Educational

Children would no longer be divided into different type schools at 11, which many believed had resulted in children at secondary moderns failing to achieve their full potential, regarding themselves as less intelligent than grammar school pupils.

Viewpoints on comprehensive schools and grammars

From the figures and from tramping the schools, I have the impression that the rise in exam passes for the middle ability children does owe something to comprehensive schools rather than only to the invention of new certificates and the lengthening of school life. But I have the impression too that this gain has to some extent been achieved at the expense of the brightest students.

Reliable evidence of this phenomenon appeared in 1978 when Richmond-upon-Thames released exam results for the whole authority. The pupils who took O-level and CSE exams in 1978 in Richmond were the first group not to have sat selection exams but to have gone instead into comprehensive secondary schools. The results showed a 57 per cent increase in CSE passes compared with the year before, and a 10 per cent increase in O-level entries. The O-level candidates did not, however, get any more passes than had O-level candidates the year before. More interestingly though there was a rise of 22 per cent in the number of CSE grade 1s, there was a 36 per cent fall in O-level grade A passes.

Source: Adapted from A Stevens, *Clever Children in Comprehensive Schools* (Harper and Rowe, 1980)

1 Has there been an overall improvement in examination results?

2 Has any particular group lost out?

3 Was there any change in examination entries in Richmond in 1978?

4 Can you think of any implications of this concerning pupils' motivation?

5 Were there changes in the proportion passing CSE with grade 1 and those passing with GCE grade A?

6 Is the author's reliance on examination results a good way to measure the performance of comprehensive schools?

There is, in short, no *evidence* that comprehensive education contributes to the breakdown of the barriers of social class which still divide adults and children alike. . . . For schools reflect the structure and culture of the society as a whole. As long as we live in a class society then the influence of social class will be felt in the schools, determining the kinds of education children receive and the results they obtain from them.

Source: J Ford, *Social Class and the Comprehensive School* (Routledge and Kegan Paul, 1969)

1 Do comprehensive schools break down social class differences?

2 According to the writer, what do schools reflect?

3 Can we therefore change society in general by changing schools?

4 Can you think of the implications of this social policy in general (the writer is a Marxist)?

1987 Some conclusions on comprehensive schools

Are comprehensive schools better?

Studies of comprehensives have not fully borne out the early hopes of the system. Much the same differences in class educational attainment appear today as in the old tripartite system.

Overall, it seems that the comprehensives offer a wider range of subjects and better facilities than the tripartite system. Late developers are not held back.

Although the majority of children attend comprehensive schools, it would be wrong to view them all as equal in the ability range they contain. There has been no demolition of class barriers, probably because of the fact that comprehensives draw their intake from the local neighbourhood. Middle-class neighbourhoods have middle-class dominated comprehensives and working-class areas have working-class dominated comprehensives. Also, some comprehensives are situated in areas that still have grammar schools. So higher ability students are often sent to the grammar school. This process, known as 'creaming', makes many comprehensive schools secondary moderns in all but name. One undisputed benefit, however, has been the increase in pupils staying on beyond the minimum leaving age of 16.

The shift to skill-training

Since the late 1970s, there has been an important change in the attitudes towards education in Britain and the way that much of the education for 16-year-olds is paid for.

The view that education was failing to train young people in the *skills* needed for jobs began to influence educationalists. The government created an agency called the Manpower Services Commission which began to pay for courses which were directly connected with training people in specific skills, rather than in the sort of general education which was typical at the time. Gradually the philosophy of skill-training, called 'vocationalism', and the large amount of money spent by the MSC changed the nature of education after the age of 16. Today, the two-year Youth Training Scheme (YTS), the Technical and Vocational Educational Initiative (TVEI) and the Certificate in Pre-Vocational Education (CPVE) all share this vocational philosophy.

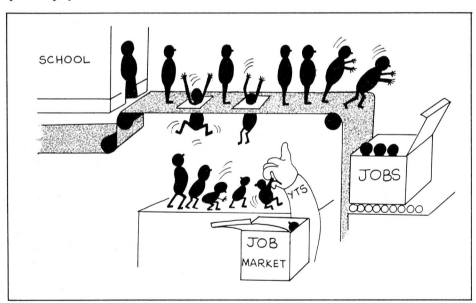

Supporters argue that as Britain has fallen behind other nations because of an unskilled workforce, the new courses will help remedy this problem, by creating new attitudes to work and new skills of working amongst young people. Critics point out that unemployment in Britain is not caused by lack of skills at all, and that increasingly it is skilled workers who are becoming unemployed. They see the new vocationalism as more of a way of creating cheap labour for employers and of keeping young people off the streets and off the unemployment statistics.

YTS – Good or bad

'We are trying, as resources permit, to work towards the point where every 16- and 17-year-old not in education or a job will be assured of vocational preparations lasting as necessary up to his or her 18th birthday. This is an extremely ambitious programme. It is nothing less than a new deal for the young unemployed!'

(James Prior, then Employment Secretary, announcing an expansion of the Youth Opportunities Programme in 1980.)

In 1976 Mr Callaghan, then Prime Minister, argued that comprehensive schools were failing to prepare their pupils for working life: that their curricula [subjects they taught] and their teaching methods were undermining the pupils' abilities to get jobs. As the scale of youth unemployment escalated, the employment problem of young people, their inability to get jobs was to be increasingly interpreted as an educational problem. In his view young people were educationally deficient and displayed a lack of willingness and poor attitudes to work.

With well over three million unemployed, the mistakes in this argument are obvious; even with appropriate skills, there are not enough jobs for the young. I would suggest that YTS has more to do with providing employers with a pool of free labour, from which they can pick and choose their recruits at the end of the year, than it has to do with meeting the training and educational needs of the unemployed.

The Thatcher Government argue that the young have priced themselves out of the labour market. Tory policy involves reconstructing youth as cheap labour.

Source: Adapted from D Finn, 'A New Deal for British Youth' in *The Social Science Teacher*, Vol. 13, No. 2

1 Where was the blame placed for youth unemployment?

2 According to the author why is this obviously wrong?

3 What did Mr Prior argue was the point of the training schemes for youth, according to the quote? What does the author think is the point of training schemes?

4 Do you think the writer has strong feelings about YTS, or is he presenting both sides of the argument fairly?

5 From the experiences of your friends, and relatives, what is your opinion of YTS?

The purposes of education

Why do we have education?

In simple tribal societies, there was no formal education system. Knowledge and the basic values of society were passed on from one generation to another quite naturally in the rhythm of everyday life.

Education in a tribal society fifty years ago

Children learn the tasks required of adults simply by doing them. They are anxious to imitate their elders, and there is never any compulsory element in the teaching of these skills. Moreover, in their education they have this advantage, that it is not carried on in an institution divorced from everyday adult activities. The child feels that he is an essential part of society; all he does is a direct contribution to the domestic economy.

General behaviour, attitudes, and values are not taught by any formal training. These are inextricably bound up with life in the society and become unconsciously adopted by anyone fully partaking in social life. . . .

One night, while sitting in a hut, we watched a girl of seven learning to cook. Fermented porridge was needed for the baby and this the girl set out to make in a small pot in the presence of her mother and several other girls somewhat older than herself who happened to be there. When the water boiled, she put in some grain, twirling the porridge twirler between the palms as she had seen her mother do. She took the comments and criticisms of the company with good grace, even when they smiled at her awkwardness. Meanwhile, her mother mentioned to us how useful it would be to have someone who could cook the evening meal on days when she came home late or tired from fetching wood.

Source: J and J D Krige, *The Realm of the Rain Queen* (Oxford University Press, 1943)

1 How do children learn to perform the economically necessary tasks?

2 Is it the same in our society? What to you think accounts for the differences?

3 Is the child an essential part of the economy? At what age does this happen in our society?

4 Who are the teachers in this tribal society? Is it the same today in our society?

What is the relationship between school and work?

Modern, industrial societies, however, are just too complex, with a wide variety of economic skills and a diversity of values and beliefs. Formal education (what is taught in schools) is used to teach people skills, to grade them by ability and to transmit certain values from one generation to the next.

Teaching skills

In tribal societies basic survival skills, such as knowledge of hunting or the gathering of edible roots and berries, are passed on from generation to generation.

In modern, industrial societies, the pace of technological change make one generation's skills irrelevant to the next. Computerisation for example is fundamentally altering office work. In ten years clerical work has changed from paperwork to information processing. Factory workers, too, are being replaced by computer robots and so they must learn new skills or face long-term unemployment.

The range and pace of skills means that it is impossible for parents to teach their children the necessary skills and knowledge. Schools perform this task.

Grading by ability

Schools should act as sieves to grade students, allowing the better ones to go forward to take the more skilful and demanding jobs. Examinations are devised to grade students and provide every level of pupil with an appropriate form and level of teaching. However, many socioligists dispute this description of the schools' grading activities. Although schools may have been created to give children the maximum learning opportunities, it is doubtful in practice that they actually do so. It seems that factors outside the control of the school, especially the social class background of pupils crucially influences educational success.

The transmission of values: A form of social control

In simple societies, basic values, such as economic skills, were transmitted (passed on) from parents to children. It would be true to say that this partly occurs in modern British society as well. However, the complexity of industrial society makes it difficult for parents to perform this task alone.

In order for our society to continue there must be some common cultural background: a common language; common beliefs; common expectations. The school system knits children from a wide range of different backgrounds into one flexible whole. Children not only learn a common culture, but just as importantly they learn the rules of society. They are taught to obey the laws and customs and to avoid any form of behaviour regarded as anti-social. Schools, therefore, impose a form of social control upon pupils through the formal lessons of the curriculum, the discipline imposed by the teachers and through the general social life of the school. This prepares them to conform later in life as adults.

How do schools teach 'social control'?

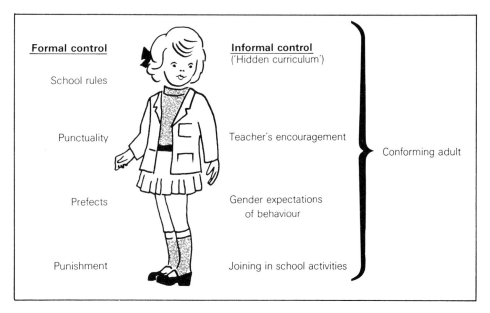

The main problem concerning the transmission of values and the imposition of social control lies in *whose values are being passed on* and *who benefits* from the social control. Radical sociologists, such as Marxists, argue that schools merely prepare the majority of pupils to be uncomplaining workers later in life, in offices and factories.

The relationship between school and work: A critical view

Two radical, Marxist sociologists, Bowles and Gintis, argue that the education system does not grade children according to their ability, but reproduces the class system from one generation to the next; that is, those in the top positions manage to place their children into similar top jobs. How is this done? Children of the better off attend public schools, where they are taught to believe they are superior, to think independently and to strive for the highest positions in society. Bowles and Gintis compare this with State schools which teach conformity and obedience both in the official and hidden curriculum. The pupils learn to arrive on time, to cope with boring lessons, and most important of all, to accept society as it is, rather than to criticise it. As a result of this working class people continue to accept boring low-paid jobs without too much complaint.

1 What does the passage mean when it states that education helps to 'reproduce' the class system?

2 Which sort of schools do the children of the better off attend?
What do they learn that helps them to be successful?

3 How do State schools, according to Bowles and Gintis, prepare working class pupils for their future jobs?

4 In your experience, do you feel there is any truth in Bowles and Gintis' argument?

5 Draw a diagram, or a cartoon, to illustrate the function of schools according to Bowles and Gintis.

The troublemakers

We have seen that the education system prepares pupils for life after school, but what about those pupils who reject the system? Will they be rebels after school? The answer in many cases is, of course, yes. But research by one sociologist, Paul Willis, has found that even troublemakers are, paradoxically, preparing themselves through their 'messing about' at school to withstand the boredom of the unskilled labouring jobs which they are bound to get. Willis argues that most working-class jobs are boring. Workers have to 'get by' as best they can, and they do this by messing about at work, 'having a laugh'. Schoolchildren who mess around in the classroom certainly confirm their condemnation to dead-end jobs, but by learning to get the best out of school through their antics, they are also learning how to cope with their future.

1 Construct a list of how pupils 'get by' in lessons. It is clear that you do not always listen to the teacher and do the set work.

2 Write a description of 'getting by' in a typical school day.

3 Ask somehow you know in employment how they 'get by' at work. Are there any similarities?

Educational attainment

How well do different social groups perform in the education system?

SOCIAL GROUPS	ATTAINMENT
Upper and middle class The middle and upper classes succeed at school, achieve the best A-level results and go on to university.	If your father has a profession or works in high-level management, you stand an eleven times greater chance of getting a university degree than if he is a semi-skilled or unskilled worker.
Working class The working class do less well from the education system. Examination results are consistently poorer for them compared to the middle class.	Percentage of children with attainment of — Father's occupation — Non-Manual / Manual: 5+ GCEs — 34 — 11 1–4 GCEs — 34 — 32 No GCE's or CSE Grade 1s — 32 — 57 Source: *Social Trends* (HMSO, 1985)
Race Certain black ethnic groups do particularly badly, such as some children of West Indian and Bangladeshi parents.	'In all CSE and GCE O-level exams 6 per cent of West Indians obtained five or more higher grades compared with 17 per cent of Asians and 19 per cent of all other leavers ... Asians ... do about as well as white children except in English language. Bangladeshis do markedly less well than all groups majority and minority.' Source: The *Times Educational Supplement*, 15 March 1985
Gender Girls perform relatively well at school, but they leave school more often at the minimum age and fewer go on to higher education or skilled forms of training (except nursing). At school they tend to study different subjects from boys.	Full-time university students in 1980: male – 143 000; female – 95 000 Percentage of school-leavers with higher grade GCE/CSE: Subject — Female — Male English — 42 — 32 French — 17 — 11 Maths — 21 — 29 Physics — 6 — 18 Biology — 18 — 12

Why do working-class children perform less well than middle-class children at school?

Working-class failure in the education system

Reasons for the relative lack of success of working-class pupils fall into two broad areas: home background and community, and school.

The home background and community

Material deprivation

The lack of amenities at home can make it difficult for the child to study or attend school. Lack of money can mean a cold and damp house, inadequate levels of nutrition, overcrowding and general deprivation. These can lead to poor school attendance through illness and inability to study at home.

The National Children's Bureau carried out a longitudinal study of all children born in England in one week of March 1958. They found that 1 in 16 children suffered from *all* the following disadvantages: poor housing, single parents, large families and low incomes.

Parents' attitudes

The degree of interest and encouragement parents show in their children's education can be a very significant element in educational success. Indeed, according to some sociologists it can overcome poverty and deprivation.

J W B Douglas led a study of schoolchildren throughout their primary and secondary schooling. He found that educational success was closely related to parental encouragement in all classes, but that middle-class parents were more likely to give help and show interest in their children's progress at school.

The effects of the home on a child's education

When housing conditions are unsatisfactory, children make relatively low scores in the tests. This is so in each social class but whereas the middle-class children, as they get older, reduce this handicap, the manual working-class children from unsatisfactory homes fall even further behind; for them overcrowding and other deficiencies at home have a progressive and depressive influence on their test performance. . . .

The conclusions are that the attitudes of children to their school work is deeply affected by the degree of encouragement their parents give them and by their own level of emotional stability. The children who show few symptoms of emotional instability and whose parents are ambitious for their academic success, have an increasing advantage during the years they are at primary school, largely because they pursue their studies with greater vigour and concentration than the less-favoured children are prepared or able to do.

Source: J W B Douglas, *The Home and the School* (Panther, 1969)

1 Do children overcome the effects of poor housing as they get older?

2 What influences does parental encouragement have on a child's school work?

3 Are your parents interested in your education? How did their attitude influence you, do you think?

Speech patterns

The ability to express oneself clearly in speaking and writing is a crucial component of success in our education system. Middle-class children are more likely to have their writing and speaking skills developed to a higher standard and at an earlier age than working-class children.

Bernstein compared groups of youths and found considerable differences in their powers of expression. Those parents who explain their actions and discuss them with their children help to develop language skills and reasoning ability which gives them success later at school. He argued that this situation was more likely to occur in middle-class homes.

Cultural deprivation

It has been suggested that children from particularly poor backgrounds, deprived inner-city areas and certain immigrant groups suffer at school because they lack an awareness of our culture and language.

The Plowden Report (1967), an official government enquiry, concluded that children deprived of culture in their home environment and community were more likely to fail at school and be labelled as 'educationally sub-normal'. To combat this 'educational priority areas' were set up. Basically these provided extra funds for schools in particularly poor inner-city areas. This idea of giving pupils from deprived backgrounds extra resources has been called 'compensatory education'.

The school

Relationships between teachers and pupils

Pupils on average spend 15 000 hours in school. Their attitudes towards school are strongly influenced by the teachers' attitudes and treatment of them. These attitudes can assist a child to educational success or condemn him to a low stream and an early exit from the system.

Colin Lacey studied a Manchester Grammar School. He found that although all the boys were generally in favour of school in the first year, by the fourth year the lower-stream pupils hated school and the upper-stream ones liked school. The reason, according to Lacey was the attitudes of the teachers. Most of them disliked teaching the lower streams and demonstrated it in their attitudes to the pupils. The pupils noticed this and so they rejected the school. The opposite happened for the high-stream pupils.

Streaming

How does streaming influence a pupil's attainment and attitudes?

The discussion on relationships throws some light on the debate over streaming. Many educationalists oppose streaming for limiting the potential of children. Defenders argue that it allows pupils to receive the correct level of teaching, at the pace best suited to the pupil's ability. According to this approach, streaming is bad as long as teachers show the attitudes discussed above. Mixed ability teaching is only successful, however, where the teacher *believes* in this form of teaching organisation.

Attitudes and streaming

> When a child was kept in the wrong stream he tended to take on the characteristics of his stream, and his academic performance deteriorated if he were in too low a stream and improved if he were in too high a stream.

Source: National Foundation for Educational Research (NFER) Report

1 What happens if a child is placed in a stream too high or low for him/her?

2 Why do you think this happens?

3 Do you feel that the class you are in influences the amount of work you do and your attitude to studying?

4 If you are in a streamed class, what do you think of the idea of mixing all the classes together, and being taught in a mixed ability class?

The importance of labelling

Teachers categorise pupils into broad groups and then treat them according to this categorisation. For example, a pupil may be 'labelled' as lazy by a teacher. Whatever the pupil does, the teacher will interpret it in this light. This labelling can have very important consequences for the pupil, especially if he/she has been labelled incorrectly or is trying to change.

Once categorised, the bad pupil can be caught in a heads-I-win-tails-you-lose-situation. The consistently rude boy who is now being polite is regarded with suspicion by the teachers; his intentions and motives come under scrutiny. His politeness may be interpreted as 'taking the mick' out of the teacher or as evidence that a crime is being concealed. The boy who turns in a first-class piece of work when normally his work is appallingly poor is suspected of copying. When such pupils behave 'out of character' and thus 'out of category' the teacher's reaction may well be preventing the process of change which the teacher is supposedly anxious to promote. What could be more devastating for a lazy pupil to find that, when he does respond to the teacher's appeal for change, his efforts are greeted with suspicion and disbelief? Would it not be reasonable for the pupil to conclude that the effort is not worth making since this is a game he can never win.

Source: Adapted from C Lacey, *Hightown Grammar* (Manchester University Press, 1970)

1 What happens to the 'bad' child once labelled as such by the teachers?

2 Why do you think the teacher reacts this way?

3 How do you think teachers build up these definitions, or 'labels', of pupils?

4 What effect will the teacher's response have on the bad pupil who is trying to reform?

5 Do you think this is a very common experience of pupils at school?
   Has it happened to you at school or college and how was the situation resolved?

Why do many Black children perform particularly badly at school?

Ethnic minorities at school

All the factors which produce poor school progress from working-class children also hit children from West Indian and many Asian homes. This is hardly surprising as the vast majority of these children are from working-class homes. But there are some problems which only black or immigrant children face. For children from immigrant homes the main language of the home is generally the country of origin. So their studies are carried out, to some extent, in a 'foreign' language. Although West Indian children speak English at home, it may be in a dialect that differs from standard English and this can cause confusion.

It is rare for teachers to be openly racist but cultural differences and poor performance in some IQ tests by black children have created the belief in some teachers' minds that black children are more likely to be slow learners. This can influence the way in which teachers 'label' black pupils and so retard their progress.

Why do some ethnic minorities do far better than others?

Differences in educational attainment between ethnic minorities

It is wrong to say that all black children do badly at school. Children of West Indian and Bangladeshi origins perform particularly poorly, whilst most other Asian children do at least as well as Whites.

Two explanations have been suggested by the Swann Report (an official government study). First, that Asians simply 'keep their heads down' and get on with their studies without attracting attention, accepting racism. West Indians, in contrast, are more likely to protest about their problems and may receive more of a negative response from teachers. Second, the tight knit, strict Asian family and culture places great emphasis on educational success and disciplines its children to achieve this.

Schooling and self-image

The West Indian child is told on first entering the school that his language is second-rate, to say the least. Namely, the only way he knows how to speak . . . is 'the wrong way to speak'. . . .

When the pictures, illust- rations, music, heroes, great historical and contemporary figures in the classroom are all white, it is difficult for a child to identify with anyone who is not white. . . .

They become resentful and bitter at being told their language is second-rate and their history and culture is non-existent. . . . The black child under these influences develops a deep inferiority complex. He soon loses motivation to succeed academically since, at best, the learning experience is an elaborate irrelevance to his personal life situation, and at worst it is a racially humiliating experience.

Source: B Coard, *How West Indian children are made educationally subnormal by the British education system* (New Beacon Books, 1971)

1 What is the West Indian child told at school about 'his language'?

2 Surely, West Indian children speak English at home, so why should there be any problems about language?

3 What does the black child discover about history?

4 What are the final results of the black child's discoveries?

5 How are black people portrayed in history, old films and novels?

*What are the
differences in the
educational attainment
of girls and boys?*

Gender differences in education

It is not true to say that females perform less well than males at school, but
they do have different educational careers. They choose different subjects
and girls are less likely to stay on at school, to train for a technical subject
or go on to university.

The reasons for differences in education between males and females can be
traced to differences in socialisation in the home (see page 51) and different
treatment at school, both of which reflect the different expectations we have
of males and females in life in general.

Childhood socialisation

It is generally believed that girls are more emotional, gentler and less
technically-minded than boys. They are valued for their attractiveness and
domestic ability (how well they can cook and keep house for instance). In
childhood, therefore, girls are brought up along these lines. If girls do not
show the traits mentioned above, then people believe there is something
'wrong' with them.

Parents care more about the looks of daughters. They buy them different
toys from boys; so that boys get soldiers and guns, while girls get dolls and
prams. They use different language to describe them; girls are sweet and
pretty, while boys are handsome and little rascals! Finally, girls are expected
to help with the housework to a far greater extent than boys.

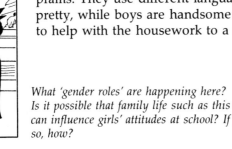

*What 'gender roles' are happening here?
Is it possible that family life such as this
can influence girls' attitudes at school? If
so, how?*

Love or learning

For girls, the pursuit of
'femininity' leads to a multitude
of distractions, such as attending to physical appearance,
fashion, boyfriends and the
sentimentalisation of love-
stories and romance. This
leads to apathy and lack of
interest in anything to do
with study and school and
influences the subsequent
nature of their life and work.

. . .
    In conclusion many work-
ing-class girls find school life
boring and irrelevant. They
look forward to leaving as
soon as they can obtain a job
that will provide money, some
interest and the freedom for
which they yearn. The education and class systems have
always discriminated against
them for being female and

working-class. They absorb a
self-image that is academically
low and their own performance may confirm this. . . .
    They have grown up with
feminine role models that
show love and marriage and
a husband and children as
more important and immed-
iate goals for a girl.

Source: S Sharpe, *Just Like a Girl: How Girls Learn to be Women* (Penguin, 1976)

1 What do you think Sharpe means when she writes about 'femininity'?

2 Why does this lead to a 'lack of interest in school'?

3 Why do you think most girls find school 'boring and irrelevant'?

4 What do most girls believe are the most important goals for them?

5 From *your* experiences, are the points that Sharpe makes true, or not?

6 Why do you think that the idea of the correct goals for women and the 'pursuit of femininity' prevent girls from going on to higher education, except for certain courses like junior school teacher-training? Why do you think that women overwhelmingly form the majority of students on these teacher-training courses?

In school

The attitudes created by the wider society about the correct behaviour for females, plus their home socialisation, is strengthened at school through the **hidden curriculum** (the underlying values of the school). Girls are often encouraged to study subjects which are more appropriate for them, such as biology and English literature, while boys are encouraged into the sciences and technical subjects. Teachers also have different expectations concerning typical patterns of behaviour for girls and boys; so girls are expected to be neater, quieter and more studious than boys who are expected to be lively and rather a handful, but to grasp technical knowledge more easily than girls.

Girls learn to lose

Research shows that science and maths are perceived as 'masculine' subjects, and that girls tend to fall behind boys in their achievement in these subjects when they reach puberty, and become concerned about their femininity. Moreover, boys are even more convinced than girls are that science and maths are more suitable for boys.

How does the way in which both boys and girls are socialised affect girls' ability to learn at school? Take these extracts from an article in *The Times Educational Supplement*, written by Judith Whyte, director of the government funded *Girls into Science and Technology Project*, based in ten Manchester schools:

'Teachers often prefer to teach boys because they are apparently more outspoken and willing to express ideas. As a number of research projects have shown, boys dominate the mixed classroom by demanding and getting more of the teacher's attention. Girls, on the other hand, tend to get ignored or lumped together as silent or uninteresting. In subjects like physics or control technology particularly, teachers tend to ask boys more questions in the belief that they are more motivated or better able to give an answer . . .'

'A science class dispersed to start practical work on heating carbohydrates. They were told that, as there were not enough safety glasses for everyone, only those actually heating the test tube needed to wear them, and the others should stand well clear. Boys rushed to collect glasses and other apparatus. In some groups of four boys, all were wearing glasses. The girls' group had no glasses and had to negotiate with the boys, or call on the teacher to help. In consequence, all the boys had started working before any of the girls' groups. This was a very interesting incident. It shows how a seemingly trivial event can lead to them appearing to work more quickly and efficiently. Girls were "learning to lose" in science as boys asserted their dominance.'

Source: *New Society*, 24 October 1986

1 Why do teachers prefer to teach boys?

2 Why do boys 'dominate the mixed classroom'?

3 In the example given, why did the girls start work on the apparatus *after* the boys?

4 Why does the author say that the girls were 'learning to lose'?

5 In your opinion, is it true that males dominate mixed classes? If you agree, what reasons could you suggest for this?

6 Many people are now suggesting that we should have single-sex schools. They claim that this would help girls. How do you think this is supposed to help girls?

7 What is your opinion?

Schools teach girls their role in society through the attitudes and language of teachers

CHAPTER ELEVEN
WORK

The changing occupational structure

What changes have taken place in employment in Britain?

There are 26 million people employed in Britain today, and approximately four million more who would like to work, but are unemployed.

There are three types of industry in which people are employed:

- primary (or extractive), which exploit our natural resources and include agriculture and fishing;
- secondary (or manufacturing), which involve making objects for our use, such as cars or electrical items;
- tertiary (or service industries), which provide services for us, such as banking, shops or restaurants.

Throughout this century there has been a move away from primary and manufacturing industries to service industries.

Forty years ago, shortly after the end of the Second World War, 70 per cent of the workforce had jobs in the manufacturing and construction industries. The vast bulk of employees were manual workers. Today, by contrast, 60 per cent of the workforce is in service industries and the majority of employees are in white-collar work. Only two per cent of workers are in agricultural occupations, reflecting the fact that Britain is one of the most industrialised nations in the world.

Automation and increasing competition from more recently industrialised countries, such as Japan, mean that fewer workers are needed for industry. There has also been a growth in the industries such as insurance and banking that employ white-collar workers.

The effects on society

What are the effects on society?

The result of these changes has been the decline of the manual workers and of the traditional working-class communities based on heavy industry such as steel, coal and the docks, with their emphasis on the extended family and trade union solidarity. As an increasing proportion of the workforce moves into white-collar jobs, they are less likely to view themselves as working-class, even if their wages are no higher than those of the remaining manual workers.

Increasingly, the new jobs in the service industries are being filled by women, for although women have only a quarter of jobs in manufacturing, they have two-thirds of service industry jobs, usually the lowest paid, it should be added. Nevertheless, it does mean more women are working than ever before. This will affect family relationships as increasingly women become the breadwinners.

Unemployment has increased strikingly in the last six years, partially as a result of these changes in industry. Those most likely to become unemployed, are those who can be replaced by automated machinery and those in the declining manufacturing and primary industries. Those most likely to be unemployed are the young who find it difficult to get work in the first place, and the older unemployed who are regarded by employers as not worth retraining.

Where have all the jobs gone?

Workers in industry

Industry	1961	1971	1979	1983
Agriculture/fishing	710 000	430 000	360 000	350 000
Manufacturing	8 500 000	8 000 000	7 200 000	5 500 000
Services	10 300 000	11 600 000	13 500 000	13 300 000

Source: *Social Trends* (HMSO, 1986)

1 What has happened to the numbers of people employed in
   a) agriculture and fishing?
   b) manufacturing?
   c) services?

2 What period has seen the fastest decline in manufacturing industry?

3 Have the numbers of jobs available in service industries risen to compensate for the decline in manufacturing?

The distribution of jobs

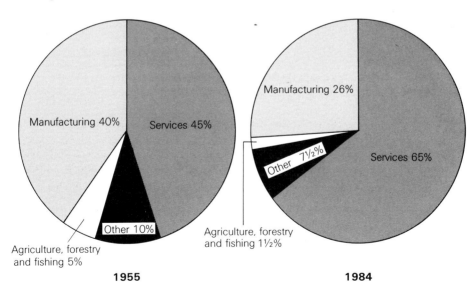

1955

1984

1 In 1984, what percentage of jobs were in
   a) services compared to 1955?
   b) manufacturing compared to 1955?

2 Can you suggest where most jobs will be in the future? Give examples of these types of jobs.

3 Can you suggest any possible consequences for society from these changes?

Industrialisation

What were the social consequences of industrialisation?

Britain was the first country in the world to industrialise. During the eighteenth and nineteenth centuries, it was transformed from an agricultural society, with the majority of the population living in the countryside and farming for their living, to an industrial society where almost all the people work in offices, shops and factories, while living in towns and cities.

But the shift from agriculture to industry was not simply an economic change, it was a profound social change too. The growth of cities as we know them now, of newspapers and later television and radio, the ability to read and write for the ordinary person, social class differences and the widespread ownership of consumer goods, even democracy as it is now, were caused, or at least influenced, by the process of industrialisation.

Factories needed a large workforce near at hand which led to the growth of towns. In turn, these attracted traders and so the towns grew into cities, and eventually into 'conurbations'. In order to work the machines and perform the clerical tasks workers needed to read and write (just as now we need to know how to use computers). Consumer goods were invented and produced at a price that eventually was within the reach of most of the employed. The overwhelming power of the employers led to the counterforce of the trade unions. Finally, the fact that huge numbers of workers were pushed together in factories and cities in a common condition of employment helped to form social classes.

Not only has industrialisation (the move from producing goods by hand to producing them by machine) produced major changes in society, but so too have specific changes in the technology of production. These changes include the move from craft production to mechanisation on to automation.

The social consequences of industrialisation in Britain

Leisure
Initially, the long hours of work in factories prevented leisure. Eventually the workers obtained shorter working hours, which led to the development of modern leisure activities.

Colonies
There was exploitation of the colonies for cheap raw materials for the factories in Britain. This led to the poverty of the Third World. It created a sense of racial superiority and eventually in the 1950s, influenced the patterns of immigration to Britain.

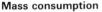

Production
This moved from agriculture to factories and machines. Working conditions were appalling – long hours for little pay. The relationship of employer and employee was one of conflict.
Now automation – consequences?

Mass consumption
Factories and machinery led to the production of cheap articles on a large scale. Eventually this caused a decline in prices and, by the 1950s, the growth of mass consumption. The majority of the population could own articles previously thought of as luxuries.

Politics
Large numbers of workers drawn together, in factories and towns in poor conditions, led to growth of political activity, notably the development of the Labour Party. The factory owners replaced landowners as the leaders of the Conservative Party.

Transport
Modern, fast means of transport, first the railways and much later cars, led to travel, holidays, suburbs, commuting and eventually the development of factories away from the towns.

Health
The growth of the cities with large numbers of people living close together forced improvements in public hygiene – sewers, water supplies, etc. Advances in medicine occurred These, plus the rise in the standard of living, improved health standards and lowered death-rates. People lived longer.

Urbanisation
The growth of cities, with their slums and social problems of poverty and crime, and later the need to improve conditions, led to redevelopment and New Towns. Decline in the inner cities later linked to riots of the 1980s.

Industrialisation in the Third World

Production
The move has been from agriculture only to providing raw materials for developed countries. Increasingly multi-national companies are setting up business here because of cheap labour, land and lack of labour laws.

Multi-nationals
Much of the production is controlled by huge companies which are based in USA or Europe. (See **Production** and **Colonialism**.)

GOOD CHEAP & FAST

Colonialism
During the last 50 years most colonies have gained their independence. However, the economy of these countries remains controlled by the developed 'rich' countries.

Politics
The extremes of poverty and wealth lead to totalitarian governments and violent protest. Often the army takes over and kills and tortures opponents. Governments are politically unstable.

Consumption
Prices are low and the range of goods is narrow. Life is excellent for the wealthy, but there is nothing available for the large numbers of the poor.

Health
It is rare to find hospitals and medical services of an adequate standard provided by the State. Conditions in the towns and countryside are very bad indeed. There are no supplies of clean water and no sewage systems.

Urbanisation
Extremely fast growth of cities, which are unable to cope with the large numbers of young people coming in from the countryside, leads to social problems, such as shanty towns, crime, drugs and prostitution, all the result of dreadful poverty.

Changing technology

Craft production

This is the normal form of production in an agricultural society, and in an industrial society the way in which complex tasks requiring great skill and judgement are carried out. Increasingly, this sort of job is being taken over by automated machines controlled by microchips. Craft work is satisfying to the worker who will make the complete product, (for example, a hand-made chair) from start to finish. However, this form of production is slow and so the finished products are expensive.

Mechanisation

What is the difference between mechanisation and automation?

Production by machines is the most common form of manufacture today, basically because it allows large numbers of items to be made at a low price, which means that people can afford to buy them and achieve a high standard of living.

There are, however, tremendous social costs involved for those who work with machines or on assembly lines. Probably the worst of these is the fact that workers constantly repeat the same task, which leads to dreadful boredom and lack of work satisfaction. Not only this, but the worker loses any control over the pace at which he works, as this is set by the management. Furthermore, as the machine produces an identical product each time, regardless of the interest or ability of the worker, then all sense of pride and craftsmanship is lost. The resulting boredom and frustration can lead to industrial action, such as strikes, as the workers try to obtain higher wages in order to compensate for the boredom of their work.

Automation

What are the consequences of automation for society?

Automation is the process where machines produce items with only a minimum of supervision by workers. Generally the machines have been programmed to repeat the same task to a high standard of acccuracy, and can even reject items which are not of the required standard. An example of automation is the simple welding machine, which is used in car production to perform a number of welds in set spots to car bodies as they pass along the production line.

The construction of complete products by machines without the need for workers has already had a considerable effect on society. However, the use of micro-chip technology, the tiny 'brains' inside home computers and calculators, is beginning to cause even more profound changes.

Technologically, the micro-chip allows machines to be controlled by computer to undertake highly skilled, as well as routine, tasks and to reach a standard of output of high quality. It is possible to manufacture virtually the whole of the car, as Fiat does, with automated machinery which needs only a few workers.

What is it like working in industry?

Working lives

The assembly line

Robert Linhart worked for a year on the Citröen production line. This is his description of assembly line work.

Each man has a well defined area for the operations he has to make ... as soon as a car enters a man's territory, he gets to work. A few knocks, a few sparks, then the welding's done and the car's already on its way out of the three or four yards of his position. And the next car's already coming into the work area. And the worker starts again.

Sometimes, if he has been working fast, he has a few seconds' rest before a new car arrives: or he intensifies his effort and 'goes up the line' so that he can gain a little time. And after an hour or two he's amassed the incredible amount of two or three minutes in hand, that he'll use to smoke a cigarette, looking on like some comfort-able man-of-means as his car moves past already welded. If, on the other hand, the worker is too slow, he 'slips back', carried progressively beyond his position, going on with his work when the next labourer has already begun his. The first car followed too far and the next one already appearing at the usual starting point of the work area, coming forward with its mindless regularity. It's already halfway along before you're able to touch it, you're going to start on it when its nearly passed through and reached the next station: all this loss of time mounts up. It's what they call 'slipping' and sometimes it's as ghastly as drowning.

Source: Adapted from R Linhart (translated by M Crossland), *The Assembly Line* (John Calder, 1981)

A craftsman

I won't say I exactly enjoy it. No, not enjoyment exactly but the time passes really quickly. ... what with so much to do, I just have to concentrate on the work. And it is satisfying – I have to say that ... just to see, say, a chair, looking lovely, and knowing what it came in like. Yes, the money is important, stands to reason but I wouldn't change to some factory job to just earn more. No.

A furniture restorer

1 In the first extract, how complex is the task that the worker has to do?

2 Do you think that his work is satisfying?

3 What does the extract tell you about the pace of the work?

4 Does this job encourage a sociable atmosphere amongst the workers?

5 Some sociologists have suggested a link between this sort of work and high rates of strikes, could you suggest some reasons why this might be so?

6 Do you think the worker in the second extract has a better or worse job than the one in the first extract?

7 What are the major differences between the two sorts of jobs described?

The spread of computers, and the fact that they are increasingly interlinked, may have many consequences for our personal as well as our working lives

The use of micro-chip technology extends far beyond manufacturing though, for it allows many services to be performed by machine alone. Examples of this are the cash dispensers found outside banks and building societies, in effect replacing bank counter staff. In offices, too, tasks like typing are being replaced by word processing (basically computer-aided typing), and skilled work such as that performed by draughtsmen is being taken over by computers. It is not an exaggeration to call this micro-chip-controlled automation the 'second industrial revolution'.

Just like the first industrial revolution, there are bound to be many social consequences. We can only guess what these may be, but it certainly seems as if unemployment will increase as machines replace people. The question then is how will society support all the unemployed, if their numbers remain permanently high?

Large numbers of people living on social security payments might lead to increasing social tension. The differences between those who are in employment and those who are not might lead to a society of 'haves' and 'have-nots'. On the other hand, if the working week is cut and the jobs are shared, without a lowering of wages, then the social consequences could be very good for society.

The social effects of automation

In itself, automation is neither good nor bad, it just depends on how it is used. We know that it could be used to eliminate boring and dangerous tasks, and to cut down the numbers of employees in offices and factories. This could be excellent for society, if workers are moved to more interesting work, or if they are given greater leisure, with the income to enjoy it.

But will this be the case? It seems more likely that rather than eliminating repetitive tasks and creating more leisure time, automation is simply replacing both skilled and routine workers, making them unemployed. There is a world of difference between unemployment and increased leisure. Leisure requires enough money to maintain an adequate standard of living. Unemployment means poverty through reliance on supplementary benefit and the loss of social prestige, even a loss of a person's identity in a society where *what* you are often determines *who* you are.

Those people who do remain employed are likely to fall into two categories: those engineers, managers and scientists who are absolutely essential, and secondly those workers needed to keep an eye on the automated machinery, perhaps simply feeding information in to the controlling computer. The majority of those remaining in work then are likely to find their work deskilled, as the computers can take over the skilled element of their work and they are left only with routine supervision. It is precisely the full use of their talents and skills that makes a job interesting and satisfying to most people. The advantages to employers in needing less skilled workers is that they can be paid lower wages.

It can be seen therefore that automation is a two-edged sword, which could free workers from the drudgery of boring work and produce a wide range of high quality articles at low prices, as well as offering new services such as armchair shopping. But it could also lead to mass unemployment, deskilling, and lower wages.

1 Can we say for certain that automation will benefit or harm society?

2 What is the difference between leisure and unemployment?

3 The extract states that 'what you are often determines who you are'. What is meant by this?

4 What group of workers are most likely to remain in employment? Why?

5 What are the advantages of deskilling to an employer?

The consequences of automation

The problems	The advantages
• Loss of skills	• Elimination of boring work
• Increase in boring supervisory work, looking after machines	• New, interesting jobs in service industries created
• Divisions between the few employed and the large numbers of the unemployed	• Better quality products produced
• Lowering of wages	
• Increasing unemployment	
• Poverty for the unemployed	
• Political tensions caused by the increase in poverty and the widening of social differences	

Write a brief account of a person's typical working day in the year 2000 if:
  a)   the very worst consequences of automation come true;
  b)   the very best consequences come true.

The experience of work

As most of our waking time is spent in work, or work related activities (such as commuting), our experience or work is fundamental to our personal happiness. Sociologists have, therefore, studied workers' attitudes to, and enjoyment of, their jobs. The results of the studies show that attitudes to work fall broadly into two categories: **intrinsic satisfaction,** meaning that workers gain pleasure from their jobs; and **extrinsic satisfaction** which means that workers find little satisfaction in their work and have to seek their pleasure outside their jobs.

Why do people work?

Intrinsic satisfaction

This is usually found in skilled or intellectually demanding jobs, ranging from craftsmen to professional people, such as doctors. Their jobs are fulfilling and creative, with a great deal of variety. Satisfaction is therefore found *inside* their employment.

Extrinsic satisfaction

This is usually found in boring, repetitive jobs, such as car assembly lines. Jobs fail to stimulate or interest workers, stunting rather than stimulating their personalities. Workers therefore turn to the wage packet for their satisfaction. They try to earn as much as possible and gain their pleasure through spending their earnings on leisure pursuits and buying consumer goods such as cars and videos. Satisfaction is therefore found *outside* their employment.

Alienation

Karl Marx, the nineteenth-century writer, suggested the term **alienation** to describe the situation where workers experience work as something to be hated. Marx argued that in an ideal world our work ought to be an extension of our personality, yet for the majority of the population this is simply not true. As two sociologists writing about work once commented '87 per cent of workers ... expend more mental effort and resourcefulness in getting to work than in doing their jobs'.

The alienated worker

Alienation at work affects a person's life outside work.

Meaninglessness

Regards work as pointless and boring:
'Why am I doing this? The only thing I get out of work is the wage. I might as well be in prison eight hours a day.'

Self-estrangement

Feels that his/her true potential is not being fulfilled:
'Anyone could do this work. I'm just like a machine.'

Isolation

Worker feels cut off from his/her companions, both physically and socially:
'It's so noisy in here, I can't hear what anyone says. Anyway, the other workers are so unfriendly, I can't be bothered being sociable.'

Powerlessness

Feels lack of control over working conditions:
'The bosses just push us around. They never listen to what we have to say. The only way of getting back at them is through the union or by "accidentally" breaking the assembly line.'

If a person is unhappy at work, how do you think it will affect his/her
   a) family life?
   b) leisure choices?
   c) general mood and attitudes to others?

Why people work

Making work more fulfilling

How do workers cope with boring jobs?

Attempts to make work more fulfilling fall into two broad categories: on the one hand, the formal methods of researchers and management; and on the other, the informal methods practised by workers of all kinds in their daily work.

Formal methods

The first method of overcoming alienation at work is simply to compensate workers for the boredom of their jobs with high wages. The usual method is for 'time and motion' experts to work out the most efficient way of doing the job and then, with the savings gained, to pay higher wages. However this may compensate, it does not actually make work itself any more fulfilling.

An alternative approach, which derives from a famous study by Elton Mayo in the 1920s, is to create a sense of community amongst a firm's workers and the belief that they are valued by the employer. This can involve working in small groups, in pleasant conditions and the firm may provide various welfare provisions such as a subsidised canteen and a social club.

Both approaches mentioned above have left the methods of work the same, but have offered some form of compensation in wages or pleasant working conditions. A third approach is to actually change the way in which the product is made. A famous example of this is the Volvo car assembly plant where the traditional assembly line has been scrapped and teams of workers build virtually the whole car. This gives the workers a feeling that they are

Most of us live part of our lives in reality, part in dreams. Why is this?

members of a team actually creating a product with which they can identify. In the traditional 'division of labour' approach on an assembly line, each individual works alone adding only a small piece to a vehicle.

Informal methods

In their daily work situation, workers are continually trying to make their work more interesting in unofficial, sometimes illegal, ways. These include daydreaming, playing tricks on workmates, taking unofficial breaks and lengthening official ones.

Strategies for fulfilment at work

Those who find work satisfying are typically found in *professional* and *managerial* occupations

Those who are alienated from work are typically found in *routine office/factory work*

Formal methods of combat alienation:

- Increase extrinsic satisfaction through higher pay to purchase a better standard of living
- Make working conditions more pleasant create sense of belonging
- Worker's participation through elected representatives in management
- Forms of employee ownership

Worker's own techniques:

- Daydreaming about life outside work and leisure activities
- Humour at work – practical jokes, humorous stories, chatting
- Work avoidance – 'skiving' at work, absenteeism, extended breaks, restrictive work practice
- Pilfering
- Getting back at management

Schools and colleges, in some ways, are similar to offices and factories in that students need to be motivated to study and accept the discipline of the school.

1 How does the school/college *formally* motivate students?

2 How do students *informally* cope with the school day?

3 Use the ideas given in the text as a basis for your answers plus your own experience.

Enriching work

Formal approach

Mayo, the researcher discussed in this extract, felt that he had found the clue to a new kind of industrial management approach that would be more humane and efficient.

His work led to the development of the 'human relations' approach in American management which stressed the creation of close ties at work and loyalty to the firm.

In 1927 at the Hawthorne plant of the Western Electrical Company in Chicago, a series of experiments were made to see how changes in the physical work environment would affect the output of the workers: in particular changes were made in the lighting arrangements for a particular small group of workers. Very curious results emerged. It was found that the productivity of the group kept climbing irrespective of the various changes. Mayo (the chief researcher) came to the conclusion that as a result of the experiment, enormous amounts of attention had been bestowed upon the group and members of the group had come to feel much closer ties with each other. Mayo decided this was the crucial factor and his work led to an appreciation of the importance of the informal group in industry.

Source: Adapted from P Berger and B Berger, *Sociology: A Biographical Approach* (Penguin Education, 1976)

Informal methods

This is an extract from a study of women working in a tobacco factory. How do women deal with their boredom?

Val: I goes to sleep. I daydream. But when we don't talk for two hours, I starts tormenting the others, pulling the rag about, muck about sort of thing. With the Irish, you know, I picks on them. About Ireland – take the soldiers back, the bombings, all that – only mucking about like, I don't mean it. But then we have a little row, but we don't mean what we says. But I get so bored, I got to do something, or I start going out the back and have a fag. (Music comes on.) It's the best part of the day when the records come on.

Source: A Pollert, 'Girls, Wives, Factory Lives' in *New Society*, 22 October 1981

All workers from managers to unskilled shop floor operatives share this desire to control their pace of work. For professionals and managers it is easy, but for assembly line workers the only method apart from trade union bargaining is the drastic one of deliberately breaking the production machinery.

Piece work employees (those paid by the number of products they make), contrary to what you would expect, restrict output and in doing so keep the price paid for each 'piece' higher. Workers who go too fast are brought back into line by sarcastic comments, practical jokes and, if all else fails, they are 'sent to Coventry'.

1 In the first extract, why were the experiments originally held?

2 What happened when they changed the working environment?

3 What conclusions did Mayo reach?

4 What is the meaning of the term 'human relations approach'?

5 In this approach to management, who would be likely to benefit most, do you think?

6 In the second extract, describe two ways in which Val keeps herself amused.

7 Could you link the fact that management play records to the 'human relations approach' described earlier?

8 According to the third extract, why do workers on piece work restrict output?

9 What happens to those who work too hard?

10 Do you think that management agree with this practice?

11 Some sociologists have talked about the 'culture of the workplace'. Using the information given in the extracts, can you explain what this term might mean?

Problems faced by women at work

What special problems do women face at work?

Women suffer from three major disadvantages compared to men in their working lives:

- They are paid less than men. On average women receive only two-thirds of the wages received by men. Remember, since 1975 it has been illegal to pay women less than men for doing the same level of job (as a result of the 1970 Equal Pay Act). The difference in earnings can be explained by the fact that women are concentrated in low-paid jobs and have less opportunity for overtime.

- They are more likely to be in part-time employment. Ninety per cent of part-time workers are women. This is because generally women regard the role of mother and housewife as the most important. Women are expected to be first and foremost wives and mothers, and secondly to go out to work. Part-time working reflects the need to be at home to look after children when they are out of school. Women tend to have higher absenteeism than men because they need to stay away from work to care for any member of family who is ill. Women, therefore, face **role conflict** at work.

- Women are concentrated in low-paid, less-skilled jobs with few holding positions of authority. Over half of all women are in clerical work or the personal services, which are usually lowly paid. When women do have professional jobs, it is usually in the lower-paid 'marginal' professions such as nursing (92 per cent of nurses are women). However, less than a third of doctors are women and less than 10 per cent of women were in the higher professions or management.

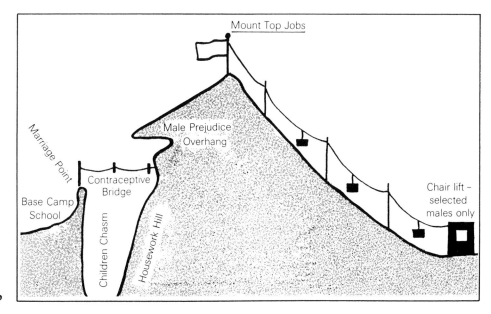

Women: the climb to the top

The pattern of women's working lives

The *typical* pattern of a woman's working life is to work from leaving school until the birth of the first child, then to give up work for the time it takes to raise her children (usually to secondary school age) and then to return to work. Of course this interrupted pattern of work means that employers are less likely to promote them or train them for a career. The employer will generally believe that the woman is less likely to remain with the company than a male worker.

The housewife

When we talk about 'work' it is usually taken to mean paid employment. However, women who do not have paid employment are usually 'house-wives', cooking, cleaning the house and caring for the family. This too is full-time work, which is often boring and seemingly never-ending. It can also be exhausting and, if there is no family nearby, the housewife can feel isolated.

(For further discussion on women at work see pages 54–8.)

Industrial relations

British society is based on the economic system of capitalism. This means that industry and commerce are owned by groups of individuals, as opposed to the State in communist societies. The owners wish to make as much profit as reasonably possible and therefore wish to keep their costs, which include wages, as low as they can. Employees wish to obtain the highest possible wage for themselves and to work in the best conditions possible. The resulting conflict between the two groups as a result of their different wishes is known as **industrial conflict**.

Forms of conflict

Are strikes the only form of industrial conflict?

- **Strike:** backed by trade union, usually with strike pay
- **Work-to-rule:** workers stick rigidly to conditions and regulations of employment; effective where workers routinely break regulations to achieve output
- **Overtime ban:** refuse to work longer than the official hours
- **Sit-in/work-in:** as response to redundancy, workers continue working and lock management out
- **Sabotage:** if striking is impossible/illegal, workers may express anger through wrecking machinery or the firm's products

The business of manufacture

Industry is organised to make profit. Most people accept this as fact and recognise that the more profit their company makes the better chance it has of providing a good standard of living and security for its employees and their families. This is not only because everybody's future earnings depend on the Company continuing to make a profit, but because a good profit encourages more investment – a good safeguard for the future.

Human resources, however, are scarce and expensive and therefore it makes sense to see that they are fully used and not misused. Just as it does not make sense to build more plants before we fully use the ones we have, neither does it make sense to keep on hiring men when some of those we have cannot make a full contribution because of bad organisation or working habits.

A Ford official publication

'It's just the situation they (management) are in. They've got to make a profit or they're finished. It's as easy as that. They've got to screw the blokes or they get screwed. That's the way it is. . . .'

A shop steward

Source: H Benyon, *Working for Ford* (Pelican, 1984)

1 What do the Ford management wish to do, according to the first extract?

2 How do they wish to do it?

3 Using the information in the quote from the shop steward, do you think that the Ford workers view the situation this way?

4 Given the different views, what sort of outcome is almost inevitable?

Reasons for strikes

The reason given for most strikes is to obtain better wages and the official view is that 90 per cent of days lost through strikes are due to pay disputes. However, sociologists are not convinced by this simple explanation. They suggest instead that strikers may express their grievances through wage demands, but underlying these there are deeper frustrations.

A British example of the way that strikes, which appear to be over pay, do in fact hide other grievances can be found in Lane and Roberts' description of a strike in the Pilkington glass works. *Strike at Pilkingtons*. The strike, which was unofficial, was eventually defined as a wage demand. However, it was really fuelled by three factors. First, the workers resented the introduction of stricter management control. Second, it was a chance for workers, who had always had to be submissive to Pilkingtons, to 'get their own back'. This resentment stemmed from the fact that as Pilkingtons were the only major employer in the area, any sign of revolt by workers would lead to their dismissal. Those dismissed would find it extremely difficult to find alternative jobs. Older workers who had less financial commitments were happy to grasp an opportunity to 'take revenge' on the management. Third, many of the strikers were resentful at the lack of interest shown by their own trade union, which was too bureaucratic and distant. The point is that in these circumstances the workers are only able to express their demands in terms of wage levels, because this is the institutionalised and accepted format for framing demands. In Britain, any other demands are regarded as illegitimate or 'political'.

Source: Adapted from S Moore and B Hendry, *Sociology* (Hodder and Stoughton, 1982)

1 Is it really true to say that 90 per cent of strikes are for better pay?

2 What were the three reasons behind the strike at Pilkingtons?

3 Why did the strikers not state the truth about the reasons for their strike action?

4 If money is not always the reason behind strikes, what implications does this have for industrial relations?

The decline in strike action

Why has the number of strikes fallen?

In the 1980s, the number of strikes, and the number of working days lost because of strikes, fell considerably from the 1979 peak (although the miners' strike in 1984–5 did break the pattern). By 1985, the number of days lost was a tenth of the 1979 figure. There are two main reasons for this.

Firstly unemployment: the fear of losing one's job frightened most workers. Secondly, government action: new, stricter laws were introduced by the Conservative Government in the early 1980s effectively limiting the power of unions to strike.

Trade unions

How have unions changed?

Trade unions represent the workforce, negotiating working conditions and wage levels with the management.

Since the 1950s considerable changes have taken place in the trade unions. The number of trade unions has declined. There are now fewer, but bigger, unions.

The total membership of the trade unions has fallen. In the 1980s alone, the trade unions have lost over 2 million members. The membership of trade unions has changed. The traditional view of trade unionists as male manual workers is now out of date. The growth area in trade union membership is in white-collar workers, reflecting the change in the whole employment structure.

White-collar workers are joining trade unions because they see themselves falling behind professional workers and some manual workers in wage levels. This has made them more militant and so more likely to join trade unions. Secondly, the old idea that clerical workers are part of the management is no longer true (if it ever was!). Working in huge numbers in open plan offices has given them a sense of 'solidarity' (a feeling of sharing a similar situation).

Professions

Are professions just middle-class trade unions?

The professions are organisations that represent the interests of the jobs which are traditionally considered as the most skilful and which carry the highest status, such as medicine and the law.

There are two views concerning professions. One group of sociologists argues that the professions are organisations which are just middle-class trade unions, protecting the interests of their members by restricting the number of new entrants. As there are few professionals about, they can demand high fees. A second group of sociologists take a slightly kinder view of the professions and argue that they exist to protect the public by placing very high standards on behaviour in these jobs.

CHAPTER TWELVE
LEISURE AND UNEMPLOYMENT

Leisure

Have people always seen a clear difference between their work and their leisure?

In modern industrial societies there is a strict division between what we consider to be 'work', that is paid employment, and what we consider to be 'leisure'. People work for a set number of hours each day and then at 5 p.m. they finish, and start their leisure.

This has not always been so. In most societies, throughout history, there was no clear distinction between a work time and a leisure time. In order to survive, people had to work in the fields or hunt. They performed these tasks until they had obtained enough food to eat, and adequate clothes and shelter. This work was not planned to happen at special times. As far as we know, there has never been a tribal society in which all the members started to hunt at 9 in the morning, stopped for an hour for lunch and then continued until 5 p.m.!

Leisure, as we know it, is related to the development of industry. Employers wanted a workforce that arrived at a particular time, so that the work of the machinery and employees could be coordinated. Work was so brutal and unpleasant that the few hours each day when people were not in the factories and offices was spent in trying to recuperate. Work then became separated from ordinary life; it became a fixed period of unpleasant labour each day. Work was time regarded as 'lost' from people's lives.

Gradually, the trade unions won shorter working days for their members and so the hours of non-work, or leisure, increased. However, the distinction in our lives between work, which is not expected to be enjoyable (for a large portion of the workforce), and leisure, which is expected to provide us with our fulfilment, has come to be seen as normal and natural.

The characteristics of work and leisure

Characteristics	Leisure	Work
Paid	No	Yes
Freedom	Yes	No
Choice	Wide	Limited
Self-imposed	Yes	No
Relationships with others based on power	No	Yes
Pleasurable	Yes	Only for those in skilled work

1 Give three examples of activities which in some situations are 'leisure' and others 'work'.

2 Can leisure occur at work? If so, give an example.

Defining leisure

Just what do we mean by 'work' and 'leisure'?

Although it may seem a very easy idea to define, leisure is a very slippery concept to grasp. It is not just *time* spent out of work, because we often have things to do which are forms of work in this time (for example, I wrote this book in my 'leisure' time). It is certainly not just *activities*, for one person's leisure is another's job. For example, some people dance for fun, others do it for a living. In the end, we have to say that there are certain characteristics more often found in leisure than in work, though these characteristics overlap.

The influences on leisure patterns

Our choice of leisure pursuits is influenced by a number of social factors. The most important ones are our social class (and within that our specific occupation, or lack of one), our age group and our sex.

Social class

Are there any social influences guiding our choice of leisure activities?

We know that social class is related to differences in: income; standards of education; amount of free time; cultural differences.

Put together these mean that middle- and working-class people often like different leisure pursuits. They read different newspapers and books, watch different programmes and films, and join different clubs.

The social differences in the wider society still remain in leisure activities

Occupation

How do our jobs influence our leisure choices?

If social class differences create broad divisions in our choices of leisure pursuits, occupational influences us in more specific ways. It has been suggested that there are three types of occupation-leisure relationships: **extension, neutrality** and **oppositional**.

Extension

This is when the job a person does is interesting and very fulfilling. In leisure, the person will often choose pursuits directly connected with work. This relationship is typical of people in professional occupations, such as social workers, teachers, etc.

Neutrality

This is when the job a person does is basically uninteresting and is seen as just a way of getting money to pay for an adequate style of life. In leisure, the person will emphasise the family and social enjoyment. Typical occupations are clerical workers and semi-skilled workers.

Oppositional

This is when the job a person does is exhausting and involves periods of intense physical effort. In leisure, the person looks for the complete opposite of work in order to refresh themselves. Typical occupations are miners and building workers.

The relationships between work and leisure

Why is it that fishermen drink so much? In many cases it is not even true to say that they do drink more than the average man, they are merely concentrating their drinking (while ashore). .... Is it that they are trying to forget the cold, black void of the Arctic which awaits them once again? Fishermen say: 'Of course fishermen get drunk. Anybody who does what we do has to drink to stay sane.'

Source: J Tunstall, *The Fishermen* (McGibbon and Kee, 1962)

This extract describes the leisure activities of workers on a production line. What often seemed to happen was that after finishing work and carrying out their various chores and family obligations, our affluent workers and their wives wanted only to 'take it easy' and 'relax', before the daily round began again.

Mr Lane, for instance, manages his own factory. He goes to work every morning at eight and often doesn't leave for home until ten or eleven at night. Mr Milner was a similar sort. An accountant in a large company he did not have such long hours in his office but almost every night and every weekend he brought papers back to work on in his study.

Some men like these work very long hours, spend a good deal of time travelling and do not necessarily share even their leisure with families, much of it being spent with business colleagues.

Source: P Willmot and M Young, *Family and Class in a London Suburb* (Routledge and Kegan Paul, 1960)

1 Parker has suggested three relationships between work and leisure – oppositional, extension and neutrality. Classify each of the extracts.

2 Overall, do you think there would be any link between these types of relationships and social class?

3 How would you classify your parents' leisure patterns?

Age group

As we pass through certain ages of life then our tastes, income and abilities alter:

- Childhood – usually spent in play, but with very limited income;

- Youth – a considerable amount of uncommitted money (no household bills to pay), which can be spent on the pursuit of style and excitement;

- Young marrieds – money is used to purchase/renovate houses and is spent on young children. Leisure is family based;

- Middle age – children leaving home and both partners working, so that this is the most affluent period of life. Luxury items and holidays are purchased;

- Over 65 – decline in income and in physical abilities. Home-based activities such as reading, watching television, going for walks.

Sex group

As the culture of our society stresses different expectations of males and females, this influences their choices of leisure. Males are far more active than females in virtually every area, particularly sport, which is regarded as more appropriate to males. Females are more likely to go dancing, engage in keep-fit and yoga. Most importantly, women have less leisure time than men as they are expected to do the bulk of the housework, even if they have a full-time job.

Leisure: The future

What will happen to leisure in the future?

In the future, the numbers of workers and the hours they will be required to work will fall as increased automation occurs. Sociologists have realised that this will make a significant impact on the role of leisure in society.

The optimists see the increase in leisure as giving us a chance to become more fulfilled. Increased time can be spent on the arts and on educating ourselves. The social class divisions caused by occupational and income differences will disappear as fewer and fewer people work.

The pessimists disagree. Where, they ask, will all the money come from for these leisure pursuits? In our society, people either receive a salary with which they can purchase leisure, or they live on state benefits which are not enough to purchase leisure. Leisure is usually provided by large profit-making companies. Unemployment will lead to boredom for the majority.

The changing patterns of leisure

In Victorian England leisure habits were sharply class-divided. Professional men and their families took no part in the street culture of working-class areas. There are still some socially exclusive pastimes. Hopeful show-jumpers need rich fathers. But the most popular leisure activities, such as watching television and taking holidays away from home, are now classless.

Paid vacations were still a middle-class perk in many firms throughout the inter-war years. Since then middle-class holiday entitlement has grown slowly, if at all, while manual workers have almost closed the gap. (On average today senior managers and the self-employed work longer than men on the shop-floor.) There is no longer any sense in which our economic and political elites can be labelled a 'leisure class'.

This trend towards a leisure democracy has been strength-ened as class differences in leisure tastes and habits have grown smaller. The middle classes still do more, but usually more of the same things that occupy working-class leisure. Class divisions in styles of holiday-making have collapsed. The main divisions now follow age, rather than class divisions. Discos cut across class barriers and it is the public in general, rather than high society, that dictates trends in fashion.

Source: Adapted from K Roberts, *Youth and Leisure* (Allen and Unwin, 1983)

1 Why do you think that leisure patterns were so sharply divided along class lines in Victorian England?

2 Is leisure now divided along class lines?

3 What do you think the author means when he talks about the 'leisure class'?

4 What divisions are now stronger than class? Do you agree?

The influence of work on our lives

Apart from leisure choices, does work influence other areas of our lives?

The impact of work on our lives does not end at the office or factory door; it spills over into many aspects of our lives. In very broad ways, our occupation determines our social status and our income. Differences in income cause different standards of living, and differences in social status influence the way people treat us. In narrower ways, too, our occupation influences our daily lives. The number of hours we work determines how much time we spend with our family, or in leisure. The demands of our job influence our personality and leisure activities.

Occupations do not only influence us as individuals, but whole communities too can be affected. A good example is the way in which traditional mining communities were pulled together by the close bonds of the miners' working relationship.

The influence of work on wider social relationships

Friendships

Maureen Cain studied the lives of policemen. She found that policemen's time outside their work is strongly influenced by the demands of their job. Policemen develop a sense of identity and inter-dependence because they need to trust one another in their work, both from physical attack and from allegations against them. Policemen are also isolated by the public who are wary about coming into contact with them. Finally, the unsocial hours caused by shiftwork adds to their difficulties meeting people from outside the police force. The result is that policemen tend to have their friends from within the force and are isolated from wider contacts.

The community

Perhaps the most striking feature of the traditional East End economy is its diversity: dockland, the many distributive and service trades linked to it, the craft industries, notably tailoring and furniture making, the markets. This diversity meant that people lived and worked in the East End – there was no need for them to go outside in search of jobs. The extended family remains intrinsic to the recruitment of the labour force and even to the work process itself. Son followed father into the same trade or industry while many of the craft and service trades were organised into family concerns. As a result of this, the situation of the work place its issues and interests remained tied to the situation outside work – the issues and interests of the community.

Source (both extracts): P Cohen, 'Subcultural Conflict and Working Class Community' (Centre for Contemporary Culture, University of Birmingham, 1972)

1 Why was there no need for the people of the East End to leave their community?

2 What result would this have for community life, do you think?

3 Were there any consequences for the family?

4 Today, the docks and the industries have closed in East London.
Do you think this has had any effect upon the community, apart from increasing employment?

5 Having read the extract on the influence of work on policemen's lives, could you make any comments on the social lives of firemen and members of the armed forces?

Copy out the diagram below so that it is large enough to write on. Complete the boxes to show the relationship between work and leisure, work and community, work and family life, work and income.

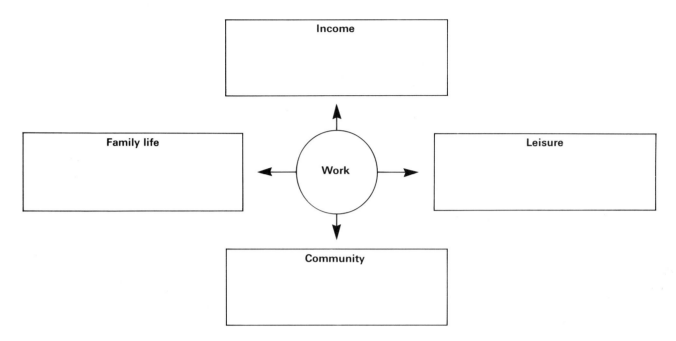

Criticism: The influence of leisure on work

Not all sociologists put all the stress on work influencing leisure: a study of Luton car workers suggests that people may choose dull and boring work in order to have a good lifestyle. In other words, the workers in the study chose boring, but better paid, work in preference to more interesting work to be able to afford to have a high standard of living.

Unemployment

The difference between unemployment and leisure

Aren't the unemployed really living a life of leisure?

There is a simple distinction between unemployment and leisure. Leisure means free time you have chosen to spend doing something you want, and having the finances to do it. Unemployment means free time not of your own choosing and with little money to spend. So the difference lies in choice and finance.

The importance of employment

Apart from the money, who cares if they are unemployed?

Employment is important to people for three main reasons: finance, status and self-respect.

Finance

Without money it is impossible to buy all the objects and the style of life that is regarded as normal. Unemployed people are usually poor.

Status

This is bought with consumer goods in our society. The latest registration car and the latest fashion in clothes indicate the position of a person, and in many people's eyes give that person status.

Self-respect

In British society the job you have is what you are (hence the opening question, 'What do you do?' in many conversations). Not to have a job is, therefore, to be nobody, not to have an identity. Clearly this is very closely linked to status, mentioned earlier.

The extent of unemployment

Why is there a disagreement over the 'real' numbers unemployed?

There is considerable dispute over the exact figures of the unemployed. The 'official' figure given by the Department of Employment in Spring 1987 was approximately 3 300 000. However, this probably underestimated the true extent of unemployment.

Only those receiving State benefits and registered to work are counted. This omits most married women. If their husbands are working they cannot receive benefit, and if their husbands are unemployed, then the benefit (and the unemployment statistic) is in his name. Secondly, people on the various training schemes (and one of the most important is the Youth Training Scheme) are not included. Thirdly, men over 60 who are long-term unemployed are omitted.

Adding all these together, the TUC (Trades Union Congress) estimated that in Spring 1987 there were really about 4.5 million people who would have liked to work, but could not.

The causes of unemployment

What are the long-term causes of unemployment?

The first point is that, in the mid-1980s, there has been a worldwide decline in employment, although some countries have been affected more than others. Japan, for example, peaked at three per cent unemployment, while it is over 10 per cent in countries such as Canada, Holland, Spain and Britain.

In Britain there are two main causes of high unemployment. Firstly, the increasing competition from abroad for manufacturing goods: a quick glance will show that the bulk of clothes, electrical goods and a large proportion of the cars are manufactured abroad. Secondly, automation: the increasing use of automation has led to the loss of traditional jobs. Initially this occurred in the unskilled labouring area, but this has now spread to skilled work.

Check a) the electrical goods in your home (stereo, washing machine, TV, etc.);
b) your clothes.
How many of these were made in Britain?

Tackling unemployment

Some European governments want to share the available work more evenly among those after a job. . . . Cutting working hours is one method . . . like the Irish who cut the working week from 48 to 40 hours and banned workers from holding two jobs. In Belgium, the government has passed laws making cuts in workers' pay in return for cuts in working time and more recruitment . . . working time cuts of 5 per cent were compensated by 3 per cent less pay and 3 per cent more jobs.

Can you persuade older people to retire early and replace them with younger workers? That's one way to redistribute work. West Germany has encouraged men aged between 60 and 65 to retire early and by 1980, only one third were working. In the Italian steel industry retirement at 50 was adopted last year.

The young come at or near the top of everyone's list for special attention. The stress throughout Europe – seen in Britain's Youth Training Scheme – on training for the young turns on two consider-ations. Training seems as good a way as any of keeping youngsters off the streets, even if there are no jobs at the end of it all. More positive is the awareness that technological change has outmoded old patterns of education and training.

With its plan to roll back dismissal rights and to water down the Wages Councils (official organisations which set wages for certain indust-ries), Britain is quite an enthusiastic backer of a dif-ferent approach, freeing the market by making it easier for employers to sack workers and pay them lower wages.

Source: Adapted from D Thomas 'Learning about job creation' in *New Society*, 23 May 1985

1 The extract mentions four methods of combating unemployment.
What are they?

2 Rank these methods in order of usefulness, in your opinion, in combating unemployment. Give reasons for your ranking.

3 Are there any alternative proposals you could suggest?

The unemployed

Which groups are more likely to be unemployed?

Unemployment hits those at each end of the labour market: the young and the old. The unemployment rate for the under 25s is about 23 per cent and for the over 55s it is about 17 per cent. In the country as a whole it is about 12 per cent. The ethnic minorities, too, have higher than average unemploy-ment rates. The rate for adult men of Asian and West Indian origin is twice that of Whites.

There is disagreement over the extent to which women are affected by unemployment. As they are generally employed in the lower-paid jobs and are more often likely to have part-time work, it seems that they are not as likely to be laid off as men. But as we saw before, the official statistics do not include many married women who would like to work but are not eligible for benefits, so they seriously underestimate the extent of female unemployment. Finally, the less-skilled worker is far more likely to be made unemployed than the skilled worker.

Unemployment

A

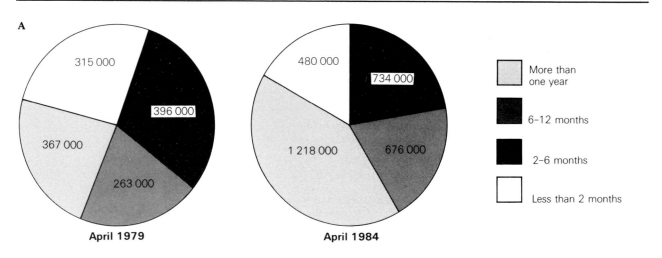

April 1979   **April 1984**

The duration of unemployment   Source: *Employment Gazette*

B

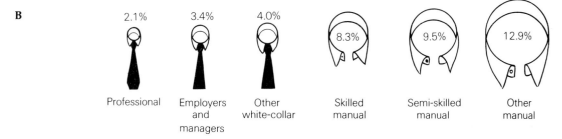

| 2.1% | 3.4% | 4.0% | 8.3% | 9.5% | 12.9% |
| Professional | Employers and managers | Other white-collar | Skilled manual | Semi-skilled manual | Other manual |

Source: Adapted from S Fothergill and J Vincent, *The State of the Nation* (Pluto Press, 1985), and the *Employment Gazette*

Unemployment by occupational groups
Note: Since these figures were calculated in 1981, *all* the percentages have risen, but in roughly the same proportion.

1 In the pie charts, A, what has happened to the proportion of people unemployed for more than one year in 1984 compared to 1981?

2 Does your answer indicate any change in the nature of unemployment and its effects on people's lives?

3 Look at B. Which occupational group
a) has been hardest hit by unemployment?
b) has been least hit by unemployment?

4 Does any pattern emerge in the relationship between class and unemployment?

The two nations

Scotland 15.2%

N Ireland
21.0%

North
18.8%

North-west
16.1%

Yorkshire
and
Humberside
14.8%

East
Midlands
12.5%

West
Midlands
15.7%

East Anglia
10.1%

Wales 16.8%

South-east 9.7%

South-west 11.7%

**Annual average rates of unemployment in the UK
in 1984**

Source: Adapted from: New Society Database' in *New Society*, 8 November 1985

Two-nation jobs shock revealed

The Government will be forced this week to confirm through its own employment figures that Britain is becoming 'two nations' – the North increasingly unemployed and the South benefiting from new service jobs.

Figures in the Department of Employment's job census to be published on Thursday – almost a year late – confirm that around 94 per cent of total jobs lost since the Tories took office have been in Scotland, the North, Midlands, Wales and Northern Ireland – where the majority of the population live.

The southern triangle – populated by the remaining 42 per cent – has suffered only 6 per cent of job losses. Publication of the census is certain to embarrass Mrs Thatcher deeply

While the depressed North has suffered massive job losses since the Tories came to power, the South-East has lost only 1 per cent employment and the South-West 2 per cent. One area – East Anglia – actually gained 3 per cent employment.

More than two-thirds of service jobs created since 1979 have also been in the more fortunate South-East.

The census reveals a 28

per cent drop in manufacturing and construction jobs since 1979, compared with an *increase* over the same period of 4.9 per cent in Japan; −2 per cent in the US; −1.4 per cent in Canada; −8.5 per cent in Germany; and −9.4 per cent in Italy.

The census paints a bleak picture of Britain's industrial decline. Manufacturing employment has fallen since 1979 from 7 067 000 to 5 126 000.

And with industry continuing to shed jobs at the rate of 14 000 a month, the number of people engaged in manufacturing by August this year is likely to fall below five million for the first time since the great depression of 1933.

Worst hit is Britain's traditional heavy industry base. Metal goods, engineering and vehicles are down just over one million jobs (a 31 per cent decline). But even

the electronics industry on which the Government pins so many hopes has suffered a 24 per cent drop of 215 000 jobs – practically double the original estimate.

The census shows a net job decline across the spectrum of industry and commerce of 1 632 000 since Mrs Thatcher assumed power, after allowing for new jobs in the service sector but excluding the growth in self-employment.

The only bright spot was in banking and finance, which posted a 34 per cent increase in employment to 560 000, a growth almost commensurate with the sharp rise in personal indebtedness.

Curiously, while so many people find it impossible to hang on to one job, others are now doing more than one. The census discloses that 373 000 people are 'double-jobbing'.

WHERE JOBS WENT

Regional breakdown of the 1.6m employee jobs lost and gained between June '79 and '86.

West Midlands	−301 000
North West	−278 000
Yorkshire/ Humberside	−266 000
The North	−215 000
Scotland	−149 000
Wales	−130 000
East Midlands	−118 000
South East	− 73 000
Northern Ireland	− 64 000
South West	− 39 000
East Anglia	+ 23 000

Source: The *Observer*, 4 January 1987

1 Using the map and newspaper extract as guides, draw your own map and fill in the numbers of jobs lost by area.

2 Which two regions have the highest unemployment rates? What are those rates?

3 Which area has the lowest rate? What is the lowest rate?

4 Which area has actually seen an increase in employment?

5 What do you think the term 'two nations' means?

6 What are the possible consequences, do you think, for the future of the north or Britain?

7 Some people have suggested that the division between north and south is now more important than that between the social classes. What is your opinion?

8 Are manufacturing jobs decreasing
    a) in Britain?
    b) worldwide?
Does this have any importance for Britain's future?

9 Which types of jobs are increasing? Can you explain this?

10 What explanations can you suggest for the variations in employment in the different parts of Britain?

The different experiences of unemployment

Does unemployment hit everyone equally badly?

The experience of unemployment will not be the same for each social group. The experience of unemployment for a man of 50, for example, who has worked since leaving school can be devastating. We know that men in particular take much of their identity from their job. When asked what we are, we reply in terms of our job. Lack of work can lead to crisis of identity. For those women workers who see their primary identity as a wife and mother, loss of employment need not be so devastating a blow to identity.

Although the majority of women workers have seen employment as an *escape* from the home and their return to the role of housewife may make them feel trapped.

Young people without a lifetime of work behind them may well find the result of unemployment very different from the middle-aged. It could be argued that living on social security, freed from the drudgery of work could be, for a short time at least, a pleasant life. However, all this is marred by a number of hidden problems that develop individually and socially the longer unemployment lasts. The first problem facing many young people is that they need to remain at home, continuing to receive financial support and are, therefore, subject to attempts at control by their parents. Friction soon develops and the traditional way out, finding a flat or getting married, is no longer available. Paul Willis in a study of youth unemployment in the Midlands has found that some girls deliberately get pregnant in order to escape from their family, relying upon the State for support.

Working-class youth, both black and white, has wholeheartedly embraced the ethics of the consumer society. Who you are is expressed through ownership of the Ford Escort XR3i and the smart clothes carrying the chain store's impressive sounding Italian labels. But unemployment is increasingly robbing working-class youth of the legitimate ways of obtaining these goods. The affluent culture of the 1970s does not change just like that. It carries on into the age of unemployment, so you cannot 'pull' a girl without a flash car, money for drinks in the pub and some smart clothes. So develops the bitter inarticulate demands of youth, who see little justification in the way money and jobs are distributed at present. If they need something and the system is unfair then it is OK to get the goods for themselves in whatever way they can.

'Consumerism' and unemployment have combined to create another feature of our current high streets, the groups of youth who are just hanging around. They have nothing to do and little money to spend. So they gather in the place where they can see and be seen by others of their age. In doing so they present a 'threat' to the middle-aged and 'respectable' shoppers. The police are called in to move the youth out and so develop the origins of resentment against the police.

1 Do all people respond in the same way to the experience of unemployment?

2 Why is it possible that at first young people may not find unemployment as 'a blow to their identity'?

3 Describe the feelings that youth have towards the possession of clothes and cars etc. What happens when they are unemployed?

4 How can unemployment lead to resentment against the police?

5 How do some girls escape from being trapped at home, according to Willis's research?

6 Do you feel this extract is an accurate description of the young unemployed that you know? If not, state your reasons.

The possible consequences of unemployment

Political unrest
In the gap between the living standards of the employed and the unemployed becomes too wide, there could be political problems as the poor look for ways out of their problems.

Scapegoating/racism
If there is no easy explanation for the high rates of unemployment, people often look for scapegoats to blame their problems on. This might increase racism.

Crime
Crime rates increase as the gap between rich and poor grows. The goods are in the shops to tempt the unemployed, but they simply cannot afford them. Therefore they may turn to crime (and political action?).

Family conflict
Women may be forced back into the mother/housewife role as jobs disappear. Alternatively, it is possible that as husbands lose their jobs, the only income will be that of the wife. Males may find this 'role swop' difficult to accept

Inner city
As unemployment rises, it appears to be youth in the inner cities who bear the brunt. The resentment and desperation is reflected in crime, riots, racism and drug abuse.

Drugs and alcohol
The despair of the young appears to be expressed by the increase in drug abuse. (See **Inner city** and **Crime**.)

Can you think of any more?
If so, include them in the boxes.

CHAPTER THIRTEEN

SOCIAL CONTROL, DEVIANCE AND CRIME

Social control: An introduction

What is social control?

When we speak and write in English, we are aware that it has a grammar (a set of rules), even if we are not sure how to explain it. We work within these rules, maybe using different words in different combinations, but always working within a framework of grammar that we have learned since childhood. We make mistakes; we have different dialects in different parts of the country and amongst different social classes. In the end, however, we know that there is a clear distinction between English and French or Italian, and you do not need to be an academic to know it.

Society too has its own 'grammar', or 'culture', which guides us in our actions, even though we may not be too aware of it. No one disputes that, in language, grammar is a good thing, but the situation is different when it comes to social rules. Sociologists are divided in their opinions of who exactly benefits from the rules and values of society. Some sociologists argue that we all benefit from having a common set of values, as life is predictable. Others disagree, claiming that the rules guiding our behaviour are to the benefit of those who are more powerful and wealthy, because they persuade us to act in the ways that they want us to. **Social control** is the process whereby people are encouraged to conform to the common expectations of society.

Types of social control

There are two types of social control: **informal control** and **formal control**.

Informal control

This form of control is based on the approval or disapproval of those around us whose view of us we regard as important, for instance family, friends and peer group (a group of people usually of similar age with whom we compare our behaviour, our classmates at school or colleagues at work, for example). If they disapprove of our behaviour we usually alter it to conform to their expectations.

How is it enforced?

People around us may tell us they do not like our behaviour, they may ridicule us, they may argue with us, they may play practical jokes on us, or they may even 'send us to Coventry'.

Informal social control is part of the 'socialisation process' by which we become a truly 'human' being, by learning the expected patterns of behaviour in society.

Formal control

Whenever we are given rules to follow, as in school or the laws which are the legal system of society, this is formal control. These rules are almost always written down.

Social control – every society needs ways of gently persuading people to obey rules

How is it enforced?

Usually, formal control is enforced through official 'sanctions', such as a fine for speeding, or imprisonment for robbery.

Social control in action

How is social control imposed on us?

We have seen that social control operates in two ways, formally and informally. In society there are a number of 'institutions', or 'agencies', which impose social control upon us. The most important are the family, the school, the peer group, the mass media, the workplace, the legal system and, to a much lesser extent, religion.

The family

The basic socialisation takes place in the family and it is here through parents and relatives that we learn the accepted morality of society, to distinguish between 'right' and 'wrong'. Delinquency has been linked to the failure of parents to socialise their children correctly. Not only do we learn what is right and wrong in general, we also learn the expected behaviour for males and females (gender roles).

The school

The process of socialisation continues, formally in the content of the lessons we are taught and informally in the expectations of us by the teachers and fellow pupils. (See pages 159 and 167 for a discussion on 'the hidden curriculum'.) Pupils are divided into the successes and the failures, and they develop appropriate attitudes to cope with these situations (see page 164).

The peer group

People of our own age to whom we look for approval are crucial in forming our attitudes to society. The peer groups develop in school and studies have shown how pupils divide themselves into those who accept the school rules and those who do not. The groups appear to develop from the different streams as a result of teachers' differing attitudes and expectations of high- and low-stream pupils.

The mass media

The term 'mass media' includes such things as newspapers, radio and television. These influence us by providing models of behaviour which we copy and by condemning other deviant forms of behaviour. Although they do not affect us directly, in the sense that seeing something on television does not immediately make us want to copy it, they do create a certain climate of opinion regarding acceptable behaviour. As the media are part of the 'establishment', they tend to reflect conservative views.

The workplace

At work, conformity is ensured by the fact that if we are troublemakers, or a bit 'weird', then we may not be promoted, or in some certain circumstances even sacked. Amongst our work colleagues, if we fail to conform to their values, then they use such things as practical jokes at our expense to show us we ought to change out behaviour (see page 182 for an example of this).

The legal system

The final, most powerful institution dealing with social control is the legal system, by which we mean the police and the courts. People breaking the law are arrested and judged. Usually the law is reserved for what many people regard as the most serious breaches of our values.

Deviance

The distinction between crime and deviance

Is a deviant act the same as a delinquent act?

As we have seen in our discussion of social control, there is a distinction between behaviour of which society disapproves, such as rudeness to others, and behaviour which is officially considered illegal, such as robbery.

Sociologists call all behaviour which is disapproved of by society, whether it is illegal or not, **deviant** behaviour. So, both robbery and rudeness are deviant. **Crime** is the word used to describe only that behaviour which is against the law.

The advantage of the term deviance for sociologists is that we can think of all behaviour of which society disapproves as the same thing. The fact that some behaviour is illegal is just another form of social control. Otherwise people tend to think of illegal acts as completely different from other forms of behaviour, which is untrue.

When is behaviour defined as deviant?

Two young men are punching each other violently. Is this a deviant act? Apparently not, for all around them men and women are cheering and encouraging them, after all it is a boxing match and the men are fighting for the heavyweight championship of the world. Now, imagine two young men fighting on the streets of London. The response of onlookers would probably be to try to separate them or call the police. Behaviour is not in itself deviant, it depends upon the circumstances and meaning of the behaviour. Sociologists have spent a great deal of time trying to explain the circumstances in which behaviour becomes labelled as deviant.

Acts are defined as deviant or not depending upon:

- place – lovemaking, for instance, is regarded as deviant if it takes place in the streets;
- society – carrying a gun is wrong in Britain, normal in the United States;
- time – hanging is now regarded as barbaric as a form of punishment in Britain, yet thirty years ago people were hanged for murder;
- who commits the act – alcohol drinking is normal for those over 18 and discouraged for those under 18.

Why are there variations in what is defined as deviant behaviour?

Why are some acts illegal and others not?

It seems that the more *powerful* a group, or person, is the more likely it is for its behaviour to be regarded as acceptable. The further away from *accepted values* an act is, the greater the chance it has of being condemned as deviant.

It is clear that if an act is strongly disapproved of by the majority of the population then it is made illegal; murder for example. There are, however, many acts which are illegal, yet there is little popular anger about them, for instance shops opening on Sundays.

Secondly, a particular 'pressure group' (see page 229) may agitate to have a certain act made illegal (or legalised), for instance the campaign against cruelty to animals in laboratory experiments. This form of pressure group activity has been called a 'moral crusade'.

Thirdly, very powerful groups in society have the laws altered to their benefit. The laws against the activities of trade unions and picketing are a good example of this. Marxist sociologists point to the way that laws in Britain seem to be mainly to protect property and that it is the least powerful groups in society, the working class, the young and the poor, who seem to be the target of the laws and police activity.

Labelling and the sad story of boy B

Labelling

Howard Becker, for example, believes that there is no such thing as a deviant act – it is merely behaviour that people so label. . . .

The essence of labelling theory is, therefore, not so much what the individual does, but the reaction of others. Often the same act of deviance is treated differently – a car theft by a middle-class youth is played down as high spirits, while a working-class youth, especially if black, might be likely to go to Borstal. . . .

Certain *master* labels, such as being declared homosexual, criminal or lunatic, tend to override all others, and, once applied, are very difficult to live down. An ex-prisoner, though he has served his sentence will find it difficult to get a job and settle back into normal life. Employers, families and friends often no longer trust him and fear being tarred with the same brush. Stigmatised and rejected by society, many such people turn back to crime, thus fulfilling suspicions about there being the criminal type – a 'born villain' – a sort of 'self-fulfilling prophecy'.

In this sense, the labellists are saying the cause of deviancy is often not the action itself, but the reaction of others to it. It is possible, they say, that social control, far from preventing crime, can help cause it.

But critics argue that it fails to explain people's actions before they are labelled. Why do some people commit crime while others do not? Marxists add the criticism that this theory fails to explain who has the *power* to label and why. In their view the power to label is an important part of the bourgeoisie's control. By labelling those who threaten its power and privilege as deviants, it can neutralise them. So left wingers are labelled 'militants', or 'loonies'.

Source: Adapted from M Slattery, *The ABC of Sociology* (Macmillan, 1985)

The story of Boy A

| *Steals a sociology textbook* | *No one sees him and he goes home to study* | *Passes all his exams* | *And is now a lecturer in . . . sociology* |

The story of Boy B: a 'deviant career'

| *Steals a sociology textbook* | *He is seen, caught and arrested* | *Given seven years in prison* | *On his release, decides he wants to be a librarian, but no one will employ him* | *So he returns to stealing, and is caught again* |

1 Explain, using the stories of boys A and B, the meaning of the term labelling.

2 According to Becker, is there such a thing as 'a deviant act'?

3 Can the same act be treated as deviant by one person and not deviant by another? Explain your answer.

4 What is a 'master label'?

5 What is a deviant career?

6 Give two criticisms of the labelling theory.

7 Can you make up a deviant career of your own to illustrate the idea of labelling?

Scapegoating and moral panic

In the mid-1960s, Stan Cohen studied the way in which the image of mods and rockers (in both the senses, of style of dress and of forms of behaviour) was created in the media as a result of some minor disturbances in Brighton and Clacton. This influenced how young people saw themselves and it encouraged them to behave in the (false) way portrayed by the media. The police and the politicians were equally alarmed by the media coverage. They insisted on very strict action against all young people who fitted the stereotype of being a mod or a rocker. The end result was a series of disturbances and large-scale arrests. There was a public outcry against the mods and for a while they were seen as a dreadful threat to law and order in Britain.

Cohen explained this 'moral panic' by saying that whenever the tensions of society start to become too great, then certain groups, usually powerless and young, are used as scapegoats on which many of society's problems are blamed. The effect of the scapegoating is to draw the bulk of people in society together in response to the supposedly dreadful behaviour of the scapegoated groups. Clearly this approach is closely linked to labelling.

Since Cohen's original study of mods and rockers (in *Folk Devils and Moral Panics*), there have been moral panics over skinheads, football hooligans, punks, and the hippy peace convoy.

1 Who created the images of mods and rockers?

2 How did the youth of that period respond to the 'labelling'?

3 How did the police respond?

4 What did Cohen call this?

5 What do sociologists mean when they use the term 'scapegoats'?

6 Why do moral panics occur?

7 Can you give an example of a moral panic not mentioned in the extract?

8 Turn to page 270 for a 'map' of a moral panic. Using this, devise some typical newspaper head-lines for an imaginary moral panic. What responses will there be from
   a) the public?
   b) the police?
   c) the politicians?
   d) the labelled groups?

Patterns of crime and delinquency

● **Delinquency:** acts of crime by those under 17; dealt with by special courts, known as 'Juvenile Courts'

Crime: for men only?

The graphs below show the numbers of people found guilty of more serious offences (indictable offences) in England and Wales by age and by gender, between 1961 and 1984.

The break in the graph at 1977 indicates that from that year onwards a new method was used to calculate the figures.

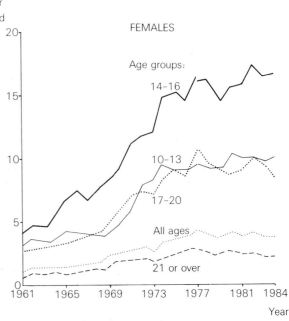

Note: The scale for this graph is five times larger than the scale for the graph of male offences.

Who commits crime, by sex and age

Source: *Social Trends* (HMSO, 1986)

1 Who has the higher rate of crime overall, males or females? (Be careful!)

2 Which age group is most likely to commit crime for both males and females?

3 What was the rate per thousand of indictable offences for males in 1984?

4 What was the rate per thousand of indictable offences for females in 1984?

5 In the age range 14–16 is it true or false to say that the number of female offences is increasing faster than that of males?

6 Some sociologists have explained the changes in the crime rate of females by relating it to their 'changing gender roles'. Could you suggest what they might mean by this? (It may help if you compare the expectations of female behaviour 50 years ago with expectations of it today.)

Who commits the crime according to the official statistics?

There are about 3½ million crimes committed each year which are considered serious enough to be judged by a judge and jury. The most common offences relate to theft and the handling of stolen goods (about 50 per cent), followed by burglary (about 25 per cent).

Four points are important when examining the statistics of crime and delinquency:

- age – the period in a person's life when they are most likely to commit a criminal offence is 14–20;

- gender – there is a marked difference between the crime rates of males and females, with the male rate being about five times higher than the female rate;

- class – crime and delinquency are directly related to social class, with working-class youth, for instance, having a crime rate eight times higher than upper middle-class youth;

- place – crime rates are significantly higher in inner cities than in the suburbs or the country areas.

Explanations for crime and delinquency

Age

Why do people commit crime?

Youth is a period when there is a great stress on excitement and 'having a laugh'. This search for a 'good time' can often lead to clashes with the law. It is also true to say that youth is a period when social control is weak. It has been suggested that the weakness of social control, coupled with the search for excitement, can lead to a drift into delinquency. People move away from delinquency as they get older because of the stability provided by marriage, family and employment. (Of course, this suggests that if rates of unemployment stay high for young people, then they may not move out of crime.)

Gender

The different expectations we have of boys and girls leave their mark on us as we grow up. Typically masculine values, such as toughness, can lead directly to fighting, for instance. On the other hand, feminine values stress conformity, domesticity and 'getting a boy' – hardly values that will lead to delinquency!

Women and crime

The criminal statistics suggest that women are less likely to commit most crimes than men, for example women constitute only 12 per cent of all offenders and in the more serious crimes such as robbery, wounding and murder, women represent only 5 per cent of offenders. In the past, this has been explained by the physical differences between men and women. However, feminists dispute this. In *Women and Crime*, Frances Heidensohn argues that much of the explanation for the conformity of women is that they are far more constrained than men, particularly by the roles they are expected to play in society:

'It's hard to bring off a burglary if you're pushing a twin baby-buggy and its contents; caring for a demented elderly relative hardly gives a woman time to plan a bank robbery. In fact women are burdened with duties which act as a constraint. . . . In public, appropriate behaviour for females is different than it is for men. For example males virtually have a monopoly over the use of force and violence in society. . . . It is unacceptable for women to be violent, yet relatively normal for men to be so.'

There is evidence to

suggest that police treat female criminals differently. They tend to think that females are 'naturally' more law abiding then males and therefore have been 'led astray' into crime. This is particularly true for female delinquency. Girls caught for delinquent acts are much more likely to be put in custody for 'care and protection' than male delinquents. Police are sometimes more lenient on females than males. For example, two girls fighting is less likely to result in arrest than two males fighting, as it is not regarded as so serious. Once again this is related to policemen's views on male and females as different.

1 What proportion of crimes are committed by women?

2 In the past, what explanations have been offered for the differences in crime levels between men and women?

3 Explain how the social role of women is supposed to explain the low proportion of crimes committed by women.

4 Given the importance of gender roles, what sort of crimes do you think women are most likely to commit?

5 Why do police treat female offenders differently?

6 What results is this different treatment likely to have?

7 Do you think that the official statistics on crime could be affected by the attitudes of police towards female crime? If so, how?

8 In your experience, have you ever been in a situation in which males and females have been involved with the police? Describe the experience and compare it with the points made in the extract.

Class

Most delinquents and criminals arrested by the police are drawn from the working class. There are various explanations for this.

Subculture of the working class

The values of the working class, such as toughness and immediate enjoyment, can easily lead working-class people into criminal activities.

Poor socialisation

This is most often found amongst the working class. Parents fail to bring up their children to uphold the values of society.

Anomie

If a society fails to provide enough ways for people to be successful, then they will feel frustrated and possibly turn to crime. This happens particularly in periods of high unemployment. The term 'anomie' refers to a situation where large numbers of people fail to follow generally accepted values, instead adopting various deviant forms of behaviour, such as theft or drugtaking.

Status frustration

Working-class youths are more likely to fail at school and be in bottom streams. They feel that everybody looks down upon them and so they express their frustration in delinquent behaviour, which helps them to 'get their own back' on society.

Criticism

One law for the rich and one for the poor: Marxist writers suggest the explanations given so far miss out the obvious and centrally important point that the wealthy and powerful pass the laws which benefit themselves, but harm the working class. If this is so, then it is bound to be the working class who commit most crime. For instance, the theft of money from a bank is quickly pursued by the police, but stock exchange swindles and tax avoidance are rarely punished or even investigated.

Place

Crime rates are higher in inner-city areas and some 'problem' housing estates, because the people concentrated in these areas are often poorer and have more social problems than the bulk of the population. Consequently, the explanations which we have just looked at regarding the working class are especially true here.

An alternative explanation put forward by many sociologists is that policing in inner-city areas, particularly in areas where there are many Blacks, is particularly strict. Indeed, it is suggested that Blacks are 'harassed' by the police. The result is higher arrest rates and greater social tension, which can lead to rioting in certain circumstances.

Why do people commit crime?: Non-sociological explanations

Psychologists have suggested there are particular types of people who are more prone to be anti-social. Some have gone so far as to argue that certain people are actually born with anti-social tendencies. Hans Eysenck, a famous psychologist, argues there are basically two personality types, the result of socialisation in childhood and natural instincts. These are the introvert and the extrovert. The introvert is quiet and reserved, he 'keeps his feelings under control, seldom behaves in an aggressive manner and does not lose his temper easily'. The extrovert is fun-loving and outward-going, but 'tends to be aggressive and loses his temper quickly; his feelings are not kept under tight control, and he is not always a reliable person'. According to Eysenck, the extrovert person is more likely to turn to crime, unless his/her parents train him to control his impulses and instil a strong conscience in him.

Bowlby, another well-known psychologist, has suggested that people who are deprived of motherly affection in their infancy later are likely to become criminal.

Sociologists are doubtful that this is the full explanation for crime. They suggest instead that cultural factors are important in two ways, firstly in helping to decide which acts are illegal, and secondly in motivating a person to commit crime. They point to such factors as feelings of frustration at being unsuccess-ful at school[status frustration], or being unable to purchase all the consumer goods advertised in the media when they have a low-paid job or are unemployed [anomie], or the values of neighbourhoods where crime is regarded as an acceptable way of life[subculture].

They question who makes laws for whose benefit. Whereas some sociologists suggest the law is the reflection of the values of the majority of the population, others argue that law is the reflection of the will of the more powerful in society. In either case, law is not something natural that people can be born to break. It is a social creation and varies from society to society.

1 Give two explanations psychologists have suggested for people committing crime.

2 Is it true or false to say that some psychologists believe that certain people are born with anti-social tendencies (and are, therefore, likely to become criminal)?

3 Do sociologists agree with these explanations?

4 Explain the meaning of the following sociological terms: status frustration, anomie, subculture. (You may find it helpful to turn to the main text.)

5 'Law is a social creation.' Why is this important in understanding why people cannot be 'born rule breakers'?

White-collar crime

When we talk about crime, most people have an image of bank robbers holding up the bank clerks and then jumping into a getaway car. However, far more money is stolen and far more injury is done by 'white-collar' crime.

Security guard shot in raid on High Street bank! Old lady beaten and robbed of her life savings by two thugs!

These are the sorts of typical newspaper headline which help to create our images of crime. Yet few people realise that these *street crimes* actually cost the nation less, in terms of injury and loss of money, than those crimes which sociologists call *white-collar crimes*.

White-collar crime often involves swindling money from companies, or even from private individuals. Sometimes it is committed by a manager who fiddles the accounts in order to steal money for himself. In cases like this, when the employers find out, they will prefer to simply sack the offender and avoid publicity, which might harm the image of their company.

But this sort of white-collar crime, although important, is dwarfed by a far more serious version, which is the deliberate breaking of the law by companies or top directors in order to swell their profits. One of the major problems of studying this sort of crime in Britain is that it is rarely uncovered and even less rarely brought to court. After all, the directors of these companies may be very important people, with a considerable number of powerful contacts in the world of finance and politics.

But one more important, point that needs to be made is that our very definition of crime is influenced by powerful groups in society. These groups can have certain behaviour branded as crime and enforced by the police,

while other activities, which *you* would consider harmful to people, are not covered by criminal law – or even if they are, they are rarely enforced.

Take the example of cigarette smoking: virtually everyone (except the cigarette companies) accepts that smoking tobacco greatly increases the risk of a person contracting cancer. Yet cigarettes are still allowed to be sold. What about the difference in attitude of most people to tax avoidance and fiddling social security? If you are self-employed and can get away without paying taxes, then well done! If you are 'scrounging' off the DHSS, then the full weight of the law falls on you.

One last example – health and safety laws at work are there to protect workers. Unfortunately for employers,

the costs of conforming with the laws can be quite high. The result? Some employers prefer to ignore them. This is a trade unionist at a toy factory talking: 'When the inspector comes to the factory we always point out the dangerous wiring, defective machines, unsafe stacking of heavy boxes, and so on. He goes in to see the management and after 20 minutes is out again. It's always the same old story – if we wish to press ahead with complaints, the factory owners will shut the place down and move production to the Far East [where the parent company is located]. If we keep quiet, production will continue here. Well, what can you do when there are hundreds of jobs at stake? We always shut up.'

1 On reading this, one student remarked: 'Law and crime – it's all about power, isn't it?' Why do you think the student said this? Give two examples to illustrate your answer.

2 Cigarette smoking is given as one example of a group that is able to avoid having its activities labelled as criminal. What

do you think about this? Is it a good example? Should the manufacture and sale of cigarettes be prohibited like other drugs? Give reasons for your answer.

3 What reasons can you suggest for the fact that street crime is heavily under-reported to the police compared to white-collar crime?

Criminal statistics

Should we believe the official statistics on crime?

All the discussion on crime and delinquency so far has made the assumption that the official statistics of crime accurately reflect the amount and type of crime committed and the people responsible. This may not be true. Sociologists studying the accuracy of official crime statistics have come to a surprising conclusion – only a small proportion of crimes are reported to the police. For example, less than a quarter of acts of vandalism are reported. The difference between official statistics of crime and what actually occurs is known as the 'dark figure'.

Three elements influence the official crime statistics: reporting of crime to the police; recording of crime; activities of the police.

The real crime rate

The chart illustrates the numbers of crimes which have taken place compared to the number of offences which have been reported to the police.

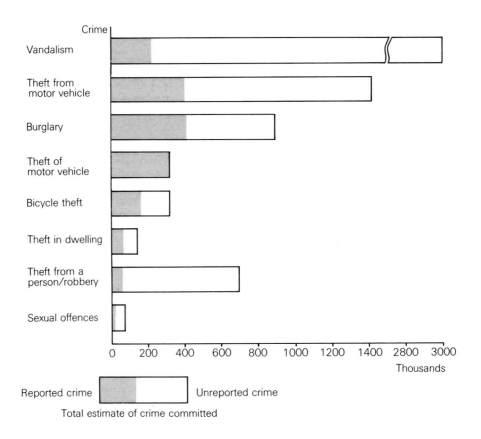

Source: British Crime Survey, 1985

Recorded and unrecorded crime in England and Wales, 1983

1 According to the information above, do people generally report crimes to the police?

2 Approximately how many burglaries were there in 1983?

3 How many of these were reported to the police?

4 Which crime is least likely to be reported to the police? Can you give a reason why this might be so?

5 Which crime is most likely to be reported to the police? Can you suggest a reason why this might be so?

6 Look at page 215. Give four reasons, each with an example of your own, why people fail to report crimes to the police.

7 Even if a crime is reported, it may not be recorded by the police as an offence. How can this be so?

8 What is a 'moral panic' (see pages 269–70)?

9 How might a moral panic influence the official statistics of crime?

10 Can you suggest a 'moral panic' that has happened recently?

Reporting of crime to the police

People often fail to report crimes because:

- they regard them as too trivial (a scratch along the side of a car);
- they do not believe the police can do anything (a wallet stolen in a busy market place);
- they regard it as a private matter (theft by a member of the family from another family member);
- they feel humiliated (rape).

But people do report crime when it is insured (car theft) and there is some evidence to suggest people make false claims in cases of burglary in order to claim larger amounts on the insurance.

Recording a crime

Police use their discretion in deciding whether an act is worth defining and recording as criminal. Sometimes they feel that they do not want to be involved, for instance, in a dispute between husband and wife. On other occasions, they regard the offence as too trivial, meriting only a warning to the person involved (riding a bicycle on the pavement).

We should be rather cautious in our interpretation of official statistics on crime.

As the law is changed, or the police interpretation of the law changes, an 'increase' or 'decrease' in a particular offence may take place. During the 1984–5 miners' strike, for instance, the police started to use the law on 'riot', unused for half a century.

Finally, the police forces in different parts of the country, record and enforce laws differently. The Metropolitan Police, for example, are reputed to be much laxer on prostitution than the Manchester police forces. This leads to different levels of official statistics on prostitution.

Activities of the police

More police are used to patrol inner-city districts. This leads some to argue that they therefore discover more crime, simply by being there! Police officers work with certain assumptions about 'criminal types'. This leads them more often to stop working-class youths, for instance, and so this might account for the high proportion of these youths in the official statistics. Similarly, racist attitudes on the part of some police have led them to 'pick on' black youths.

A final point is that the police are often influenced by the media and may become 'sensitised' to certain types of crime (or suspect). This leads to a 'blitz', or 'moral panic' on these crimes or those suspected of committing them, and so the figures for this form of offence grow alarmingly. A famous example of this is the rapid increase in mugging which took place from the mid-1970s, as the police responded to a number of lurid newspaper articles.

Acts of delinquency

Below is a list of statements about deviant acts. It is called a 'self-test' as it is normally given to a group of people who then tick each deviant act they have committed. It is useful in that it avoids the embarrassment of an interview. The results allow researchers to measure the extent of criminal acts committed by people who have never been arrested or charged by the police.

1 I have ridden a bicycle without lights after dark.
2 I have driven a car or motor bike/scooter under 16.
3 I have been with a group who go round together making a row and sometimes getting into fights and causing disturbance.
4 I have played truant from school.
5 I have travelled on a train or bus without a ticket or deliberately paid the wrong fare.
6 I have let off fireworks in the street.
7 I have taken money from home without returning it.
8 I have taken someone else's car or motor bike for a joy ride then taken it back afterwards.
9 I have broken or smashed things in public places like on the streets, cinemas, dance halls, trains or buses.
10 I have insulted people on the street or got them angry and fought with them.
11 I have broken into a big store or garage or warehouse.
12 I have broken into a little shop even though I may not have taken anything.
13 I have taken something out of a car.
14 I have taken a weapon (like a knife) out with me in case I needed it in a fight.
15 I have fought with someone in a public place like in the street or a dance.
16 I have broken the window of an empty house.
17 I have used a weapon in a fight, like a knife or a razor or a broken bottle.
18 I have drunk alcoholic drinks in a pub under 16.
19 I have been in a pub when I was under 16
20 I have taken things from big stores or supermarkets when the shop was open.
21 I have taken things from little shops when the shop was open.

22 I have dropped things in the street like litter or broken bottles.
23 I have bought something cheap or accepted as a present something I knew was stolen.
24 I have planned well in advance to get into a house to take things.
25 I have got into a house and taken things even though I didn't plan it in advance.
26 I have taken a bicycle belonging to someone else and kept it.
27 I have struggled or fought to get away from a policeman.
28 I have struggled or fought with a policeman who was trying to arrest someone.
29 I have stolen school property worth more than about 5p.
30 I have stolen goods from someone I worked for worth more than about 5p.
31 I have had sex with a boy when I was under 16.
32 I have trespassed somewhere I was not supposed to go, like empty houses, railway lines or private gardens.
33 I have been to an 'X' film under age.
34 I have spent money on gambling under 16.
35 I have smoked cigarettes under 15.
36 I have had sex with someone for money.
37 I have taken money from slot machines or telephones.
38 I have taken money from someone's clothes hanging up somewhere.
39 I have got money from someone by pretending to be someone else or lying about why I needed it.
40 I have taken someone's clothes hanging up somewhere.
41 I have smoked dope or taken pills (LSD, mandies, sleepers).
42 I have got money/drink/ cigarettes by saying I would have sex with someone even though I didn't.
43 I have run away from home.

Source: A Campbell, *Girl Delinquents* (Blackwell, 1981), which was based on H B Gibson, 'Self-reported delinquency among schoolboys and their attitudes to the police', *British Journal of Social and Clinical Psychology*, 6, 168–73

1 Tick the activities you have done. How many have you ticked?

2 As a class exercise, compare the results of the males versus the females. Are there any differences?

3 Do you have any criticisms of the questions, or do you think they are a representative selection of deviant acts that might be performed by young people?

CHAPTER FOURTEEN
POWER, POLITICS AND GOVERNMENT

The nature of power

What do we mean by power?

When we talk about 'power', we generally think only of politics. However, power is something that is used and experienced every day by all of us. If we obey someone else, we do so because they have power over us. So parents, teachers, police officers, bullies at school and referees in hockey games all make us obey them.

Sociologists are interested in power in all its senses, not just as something related to politics and government. At the beginning of this century, Max Weber suggested that to understand how some people get others to obey we ought to distinguish between *power*, which is when we obey people because they can threaten us if we ignore their wishes, and *authority*, which is when we willingly obey people because we believe it is right for them to boss us around. Examples of power include the power of prison officers over the inmates (from the prisoners' viewpoint), and the power of kidnappers over their victims. Examples of authority include the authority of parents over their children, and the authority of managers over their employees.

Power or authority?

Power and authority

The whole idea of social relationships involves the notion of power. Whenever two or more people are engaged in some activity, potential conflicts will arise and will have to be resolved.

Questions of obedience and disobedience arise in families, in the classroom, between couples and at work, as well as in dealings with the law.

In our own system of government, which we regard as democratic, power is usually invisible. But, as with personal relationships, this does not mean that it is not there. If a peson breaks the law or challenges the state in some way (as in Northern Ireland), then the whole weight of the law can be used to ensure that the person does what he/she is told.

Source: Adapted from 'Power and Authority' in *New Society*, 21 February 1985

Power can be divided into two broad categories. First people do what others tell them because they have to, otherwise they may be punished or face penalties of some kind. This is known as *coercion*. Secondly, people do what they are told because they believe the person giving them an order has the right to do so. This is known as *authority*.

The nature of the power in totalitarian societies is usually coercion, as people have not freely chosen the government. In democracies the nature of power is generally accepted to be based upon authority.

However, Marxists argue that western democracies are really based on coercion, but the ruling class have managed to trick the population into accepting that the political and economic system is really to the benefit of everybody. Consequently they rarely have to resort to open threats and violence. The task of persuading people to believe in the system is usually dealt with by the education system and the media. If these fail then the police or the army are used, as happens in Northern Ireland or in the serious industrial disputes such as the 1985–6 miners' strike.

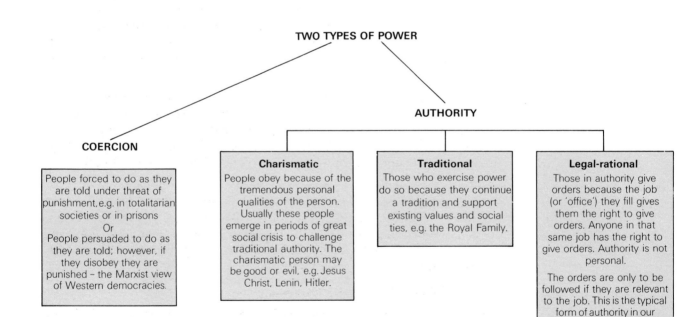

TWO TYPES OF POWER

AUTHORITY

COERCION

Charismatic
People obey because of the tremendous personal qualities of the person. Usually these people emerge in periods of great social crisis to challenge traditional authority. The charismatic person may be good or evil, e.g. Jesus Christ, Lenin, Hitler.

Traditional
Those who exercise power do so because they continue a tradition and support existing values and social ties, e.g. the Royal Family.

Legal-rational
Those in authority give orders because the job (or 'office') they fill gives them the right to give orders. Anyone in that same job has the right to give orders. Authority is not personal.

The orders are only to be followed if they are relevant to the job. This is the typical form of authority in our society, e.g. any 'bureaucracy', such as the Civil Service, a commercial company or a school.

People forced to do as they are told under threat of punishment, e.g. in totalitarian societies or in prisons
Or
People persuaded to do as they are told; however, if they disobey they are punished – the Marxist view of Western democracies.

The nature of power

1 Give two examples of power in everyday life.

2 What does coercion mean?

3 Give an example of a country/area where coercive power is used.

4 What is the major difference between coercion and authority?

5 What are the three types of authority?

6 What is the difference between the reason for obeying a figure like Hitler and obeying your boss in the office?

7 Why do people listen to what Prince Philip or Prince Charles have to say?

8 Why do Marxists disagree with the argument that the form of power in democracies is 'authority'?

9 Why do you obey
   a) the teacher/lecturer?
   b) the police officer?
   c) your parents?

Political systems

What do we mean by the terms 'democracy' and 'totalitarianism'?

Societies vary in the amount of power ordinary people have to influence the decisions of the government. In some societies the people have very little say indeed and these are generally described as 'totalitarian', On the other hand, societies which try to give ordinary people a strong influence in what decisions are made, are known as 'democracies'.

A true democracy would be a society in which every decision made by the government was voted on by the members of society, but this is not practical as it would be too complicated. Instead, most democratic societies have a system called 'representative democracy', in which certain people (MPs in Britain) are elected to represent the interests of communities (known as 'constituencies' in Britain). This is the model used in Britain and Western Europe. We elect Members of Parliament to represent constituencies of about 60 000 people.

But a democracy is more than just voting once every five years for an MP. It also involves freedom to express opinions critical of the government, to have an uncensored media, free from government control, and an independent legal system. If all these things exist then it is likely that the laws passed by the government and the decisions made by it will reflect the will of the people.

Totalitarian societies, on the other hand, are those controlled by a very few people who usually arrange the society for their benefit. The rulers refuse to allow the population any say in the important decisions that affect them and they may well ensure their view holds by controlling the police, courts and the mass media. Criticism is forbidden.

Types of totalitarian societies include:

- monarchy, where a king or queen has absolute power, as in Britain in the Middle Ages;
- dictatorship, where one person (the dictator) holds absolute power, for example in Germany in the 1930s and early 1940s under Hitler;
- oligarchy, where a few people rule, as in the case of the People's Republic of China.

A checklist of the elements of a democracy

	Yes	No
Is there more than one political party competing to gain power?		
Are there regular elections?		
Do the majority of people have the right to vote?		
Is it possible to express criticism of the government openly?		
Is there a range of opinions expressed in the newspapers, on radio and television?		
Are the mass media free of government control?		
Is there any way in which ordinary people can communicate with the decision makers (such as MPs) between elections?		
Are the police and the courts free of direct government control?		

For a society to qualify as democratic all the answers ought to be Yes.

1 According to the checklist above is Britain a democracy?

2 Give two other examples of democracies.

3 Find two other nations where the majority of the answers to the checklist are No. (The *New Internationalist* magazine has a useful section on political rights. Your school/ college library should have copies.)

Political parties and philosophies

What political parties exist in Britain, and what do they stand for?

A political philosophy, or ideology, is an explanation of how society works and a prescription on how to act based upon this explanation. Political parties are organised groups who share a common philosophy and who try to win political power, usually aiming ultimately to form the government of a country.

The main political philosophies are communism, socialism, conservatism, liberalism and fascism.

Communism

This is the belief that those who control the economy control society. It argues for ownership of all the economy by 'the people'. In practice this has meant ownership by the government, which is usually not representative of the people, nor democratic.

The political party associated with this philosophy is the Communist Party.

Socialism

This is also the belief that ownership of the economy leads to political control. Socialists argue for an elimination of the extremes of poverty and wealth through the goverment keeping some degree of control of the economic life of a country.

The political party associated with this philosophy is the Labour Party.

Conservatism

This is the belief that the government should not interfere in the economic life of a country and that it is not the job of government to iron out the extremes of wealth and poverty. Private individuals, rather than the government, ought to own industry. (This is known as capitalism.)

The political party associated with this philosophy is the Conservative Party.

Liberalism and social democracy

This philosophy accepts the inequality of capitalist society and the fact that the ownership of economic enterprises should not be taken by the State. However, they see the government as having some role to play in caring for the worse-off.

The political parties associated with this philosophy are the Liberal Party and the Social Democratic Party. They are closely linked and are known as the 'Alliance'.

Fascism

This is the belief that some groups are racially superior to others and the superior group ought to have preferences in social and economic affairs. Where fascist parties have come to power they have always eliminated democracy.

The political parties associated with this approach are the British Movement and the National Front.

Political socialisation

Where do people get there political beliefs from?

Just as individuals learn about the general beliefs and values of society and the correct forms of behaviour, they also learn about political values. We talk about **political socialisation** as the term for this process of learning political values and preferences. In Britain, most people are socialised into an acceptance that the democratic process which we have is the best political system. Within this, however, they are socialised differently in their preferences for political parties.

People learn their political preferences through the media, the family, the school and the peer group/social class, in just the same way that they learn ordinary social values (see Chapter 1).

Media

Newspapers in Britain generally support the Conservative Party. This is hardly surprising as the newspapers are usually part of large companies, precisely the sorts of institutions that would lose out under a Labour government and would benefit from a Conservative government. The radio and television are not allowed to support any particular political party and they could best be described as supporting the 'establishment' view of the world, which is basically to keep things as they are.

There is little evidence to show that people's voting choices are determined by the media. However, it is clear that general opinions about political events are formed by the way in which they are portrayed by the media. Support of the British capitalist, democratic system is constantly expressed in the way world events, the Soviet Union, and the United States are described. So people learn to interpret the world around them through the framework provided by the media.

The family

The most important agency of socialisation is the family (see pages 5–7). It is where we first learn the expectations society has of us and these lessons stay with us throughout our lives. It is hardly surprising therefore that political attitudes are also learnt in the family.

The school

At first it may seem surprising that the school has any political influence on us. Yet here we learn a particular version of history, one in which Britain plays the part of the 'goodie', a belief in the value of British society as it is, the habit of obeying rules, the need to compete against each other, and the acceptance that the more successful ought to take higher rewards. These may not appear to be political at first sight, but they are all values on which our political system is based.

The peer group/social class

The people we mix with in our daily lives are very influential in reinforcing or weakening our own opinions. Usually the people with whom we mix (peer group) are drawn from the same social class and as the experiences of social classes are so different, people in each class develop very different views on political events.

Voting behaviour

Why do people vote the way they do?

In a representative democracy such as Britain, the government is chosen by the electorate and people vote for the party which they prefer. Sociologists have tried to uncover the reasons for people's choices. They suggest that the most important factor is social class. Other less important factors are party images, the influence of the mass media, the role of the family, and geographical location.

Social class

The two traditional political parties in Britain, Labour and Conservative, are class-based parties. The Labour Party is seen as the party of the working class and the Conservative Party is seen as that of the middle class. This is still true today. However, although the bulk of working-class people vote Labour, and the bulk of middle-class people vote Conservative, a considerable minority do not.

The working-class Conservative vote

Why do working-class people vote Conservative?

There have been a number of explanations for the fact that over a third of working-class people vote for the Conservative Party.

The deferential voter

It has been suggested that certain people regard the upper class as 'born to rule' (this sort of voter is described as 'deferential'). Just as many people regard royalty as somehow superior to ordinary people, so these voters regard those with an upper-class background as superior. As the Conservative Party is associated with this type of person, the voter gives his/her support to that party.

The deviant voter

It has been argued that as virtually all the media and important institutions of society support conservative parties, it is only those who can reject their influence, that vote socialist (Labour). Where large numbers of working-class people live and/or work together, they develop a more critical view of the media, as they are able to support each other's views and vote for a party which is generally criticised in the press.

Sociology does not attempt to explain every voter's choice

Why do middle-class people vote labour?

What relationship is there between class and the Alliance?

The changing class structure

In recent years, a division has occurred between what is now called the 'new working class' and the 'traditional working class'. The new working class are the people in better-paid, more secure work who have bought their own houses away from the inner cities and who enjoy a lifestyle which appears fairly similar to that of the middle class. The 'traditional working class' are those workers in the older, declining industries (generally of manufacturing) who rent their homes and live in small one-occupation communities (such as mining villages) and the inner cities. The new working class have less class loyalty and prefer to vote for the party which will directly benefit them. The traditional working class tend to vote Labour as a matter of course.

Middle-class origins

People who came from middle-class homes but have moved into the working class may still vote according to their origins (see the section on the family on page 227).

The middle-class Labour vote

About one fifth of middle-class people regularly vote for the Labour Party.

Working-class origins

People from working-class homes who have succeeded in entering the middle class may still retain their loyalty to the working class.

Changing class structure

Since the 1960s there has been a massive increase in routine clerical work and a shrinking of manufacturing manual jobs. People who would once have been employed in manufacturing, now work as low-paid clerks. Their new jobs may appear to be middle-class, but they are still really working-class people, and vote accordingly.

The Alliance

It is true to say that the Alliance has been successful in drawing its support right across the class structure, although membership of the SDP, for instance, is mainly drawn from the middle class; only seven per cent come from the working class.

Party images

One recent survey showed that over 20 per cent of Labour voters actually agreed more with Conservative policies than with Labour ones, while seven per cent of Conservative voters preferred Labour policies. Ask anyone (including teachers of sociology) exactly what the *specific* policies of the Labour and Conservative Parties are in a forthcoming election and they are unlikely to know!

It seems that people have a general image of the main political parties: Labour is for the working class, the trade unions and the Welfare State; Conservatives stand for business, law and order and the better-off; the Alliance stands for a restricted degree of reform, but no radical changes.

These party images may not be accurate, but they are the main guides people have to help them decide which party they are going to vote for.

Do the media influence political attitudes?

The influence of the mass media

The mass media are the newspapers, radio and television. The mass media do not appear to have any direct influence on voting behaviour. It appears that people *select* information which *reinforces* the views they already hold and ignore other information. What the media does, though, is to *set the agenda*, by which we mean that they decide which issues are regarded as important and newsworthy.

One study found that 33 per cent of Labour voters read a newspaper that supported the Conservative Party, yet they continued to support Labour. They ignored the information in the newspapers that did not fit their views. The researchers also found that television coverage of general elections neither made the public better informed on key issues, nor influenced people's minds on which party to support. (There is further discussion on the media and politics in Chapter 16.) What the media do is to create a general 'climate of opinion' about issues which fits in better with the political stance of one party rather than another.

The family

This most important agency of socialisation teaches us to be a social being, accepting the rules and values of society. Amongst the values we learn are political values, both general, in the sense that we learn to support democracy, and specific, so that we learn to support one particular party. This sympathy for one particular party often stays throughout the whole of a person's life, especially if reinforced by social class.

A study of the influence of the family on voting behaviour found that over 80 per cent of people's original political preference is the same as their parents. This gradually fades over time, but, later in life, two-thirds of the electorate still vote as their parents did. Fading of party loyalty only takes place when the voting loyalty learned from the parents is contrary to the normal political support of the children's class. So if the children are middle class and they have learned to support the Labour Party, they may change their voting habits to Alliance or Conservative.

Geographical location

People in the north of England, Scotland and Wales are more likely to support the Labour Party. In the south, the Conservatives and Alliance receive more support. Also, Labour voters are more likely to live in the inner cities.

The reason is partially that there are more working-class people in the north and inner cities, and these face greater problems than those in the south and in the suburbs or New Towns.

The influences on voting and political attitudes

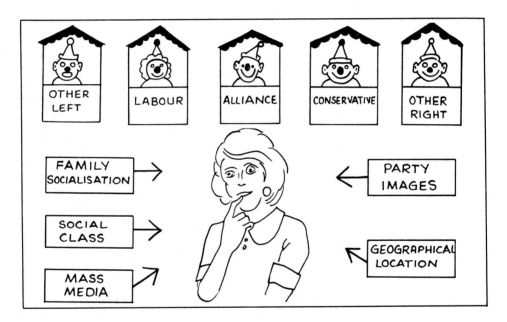

The diagram above shows the main factors influencing voter's choices of political parties in elections.

Write a very short explanation of each influence using information given in the main text.

Women and political power

In May 1987 there were 635 MPs in Parliament. Of these, only 26 were women; 11 Labour, 14 Conservative and one Liberal. Fifty-one per cent of the electorate are women.

What has happened since May 1987?
Find out how many women MPs there are now. To which parties do they belong?

Democracy in action: The activities of pressure groups

What are pressure groups?

As we saw earlier, democracy involves more than just the right to vote in elections every five years. Most important of all, it involves a constant flow of communication from the people to their representatives in Parliament. In many cases this simply involves MPs meeting their constituents (the people who elected them) and listening to their views.

However, far more important are the activities of organised groups who agitate in order to persuade Parliament to pass laws which benefit them or they believe would improve society. These groups are known as interest groups or pressure groups.

Types of pressure groups

There are two types of pressure groups: those which defend their own interests, such as trade unions or the Confederation of British Industry (representing the owners of industry), these are known as protective, or defensive, pressure groups; and those which promote new initiatives which they argue will benefit society, known as promotional groups, examples of which include the Child Poverty Action Group, which campaigns for better benefits for low income families, and the Royal Society for the Protection of Birds.

In reality the division between the two groups is not completely clearcut. Some pressure groups might wish to promote change in order to benefit themselves. For instance, those groups who campaigned for Sunday shop opening were mainly linked to the major chain stores who saw great financial benefits from Sunday opening.

Pressure groups and political parties

How do pressure groups differ from political parties?

There are two main differences between pressure groups and political parties. Firstly, pressure groups generally do not try to win electoral power, they just wish to influence MPs or those in authority. Secondly, they generally concentrate on one issue rather than the wide range of issues supported by political parties.

Pressure groups and the decision makers

How do pressure groups influence the decision-makers?

Lobbying

This involves sending representatives to see MPs, or whoever is in authority. The representatives try to persuade those in authority of the sense of their campaign. This is usually supported by leaflets, letters and documents. In recent years, there has been the growth of professional lobbying firms, who will lobby for any pressure group if paid to do so.

Retaining the services of those in authority

A number of Labour MPs are 'sponsored' by trade unions to look after their interests. On the Conservative side, a considerable number are paid 'retainers' (a yearly salary) to represent the interests of groups of companies or commercial interests. In the 1985–6 scramble to obtain the contracts to build the Channel tunnel, a number of companies took on MPs as 'advisers'.

Publicity

For many groups who have few contacts with those in authority, the best way of gaining attention is to attract publicity. Pressure groups may give stories to the press or engage in newsworthy exploits. Greenpeace, the environmental group, is particularly good at this. The aim is not just to attract attention, but also to win public sympathy.

Protest

Demonstrations and public meetings within the law, as well as direct action outside the law, may attract publicity and bring pressure to bear on the authorities to change their attitudes. Protest is usually the method of the weakest, as the powerful generally have direct access to the politicians and civil servants. One group which has moved towards illegality in recent years is the Animal Liberation Front, which protests against the use of animals in experiments. Its members break into laboratories and free the animals.

'Yes, minister, this would be in the interests of Britain . . . and, of course, Hardcake Construction Company'

Criticism

The idea that the activities of pressure groups guarantee democracy has been most strongly criticised for the fact that it overlooks the real differences in *resources* that various pressure groups have at their disposal. The Confederation of British Industry, which represents the owners of British industry, employs over 400 people and is very rich. Yet other groups such as Help the Aged, a pressure group to look after the needs of pensioners, has only a tiny staff and little money.

Pressure groups in a democratic society

In 1986 the Conservative Government introduced a bill (a proposal for a new law) into Parliament to allow unlimited opening of shops on Sundays. The bill was defeated and the law remained which prohibits many shops trading on Sundays. It is a good example of the activities of pressure groups in action.

By the Autumn, Mrs Thatcher hopes to hang an 'Open All Hours' sign above every retail outlet in the country. The Shops Bill due before the Commons in three weeks will sweep away laws banning Sunday trading, but only if it can overcome opposition from at least 70 Conservative MPs.

So far there have been 40 000 letters delivered in protest (compared with only 7 500 letters of support) and petitions bearing more than 1 million signatures. The Prime Minister was won over by the lobbying of five big retailers. Woolworth, W H Smith, Harris-Queensway, Asda-MFI and the Mothercare-BHS-Habitat group commissioned research in 1984 which showed that the overall volume of business would grow if Sunday trading was legalised.

What the government overlooked was the report's finding that there was no public clamour for Sunday trading, a point that no public opinion poll has seriously been able to question. When the government published its bill, the Home Office and scores of Tory MPs were startled by the speed with which the Keep Sunday Special group, formed by a broad alliance opposed to Sunday trading based mainly on the churches, organised protest meetings in about 250 constituencies.

One organiser for the shopworkers' union USDAW says that staff will strike rather than work on Sundays. 'We are doing everything except sleep here (at a Tesco supermarket) six days a week as it is,' she says.

Source: *The Observer*, 30 March 1986

1 What was the aim of the proposed bill?

2 Which group would have benefited most from it?

3 Which groups first proposed the idea?

4 How did they manage to get a bill introduced?

5 Which groups joined together to oppose the bill?

6 What was the name of their pressure group?

7 How did they bring pressure to bear against the bill?

8 What happened in the end?

Not all pressure groups are equal

On the same day as the Government was condemned by the Royal College of Physicians for failing to prevent 'an avoidable annual holocaust' of 100 000 premature smoking deaths, the junior Minister of Health, Mr John Patten, met a delegation from the Freedom Organisation for the Right to Enjoy Smoking Tobacco (financed by the tobacco industry to the tune of £100 000 a year). This casts a revealing light on the Government's real attitude towards smoking and health.

Its complicity with the tobacco industry in perpetuating an epidemic that kills prematurely (many) young male smokers is rarely seen in its stark, true colours.

Another revealing chink of light came recently when the Health Education Council, which is funded by the Government to promote better health care, advertised for a new head of public affairs.

It soon became evident that one of the applicants, Mr Michael Daube, a senior lecturer in health education at Edinburgh University, was not only the best qualified but had majority support. At this point, however, the chairman said that Mr Daube was unacceptable to Ministers.

Why was Mike Daube blacked? Precise answers to such questions are difficult to establish, but it is easier to understand why Ministers were less than keen on Mr Daube. As a former very energetic director of the anti-smoking campaign, Action on Smoking and Health, he was no friend of the cigarette manufacturers. And there is considerable evidence to suggest that the tobacco industry lobbied hard within the department in a deter-mined attempt to block the appointment.

The Tobacco Advisory Council, the industry's lobby-ing arm, is a lavishly financed body whose writ runs much further than is generally realised. Two years ago it persuaded Mrs Thatcher to shift the then junior Minister of Health, Sir George Young, whose tough, anti-smoking campaigning policies had incurred its bitter hostility.

Sir George's removal to the Department of the Environ-ment was secured through industry pressure exercised via the Tory Whip's office. Afterwards a senior civil servant in the Department of Health commented: 'I never knew the tobacco industry was so powerful.'

Source: *The Observer*, 4 December 1983

The Government's decision to scrap the Health Education Council, announced yesterday, will mean the end of the quango's political campaigns against tobacco and alcohol, senior council officials said yesterday.

Colleagues of the council's influential director, Dr David Player, fear there is unlikely to be a place for him in the new special health authority which will come under the direct control of the Social Services Secretary, Mr Norman Fowler.

Dr Player has been an effective critic of the Govern-ment's failure to curb alcohol-ism and its policy on the tobacco industry's sponsorship of sport.

It was under his direction that the council persuaded the BBC to clamp down on cigarette advertisements in televised snooker competitions, motor racing, and tennis. . . .

He arrived four years ago from the Glasgow-based Scottish Health Education Group with a reputation as a 'tough cookie'. Ever since, he has been a thorn in the side of the tobacco and alcohol industries.

In September an HEC report showed that the BBC was broadcasting the equiva-lent of more than 500 cigarette advertisements a year.

Last month Dr Player embarrassed ministers by publicly blaming pressure from the drink industry for the refusal of the DHSS to fund alcohol education programmes.

'The alcohol industry is even more powerful in its effect on government decisions than the tobacco industry', he said on the BBC 2 television programme, Brass Tacks.

Source: *The Guardian*, 22 November 1986

1 Name two pressure groups mentioned in the extract from the *Observer* above.

2 Is there any financial link between them?

3 Give two results of their lobbying of senior politicians.

4 In the earlier extract we saw the way in which the Keep Sunday Special pressure group operated. Contrast the differences in approach between the tobacco industry and the Keep Sunday Special group.

5 It has been argued that pressure groups are both the backbone of democracy and a danger to it. How do the three extracts on pressure groups help us to understand this statement?

6 Do you think that pressure groups which fail to persuade people peacefully should ever turn to violence? The Animal Liberation Front is an example of this.

Opinion polls

Are opinion polls a good thing in a democracy?

Opinion polls are generally used to find out people's opinions on topical subjects, or to carry out market research on consumers' preferences. They involve asking questions of a typical cross-section of the population, and the results are then assumed to be generally true for everybody. Opinion polls are widely used by political parties and newspapers to find out voters' intentions at elections. However, they have been criticised for possibly having an effect on the outcomes of elections.

Why? Voters, who realise that the party of their first choice has absolutely no chance of winning according to the opinion polls, may decide to switch votes to another party in order to defeat the third party that the opinion polls put in the lead. For example, there is some evidence that in seats where the Labour Party is clearly in the lead, Conservative voters may switch to the Alliance in order to defeat Labour. Opinion polls are then actually influencing the outcome of the elections, not just informing people of the situation.

Clever use of opinion polls by political parties becomes an important weapon in the electoral battle. The result is that people vote into power not the party of first choice, but the one *least disliked*, a rather different matter. Of course, this all assumes that the opinion polls have actually predicted correctly the voting intentions of the electors. As we discussed on pages 13–20, it is possible that opinion polls (which are a type of survey) may be inaccurate.

Opinion polls – an unfair political weapon?

In constituencies where the Labour party had little chance of winning in opposition to the Tories, and where the Alliance candidates' vote was fairly high, it was claimed in a New Statesman article that:

Local Liberal and SDP candidates in a number of constituencies tried to boost the Alliance's support by circulating misleading information about the local state of the parties. . . . For example, leaflets distributed on behalf of Malcolm Dean stated that 'Our polls show we need just a few hundred more votes to win'. The Conservative majority was 5304.

Source: *New Statesman*, 8 July 1983

1 When there are three parties running together and a leaflet bearing the above information is distributed, how is it possible to affect the result?

2 If the information above had stated that the Conservatives were so far ahead that it was impossible for the other parties to catch up, what effects might the poll information have had?

3 In France, opinion polls are banned immediately before the polling day. Why is this? Do you think the ban ought to be introduced in Britain?

Opinion polls can be misleading if not examined closely

The State

The State is the decision-making agency of British society. It consists of three elements:

- a decision-making body – Parliament;
- a bureaucracy that carries out the decisions – the civil service;
- an organisation that enforces the law – the police and judiciary (the courts).

Parliament

The House of Commons is the elected body of representatives. The members of Parliament (MPs) are divided along party lines. Normally the largest party forms the government. There is also the House of Lords which is not elected. Proposed laws (known as 'bills') have to be passed three times to become law and are then passed to the Queen for her assent.

Many critics have pointed out the unrepresentative nature of MPs. They are overwhelmingly male (only 26 of 650 MPs are women), white and middle class. Is it therefore possible for them truly to reflect the will of the people?

The Civil Service

The civil service is the bureaucracy that runs the State on behalf of the government. In total there are over 600 000 civil servants.

Some sociologists have commented on the power of senior civil servants over ministers. They have argued that ministers, who are the politicians appointed by the Prime Minister to run civil service departments, are themselves controlled by the civil servants.

Whereas ministers rarely stay in one ministry (government department) for more than two years, civil servants spend their whole careers there. They are, therefore, able to manipulate the ministers into taking the decisions that they want them to. The result is that the country is run more by the civil service than by elected politicians.

A second point of concern is that top civil servants come largely from a very exclusive social background. In 1984, for example, over half of all recruits to the top jobs in the civil service came from public schools, which are the sorts of schools attended mainly by the British upper class.

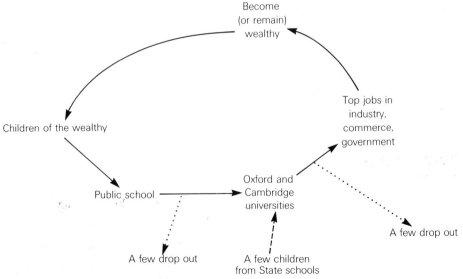

The circle of power and wealth

Are the top positions open to all, or is the diagram opposite untrue?

The police and the judiciary

There are about 145 000 full-time police officers in Britain, concentrated mainly in the large cities.

The judiciary, composed of judges and magistrates (who judge lesser offences), have the role of interpreting and fairly applying the law passed by Parliament. It should be noted that judges too are drawn from a very restricted social class background, just like senior civil servants and have generally attended public schools.

Top schools for top jobs

Holders of elite jobs educated at public school

Top jobs	Percentage
Conservative cabinet 1982	73
Conservative junior ministers 1982	88
Conservative MPs 1979	67
Labour cabinet 1979	21
Labour junior ministers 1979	21
Labour MPs 1979	8
Senior civil servants 1970	62
Judges of the High Court and Court of Appeal 1971	80
Bishops of Church of England 1971	67
Professors etc at Oxford and Cambridge 1967	49
Professors etc at universities, England and Wales 1967	33
Directors of 40 major industrial firms 1971	68
Directors of major insurance companies 1971	83

Directors of the 'big four' banks educated at public school

Year	Percentage	Number
1927	76	62
1961	71	94[1]
1980	72	67[2]

[1] Includes 38 from Eton, [2] Includes 25 from Eton.

Approximately 5 per cent of secondary school pupils attend private schools.

Source: J Fothergill and S Vincent, *The State of the Nation* (Pluto Press, 1985)

1 What links all these 'top' people?

2 Find out the background of the powerholders of today. First, research the names of the members of the Cabinet and other top political and business leaders. (You could look through old copies of newspapers and magazines in your school/college library.)
Once you have made a list, find a copy of *Who's Who* and look up the backgrounds of these people.

Does the State reflect the will of the people?

There are two basic views on this, put forward by pluralists and neo-Marxists.

Pluralists

This approach suggests that power is spread right across society and that everybody, in some way, is able to influence government decisions. They can join a political party or pressure group, vote in elections and see their local MP if they have any views or problems. The term 'pluralism' simply means that there is more than one (plural) centre of power. According to this approach the government reflects the will of the people.

Neo-Marxist

This approach argues that power lies in the hands of very few people, the rich, and that the vast majority of the population really have no effective way of influencing the decisions of the government. Supporters of this view point to the great differences in resources and contacts between the pressure groups representing the interests of industry and those representing the ordinary person. They also point out how control of the mass media by very few people can lead to their views (generally in support of the rich) being imposed upon the majority of people.

The distribution of power in society

The dominant feature of advanced industrial societies appears to be an elitist distribution of power (that is, a small group of people who are very powerful). Specialisation has given rise to a large number of elites in every walk of life – top politicians, businessmen, and civil servants. The question sociologists have tried to answer is whether these elites form a ruling class governing in their own interests (the Marxist view). Or is it a large number of elites like a market place competing against each other, so that no one single group has overall power (the pluralist view)?

The case for the Marxist view:

On the face of it, we are a grossly unequal society, with the top 10 per cent, for instance, owning 60 per cent of all personal wealth. . . .

Our top institutions are dominated by people from privileged social backgrounds, educated in the main at public schools and the universities of Oxford and Cambridge. Only about 5 per cent of the population go to public schools, but 47 per cent of MPs did, over 60 per cent of senior civil servants, over 80 per cent of judges and army officers, as well as 65 per cent of the chairmen of major companies. . . .

The mass media are controlled by fewer and fewer hands. One man, Murdoch, owns four Fleet street newspapers, for instance. In their studies of television news, the Glasgow University Media Group have argued that by careful selection it presents a pro-establishment point of view while appearing to be neutral and objective. Strikes, for example, are given a bad image and controversial topics carefully vetted.

The case for the pluralists:

But pluralist writers are not convinced by these arguments. This evidence might prove the existence of a British establishment, but it fails they say to prove 'that it rules'.

A study by Christopher Hewitt of 24 major policy issues faced by successive British governments over a 20-year period found that no one significant group managed to get its way on most issues. Indeed on only one issue did Parliament go against public opinion and that was when it stopped capital punishment for murder.

In a detailed study of the influence of the Confederation of British Industry, the organisation which speaks for most of the large British companies, Grant and Marsh, found that 'the CBI's ability to influence events is limited by the government's need to retain the support of the electorate and by the activities of other pressure groups.

The debate continues:

But the reply of many of those who believe in the idea of a ruling class has been to develop the idea of 'non-decision making', which is the ability of the powerful to ignore or suppress all but the safest of issues, and to ensure that threats to their own most important interests (such as redistribution of private property) are never seriously debated in parliament.

Source: Adapted from *New Society*, 21 February 1985

1   What does the term 'elite' mean?

2   What is the dominant feature of industrial societies according to the extract?

3   What do sociologists mean by the term the 'ruling class'?

4   Briefly summarise the Marxist viewpoint.

5   What evidence do pluralists put forward to refute this?

6   So, what do pluralists suggest is the best way to understand the distribution of power in British society?

7   What does the non-decision-making approach argue?

8   Whose argument, the pluralists' or the Marxists', does it support?

---

1   Find out who the MPs for your town are. What party do they belong to? What is their majority of votes over their opponents? Check the local papers to see what their views are on major topical issues. Are there any clear influences of pressure groups on them?

2   Delegate a small group to arrange a visit with your local MP. Devise a questionnaire for him/her concerning such things for example as the rights of women, education, the public service, the power of the civil service, whether an establishment exists.

3   Is there a local issue of great importance currently being debated in your town? If so follow the history of it, find out which groups are influential and what the outcome of the issue is.

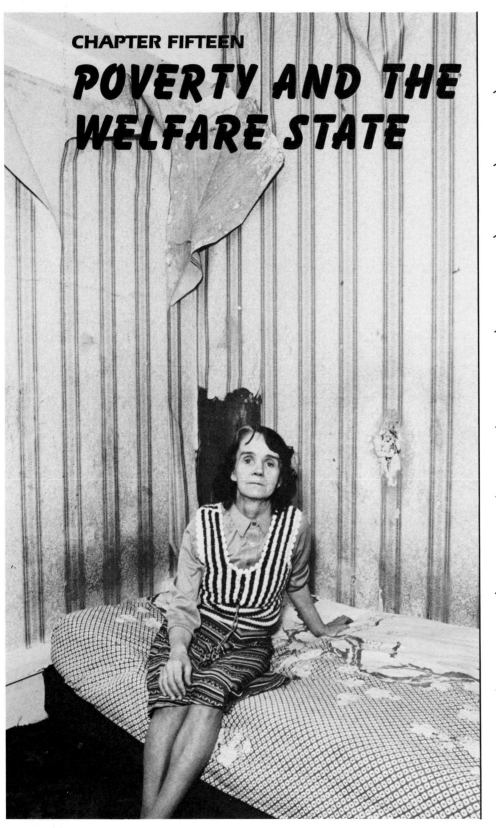

CHAPTER FIFTEEN

POVERTY AND THE WELFARE STATE

Defining poverty

What exactly do we mean when we say a person is living in poverty?

Britain is one of the richest nations in the world, yet one in seven of its inhabitants live in poverty.

In order to understand the extent of poverty and its causes we first need to agree on what we mean by the term. Sociologists have defined it in two basic ways: **absolute poverty** and **relative poverty**.

Absolute poverty

Towards the end of the last century, a number of concerned people began to argue that something ought to be done about the dreadful problem of poverty that existed. Most powerful people laughed at this, denying there was any serious problem (just as happens today).

In order to prove just how bad the situation was, Seebohm Rowntree decided to conduct a survey to discover the extent of poverty in Britain. First, though, he had to provide a clear guide to the point at which people fell into poverty. In order to do this, he created a poverty line with which nobody could disagree. To do this, he decided that the line was the income needed to ensure that a person was able to live healthily and work efficiently.

To find the amount of income to reach this point, Rowntree added together: the costs of a very basic diet; the costs of purchasing a minimum of clothes; the rent for housing. The poverty line was then drawn at the income needed to cover these three costs.

Criticisms

The main problem with this sort of definition is that it fails to take into account the fact that what is regarded as poverty *changes* over time. What is a luxury today may be a necessity tomorrow. For example, a basic diet today is very different from a basic diet of 100 years ago.

1 Make a list of necessities for two adults and two children for one week. What total sum of money would they add up to?
2 Can you agree exactly what necessities are?

Relative poverty

Relative poverty suggests that people are poor if they do not have what is normally expected in society. There are some problems with this definition.

The criticism of Rowntree's definition led sociologists to create a different definition of poverty. This is based on the idea that poverty is really the situation in which some people are denied what most people normally expect to have. For instance, 30 years ago central heating in homes was a luxury for the better-off. Today it is regarded as a normal convenience for

the majority of households. At that time televisions, telephones, and cars were all luxuries. Are they today? Rowntree allowed a set of warm clothes, but surely a degree of fashion is important today?

The result of this was that sociologists began to search for a poverty line reflecting the fact that poverty was closely related to the general standards of living of the population. In different surveys, sociologists have used:

Supplementary benefit levels

This is the lowest level that the government will let anybody sink to, it reflects the politicians' view of poverty and is roughly related to the changing standards of living.

The threshold of deprivation

Recent surveys on poverty have listed what most people regard as necessary in our society (such as decent heating and three meals a day for children, etc) and then found how many people actually go without these 'necessities'. The poverty line or 'threshold' is therefore lack of socially agreed necessities.

The different definitions of poverty

'When I use a word,' Humpty Dumpty said in a rather scornful tone, 'it means just what I choose it to mean – neither more nor less.'

A
'A family is poor if it cannot afford to eat.' Sir Keith Joseph and Jonathan Sumption

B
'People who are living in need are fully and properly provided for.' Margaret Thatcher in the House of Commons, 22 December 1983

C
Defining as poor those whose incomes were too low to provide them with three or more necessities (as defined by a survey of public opinion), the researchers estimated that 7½ million people were living in poverty. The survey found three million people unable to heat the living areas of their homes and six million go without some essential item of clothing (such as a warm waterproof coat) because of lack of money. Three million people cannot afford Christmas celebrations or presents for the family.

Source: J Mack and S Lansley, *Poor Britain* (Allen and Unwin, 1985)

1 The quotes above reflect different definitions of poverty. Which is absolute and which is relative?

2 According to A, do you think that there would be as many people in poverty as C?

3 Defining poverty in different ways means that:
   a) the numbers of people in poverty will be different;
   b) that the amount of money or assistance needed to combat poverty will vary.
   Can you explain these two points?

The importance of different definitions of poverty

Why are sociologists interested in defining poverty?

Sociologists are concerned about defining poverty because the outcome of their work has very important results for poor people.

If poverty is simply the level below which people cannot live and work efficiently, as Rowntree suggests, then very low levels of financial support are needed from the government, and the number of people considered to be in poverty is very low. On the other hand, if poverty is not having what is regarded as normal and desirable, as the relative poverty group argues, then the level of financial support required from the government is high and the numbers of people defined as poor are very high too.

The poor

The low paid

Forty per cent of households in poverty have a head of household in full-time work, but who earns such a low wage that he/she is unable to support the family. This affects 1.75 million adults and 1 million children.

The unemployed

As unemployment increases so too does the number of those in poverty. Overall, there are 1.65 million adults and 1 million children in poverty as a result of being unemployed. Two-thirds of families in *intense* poverty have a head of household who is unemployed.

Those unable to work

The elderly

About 1.5 million elderly people live in poverty. In recent years, the elderly have formed a smaller proportion of the poor than in the past. This is because there are many more poor, because of the rise in unemployment, and because pensions have kept slightly above the general rise in the standard of living.

The sick and disabled

There are about 800 000 sick and disabled people (under retirement age) who are unable to work. These mainly live on State benefits.

Single-parent families

At least half the children under 16 in single-parent families live in poverty. Usually these families are headed by women.

Poverty and region: Where do the poor live?

There is a sharp north/south divide. Over two-thirds of those in poverty live
in Scotland, the north of England and the Midlands, with half of the poor
coming from the large cities of the north, such as Merseyside (the area
around Liverpool).

The extent of poverty in Britain today

Who are the poor?

Are the poor a distinct group cut off from the rest of society?

5 million adults
$$+ \qquad = \text{7.5 million people, or 1 in 7 of the population}$$
2.5 million children

No. When we talk about the poor, it would be better to talk about those
groups in risk of poverty. For those with little money, certain periods of
their lives will be difficult ones when they will fall into poverty and then
other periods when they will climb out again. For example, those with
young, dependent children who have a low wage, will probably be in great
financial difficulties because of the great costs of the children and they will,
therefore, be likely to go into poverty. Only a few years later as the children
leave home, and possibly both parents are working, they will move out of
poverty (just!). As they grow old and their incomes decline again, they may
fall back into poverty. There is then a **cycle of poverty**.

The cycle of poverty

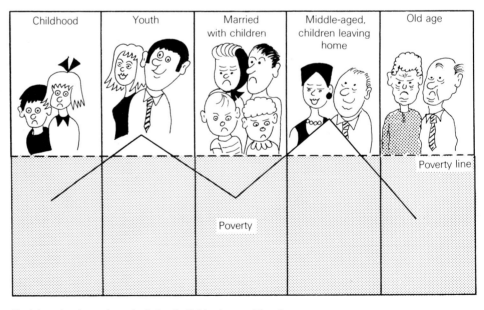

Explain why, in each period, the individuals are either in
poverty or out of poverty.

Living in poverty in Britain today

'I cannot go for a job interview even if I could get one, as after three years of unemployment my clothes are virtual rags, and I cannot buy any more, as it costs so much to keep my son decent – scruffy children have their lives made a misery at school and whatever else I do without, he will not have to go through that.

He wets the bed and has to wear nappies. His sheets and bedding must still be washed every day. When my washer broke, I asked if the DHSS could help and was told that the washer was not regarded as a necessity, and I should use the laundrette.

He has not had either birthday or Christmas presents since he was two. He asks for Lego and cars from Santa, but Santa is dead in this house; how does one explain that to a child of five?

I have no chance of getting out to meet people; a babysitter here costs £1.50 an hour. I have no relatives to help out and since I can no longer entertain or go out, I have literally no friends. So I spend every day alone and every night.

I sat down and worked out roughly what you spend per week. And now you've got washing-up liquid, you got toilet paper, you got soap to wash with. Well, what is it, you go out and you think to yourself, now if I buy washing-up liquid I can't have a loaf of bread. Which do you do? Buy the loaf of bread or the washing-up liquid? You've got to keep yourself clean and you've got to eat. So which way do you sway?

Some days I just go into a corner and won't let anybody come near me. I just sit in a corner and bang my head against the wall. And say why me?'

Source: J Mack and S Lansley, *Poor Britain* (Allen and Unwin, 1985)

'It just seems to get worse, no matter how hard we try. Jack (the husband) works all the hours he can, but the bills always seem to beat us. On Thursdays we sometimes don't have a thing to eat except bread and beans in the house. It breaks my heart seeing the children eating the rubbish I give them, but what more can I do?

Shopping is the worst thing, because it's so public. In the supermarkets I feel so stupid buying only a couple of things while everyone else has those trolleys filled to the top. Anyway I can't go anymore to Tesco's as it's been moved to a bigger superstore out of town and without a car you can't get there. So I go around the corner (to the local small shops). Everything is more expensive . . . then there's these special offers you get for buying the really big packs of things, but I haven't got the cash so I always end up with the small jars and packets . . . costs a lot more.

Clothes for the kids – oh, it's always the Oxfam shop – the one place I am a regular! I've tried buying from the mail order catalogues as you can pay the clothes off weekly, but the prices were much higher than in the shops.

Holidays? You must be joking! Our kids have never been anywhere.

Oh, the house is just awful. It's damp and it never gets warm. Well, we just can't afford the heating for more than this room. We only got the fridge because a friend of my sister was chucking it out.

Life, well it's just a struggle. I feel like giving up sometimes . . . but then there's always the kids.'

1 Why do the poor have to pay more for the goods they buy?

2 Can you suggest reasons why, once a family is poor, it becomes increasingly difficult to escape from poverty.

3 Apart from lack of money, what other problems does poverty cause?

Why poverty continues in our society

Why are there still people in poverty in Britain, even though we have health and social security systems?

By 1950, it seemed to most people that the introduction of the Welfare State, with its benefits of health care and social security, had defeated poverty. Yet a famous survey in 1965 by Abel-Smith and Townsend found that poverty still existed in Britain and had never gone away. Since then numerous studies have confirmed the continuing existence of poverty, to the extent that we know there are still 7.5 million poor people today.

Why has it continued? Three explanations have been put forward: the cycle of deprivation; the culture of poverty; power.

Cycle of deprivation

This explanation is based on the fact that those who are born into poor families tend to have many disadvantages in childhood. They live in inner-city areas, in poor housing, have inadequate diets and are more often ill. As a result of all this, they do badly at school, leave without qualifications and enter poorly-paid work themselves. Their children are then brought up in the same poverty and so suffer the same problems. The cycle begins all over again.

Criticism

This explanation, of course, fails to explain why some groups are in poverty in the first place.

Culture of poverty

Linked to the cycle of deprivation is the culture of poverty. This explanation, that poverty is passed on from one generation to another, agrees that the disadvantages mentioned above are important, but also adds that the *values* of the poor actually prevent them escaping from their poverty. The idea first came from Oscar Lewis in 1961 in his study of very poor Mexicans, *The Children of the Sanchez*. He found that in order to cope with the hopelessness and misery of their lives they had developed a particular set of values (a culture) which helped them to get through their daily lives. The culture stressed enjoying life today, as there was little chance of a decent future, and to make the best of things as they were. But these very values prevented them from escaping their poverty. Why go to school or save any money, better to have fun now surely?

Criticism

The culture of poverty, just like the cycle of deprivation mentioned earlier, is really a *result of poverty* not the original cause. Indeed it just reflects a realistic appreciation by poor people of their lives; they know they are not going to be successful, so they make the most of things. Secondly, whenever sociologists have studied the lives of poorer people in society, such as Paul Willis's work on unemployed youth in the Midlands, the conclusion is that they share just the same dreams and hopes as the rest of society. Their dreams may be the same, but they appreciate that they are unlikely to be successful.

The cycle of deprivation and the culture of poverty

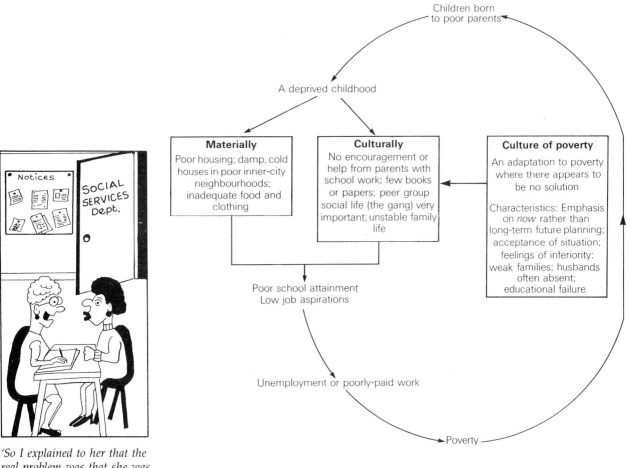

'So I explained to her that the real problem was that she was suffering from the culture of poverty. She looked surprised and said that as far as she could tell she was suffering from lack of money.'

This explanation ignores the reason why some families start off poor.

Could it be that an unfair proportion of the wealth and resources of society are taken by the rich and powerful?

Power

More radical writers, including Marxists, have suggested that the real reason for the continuation of poverty is that the poor lack the power to grab more of society's wealth for themselves. They are the ones who perform the jobs others do not wish to do, and because of their low wages they provide profits for owners of offices, shops and factories. They also keep down the prices of the goods the rest of us buy.

The unemployed play a particularly important role. They act as a threat to the employed; 'If you don't like the job, there are plenty of others willing to do it for less money', say the employers.

Poverty and deprivation

'Poverty is not simply about lack of money. . . . Poor people suffer from deprivation in most aspects of their lives.'

Housing and neighbourhood
Damp, unheated or modern high-rise developments with expensive central heating; bleakest inner-city areas with general lack of facilities, parks, etc; rent housing, no chance to buy. Inner-city areas have high crime rates and social problems.

Health
Few doctors practising in inner-city areas. Often poor do not know their rights from Welfare State (dentists, doctors, hospitals, etc). Poor, inadequate diets lead to ill-health.

Shopping costs
Increasingly, supermarkets are moving to out-of-town sites, where a car is needed. Smaller local shops tend to charge higher prices. Poor can only buy small quantities which work out more expensive; need to buy on credit (if allowed to) and so pay HP costs.

Education
Children tend to lack a home environment which stimulates (books, high level of parental encouragement). Generally, parents left school early themselves. Stress on leaving school to find work.

Family life
Poverty causes family problems – depression, feelings of despair and hopelessness lead to arguments and violence.

Attitudes to poverty

In an opinion poll conducted by the research organisation MORI in 1985, 1 in 5 people *disagreed* with the statement: 'people living on supplementary benefit are in real need'.

What is the opinion of your class?

Below is a letter written in reply to a letter published the previous week in a local newspaper. Read it carefully.

There is only one part of Mr "Paw's" letter that makes any sense and that is his statement that there is a link between illness and bad diet.

His suggestion that people on low incomes are more likely to consume a poor diet is nonsense. A good diet is a simple diet and such foods are cheap compared to expensive 'convenience' foods.

Let's look at Mr "Paw's" low income group – most people in this category are unemployed, but that is no reason to be unhealthy. In fact, the opposite should be the case because these people have the time to keep themselves fit and well.

The eight hours a day the unemployed don't work should be occupied in useful activity. Shopping for bargains in good wholesome food can be both stimulating and educational.

The basis of any sound diet is fresh fruit and vegetables and when these are bought in season they are quite cheap. New potatoes are 10p per pound at present, bananas 32p per pound.

Another important food is wholemeal bread and my local supermarket is selling a large wholemeal loaf at 38p – a penny cheaper than five years ago.

For protein, minced beef can be bought for less than £1 per pound. Fresh milk, another nourishing food, is much cheaper if bought from a supermarket than a doorstep delivery.

Mr "Paw's" glib phrase 'poverty trap' emphasises his negative thinking on this subject. Any trap is a self-imposed one created by people squandering their dole money on non-essentials like beer, baccy and junk food.

Used sensibly, the current supplementary benefit allowance can even provide the occasional luxury like a bottle of good wine.

Source: Adapted from the *Southend Standard Recorder*, 19 September 1986

1 What do you think the letter writer's response would be to the MORI poll mentioned above?

2 Briefly, summarise the letter writer's viewpoint.

3 This is a reply to a previous letter. What do you think it said? Try to reconstruct the original letter by Mr 'Paw', as he wrote it to the newspaper.

The poverty trap

What do we mean by a poverty trap?

Once in poverty, a person is often trapped in it. Being poor actually costs you money. A poor person has no car to go to the large out-of-town supermarket and so shops locally in small shops where prices are high. The poor cannot afford to buy in bulk, so they buy the smaller packets or jars (for example, of soap powder and jam) which cost more in the long run. They have lower standard housing which is usually more draughty and damp, so it costs more to heat.

Combating poverty

What attempts have
been made to do
away with poverty?

The Welfare State

Poverty continues to exist in Britain, even though there have been efforts to wipe it out. Clearly, the most important project ever undertaken to eliminate poverty was the introduction of the Welfare State after the end of the Second World War. (We will look at this as a topic in its own right on page 249.) It was decided that the dreadful poverty that had existed in the 1930s should never happen again. Today there is a National Health Service which gives free health care (although most people have to pay for prescriptions). There is a system of State payments for the unemployed, the elderly, and the severely disabled, as well as a weekly allowance for children.

Criticism

The level of payments by the State is very low, and people living on supplementary benefit, for example, can still be described as living in poverty. Also, many people who are entitled to claim benefits from the State do not realise this and go without.

Community development projects and educational priority areas

People seem happy to believe that poverty no longer exists in our society

The influence of the cycle of deprivation and culture of poverty as explanations for the continuation of poverty was very great in the 1960s. As a result, the government decided that the best way to get rid of poverty from the inner cities was to send in teams of social workers and teachers to help the poor change their attitudes towards work and learning. The hope was that, by organising a feeling of community and giving the people a sense of purpose, they could break out of poverty. Millions of pounds were spent.

Unfortunately, by the mid-1970s the results were disappointing. It was clear by then that if there were no jobs available, no amount of community spirit could help the poor to find well-paid work. The main cause of poverty was the move out of inner cities of the factories and workshops, and even some offices, that had provided what jobs there were. The community development projects were wound down and the social workers left.

Pressure groups and voluntary agencies

Although the Welfare State and the government play an important part in the fight against poverty, it is often felt that the government prefers to listen to the powerful voices of business and the trade unions before those of the poor. As a result, a number of pressure groups have developed (see

Chapter 14) which try to persuade the government to make more efforts to look after the interests of the poor, by raising benefits or by ensuring that all those who are entitled to benefits actually get them. Examples of pressure groups looking after the interests of the poor include the Child Poverty Action Group, who look after the interests of children in poor families, and Shelter, which specialises in housing.

Voluntary agencies (see page 253), or charities, also play a most important role in caring for the poor and plugging the holes in the State system. The most obvious group looking after the poor is the Salvation Army with its soup kitchens and hostels. Other voluntary agencies include War on Want, Help the Aged, NSPCC, National Association for the Resettlement of Offenders and the Church of England Children's Society.

The origins of the Welfare State

How did the Welfare State develop?

There has always been poverty, unemployment and chronic ill health in Britain. Historically, there have been various organised attempts to combat these evils, as long ago as the seventeenth century. But overall people believed that it was the job of the family to look after its members who were in ill health or in trouble of whatever kind. In the last century, with the massive growth of towns and industry, the rich could not fail to see the absolutely desperate conditions of the British working class. Most of the better-off managed to push the problems of the poor out of their minds (as most of us today manage to forget the situation of the poor in the Third World), but some philanthropists (people who wish to help others) studied the situation of the poor and tried to improve their lives. These philanthropists included Rowntree whose work we discussed when we studied poverty.

At first, help for the poor took the form of charity, organised by individuals and voluntary groups. However, the State was gradually persuaded to intervene. Between 1906 and 1919 the Liberal governments of the time introduced limited schemes introducing old age pensions, sickness and unemployment benefits, as well as some health services.

The dreadful poverty and unemployment that followed the First World War and lasted until the outbreak of the Second World War persuaded many reformers, particularly in the Labour Party, that the limited reforms of the Liberals were not enough. What was needed was a system that provided a decent standard of living for everyone *as a right*. As a result, at the end of the Second World War, the new Labour administration introduced a massive package of reforms in the areas of health, education, unemployment, poverty and housing, based on a report by Sir William Beveridge:

- a National Health Service was introduced, giving everybody the right to free medicine;

- an education system was introduced that aimed to give every child a right to the very best education;

- a system of social security was introduced that gave people an assured amount of money if they were unemployed or had great financial problems;
- a housing programme was started to eliminate the slums and give everybody a decent house or flat as a right.

This system has become known as the Welfare State.

The debate over the Welfare State

Why do some people criticise the Welfare State and wish to see it dismantled?

The Welfare State is the centre of a great debate. On the one hand, there are its supporters whose only complaint is that not enough money is spent on welfare. On the other hand, there are a number of very powerful critics, usually associated with the Conservative Party, who put forward the following points: that the Welfare State is no longer needed; that State benefits should be paid more selectively, and that the Welfare State makes people lazy.

The Welfare State is no longer needed

In the 1940s, standards of living were low and there was still great poverty and deprivation. This is no longer the case. Standards of living are higher than ever before and people can afford to look after themselves without the State interfering.

Universalism vs selectivism

What do we mean by the terms 'universalism' and 'selectivism'?

The present system of paying everyone certain of the State benefits, or of providing everyone with free hospital services, known as universalism, is wasteful. Many people have no need of the benefits, it is argued, and could well pay for the services. The critics go on to suggest that the best thing would be to be very selective about giving free benefits. Applicants for State help ought to have their incomes checked to see that they really are in need.

The results would be fewer people receiving benefits so the costs to the taxpayer would be less. As fewer people would be receiving benefits, these could be at a higher level because the government's resources would not be spread so thinly.

The Welfare State makes people lazy

The final (and rather feeble) argument against the Welfare State is that it robs people of their desire 'to stand on their own two feet'. So, the argument continues, they prefer to stay on social security rather than go out to work. No evidence is offered to support this point.

The state of the Health Service

For almost two decades successive governments have been confronted by the problem of trying to meet an ever-increasing demand for health care in a contracting economy.

The policy of the present Conservative government (1986) with its strong ideological commitment to reducing public expenditure, has been to try to restrict increased spending on the NHS and encourage the further development of private sector health care.

To supporters of this policy, private practice will act as a 'safety valve' for an overworked NHS. However, it is important to realise that what private health is willing and able to achieve in this direction is strictly limited.

Very few people are rich enough to be sure of being able to pay for the medical treatment they might need. Most people wanting private health care are, therefore, dependent on a health insurance scheme. The problem here is that insurance schemes are restricted. They frequently do not cover, for example, long term care of the elderly or chronically sick. There is some justification in the cynical observation that private health insurance works well providing you do not get ill.

The result of this is that those groups in society who tend to be in most need of health care, such as the elderly, mentally ill, chronically sick, the low paid and the unemployed are still going to be dependent on state health care. The experience of countries such as the United States, where private health insurance schemes flourish, suggests that such a health policy tends to produce a rigid 'two-tier' system of health care, where the affluent and insured monopolise the best health care facilities and medical personnel at the expense of the rest of the population.

Source: S Taylor and L Jordan, *Health and Illness* (Longman, 1986)

Source: *The Guardian*, 1 November 1986

Hospital 'must make cuts or go bankrupt'

By Michael Morris
One of Britain's leading teaching hospitals is expected to close an operating theatre block and two surgical wards in the next few days so as to avoid the threat of bankruptcy within months.

132,000 in NHS queues for year

MORE than 132,000 chronically ill patients have been waiting more than a year for hospital treatment, according to confidential figures gathered by the Department of Health and Social Security.

The waiting list for the five major surgical specialities, due to be published at the end of the month, shows that the queue for treatment has changed little since this time last year, senior sources said yesterday.

1 The extract says that private medicine would act as a 'safety valve' for an overworked NHS. Do the newspaper headlines provide any information on this point?

2 Would private hospitals deal with the majority of health care problems?

3 What is meant by a two-tier system of health service?

4 What do you think is the opinion of the authors of this extract? Are they supporters or opponents of private medicine? Can you provide any evidence to support your answer?

5 What is your opinion of private health care? Should it be encouraged? Should it be banned? Should there be a system by which those who could afford it are treated privately and those who cannot are treated by the NHS?

6 Is your family covered by private health care insurance?

7 If possible, you could draw up a simple questionnaire and ask people in the out-patient/waiting areas of your local hospital their opinions on the NHS and on private medicine. (You had better ask permission from the hospital authorities first!)

Alternatives to the Welfare State

What alternatives are proposed in place of the Welfare State?

What are the advantages and disadvantages of these alternatives?

"Well, there are two possibilities - either sign up on our "Pay as you die" plan, which means we take everything you have. Alternatively, we could dump you out in the gutter!"

It has been suggested that hospitals would be far more efficient if patients had to pay for their care

Those who criticise the Welfare State have proposed alternatives to it. One of these is privatisation which means that instead of the State providing education, health and housing, private companies would run these services in order to make a profit, just like any other commercial company. Hospitals, for example, would belong to private companies who would then charge for their services. People would have to pay for their hospital treatment just like they pay for a car or television.

This would be linked to insurance schemes that people would pay into to cover them for unemployment, sickness and old age. Those who save more will receive higher benefits. However, those groups who are too poor or ill ever to be able to contribute would receive a limited amount of State help.

Voluntary organisations would be encouraged more than today, with government grants to help them. They would take over many of the tasks that State employees do at the moment, such as social work.

The advantages

The advantages claimed would be those of *lower taxes*, because the system would cost less and that people would have the *choice* of which school to send their children to, or which hospital/doctor to be treated by.

The disadvantages

There is no convincing evidence that this system would be cheaper. Indeed, the National Health Service is remarkably good value for money. Also, the costs for the less-affluent may simply be too great for them to afford hospital treatment. So a two-tier system would develop, a high standard of services (schools and hospitals for example) for those who are in well-paid, secure jobs, and a very basic standard of services for those who cannot afford to pay the high insurance premiums. And, of course, these are just the people most in need of social security provisions.

Social policy and the Welfare State: A conclusion

In essence the debate over the Welfare State is one over the nature of British society. On the one hand, we can have a society in which individual pleasure and well-being is most important and little thought is given to others, which is the ideal of those who criticise the Welfare State. Alternatively, we can have a society that stresses that we all owe a duty to help the less fortunate, and that giving up some of our income in tax is a recognition of this duty. We also accept that as a *right* people are entitled to the best medical treatment possible for their illness, irrespective of how much money they have.

Voluntary organisations

Long before the State entered the field of social services, various charities were helping those in need. One such organisation is the Salvation Army. Voluntary organisations are groups of people who try to help others, less fortunate than themselves, and who seek no payment for their work. They fill an important hole in the Welfare State. The 'meals on wheels' service, for instance, run by the WRVS and local authorities, would be too expensive for local authorities to provide on their own without the help of the women volunteers who actually deliver the food.

Some groups, apart from providing help, also act as pressure groups, trying to put pressure on the government to provide more resources to the particular problem they are involved in. For instance, Shelter has been very active in actually helping people to find accommodation, but also they are constantly hammering away at the government to do more for the homeless.

An unintended consequence perhaps of the activities of voluntary organisations is to involve many people in helping solve problems they would otherwise be unaware of or uninterested in. When the State gets involved people usually prefer to 'leave it to the professionals', but voluntary organisations go out of their way to attract new recruits and so involve a wide section of the community in the problems of their fellows. This helps to create a sense of belonging and caring in the community.

CHAPTER SIXTEEN
THE MASS MEDIA

The mass media and social control

What do we mean when we speak of the mass media?

- **Mass media:** refers to *all* forms of written communication to the public, such as newspapers, magazines and books and to *all* forms of transmitted communication, such as radio, television and cinema

(Incidentally, the word 'media' is the plural of 'medium' and we say such things as 'the mass media *are* . . .'.)

How do the media help to maintain order in society?

Every society needs order and predictability: this involves persuading people to behave in certain socially acceptable ways, and punishing those who refuse to do so. This is the process known as social control. As the mass media are one of the main sources of information about the world for most people (virtually all of us watch television, read newspapers and magazines for instance), they play an important part in making people conform. They give us correct models of behaviour to follow, at the same time criticising anti-social behaviour.

Of course, the media are not *always* acting to promote social control. They also act as critics of current trends in society. Newspapers can promote alternative values just as much as they do traditional conservative ones.

Examine the newspapers over the last week. *Underneath* the actual stories, can you uncover a number of values?

The mass media and behaviour

How do the media influence our behaviour?

We know that the media play an important role in society by channelling social behaviour into socially acceptable patterns, but specifically *how* do the media affect individuals?

Sociologists have suggested two ways of understanding the effects of the media on individuals: the personal approach and the cultural approach.

The personal approach

This approach stresses that the media have a very direct effect on the individual. They are said to respond to the 'stimulus' (message) of the media. For instance, a child watching a television programme containing violence is likely to be influenced into violent acts him/herself.

However, the media can only *reinforce* attitudes to which the person is already sympathetic. Secondly, people are selective in what they choose to listen to, or read only information that appeals to them. Thirdly, the attitudes of others around us influence the extent to which the information affects us.

The cultural approach

This approach follows on from the 'personal approach', but goes further in exploring the culture within which the media exist and influence people. The media are not seen as having an immediate effect on individuals, but they have instead a very slow effect, building up a climate of opinion and expectations about society.

Attitudes towards women, for instance, are strongly influenced by the way they are portrayed in the media. The daily 'page 3' photograph does not directly drive men into raping women, but it does strengthen (or create?) the way in which they see women as sexual figures whose looks count more than their personalities.

What is your view of 'pin-up' photographs of women: an insult or a 'bit of fun'?

Democracy and the mass media: The debate on ownership and control

Whose views do the media reflect?

There has been a debate for a number of years about the role of the media in a democratic society. Basically there are two approaches, the pluralist sees the mass media as performing a vital role in reflecting the wide range of views on political and social issues. The alternative, Marxist-derived view holds that the media reflect the views of only a few powerful people and critical views of our society are smothered.

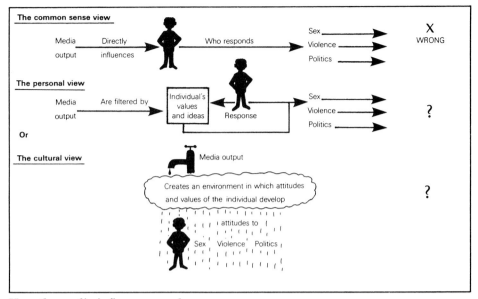

How the media influence people

The pluralist view

This holds that the mass media, apart from promoting social control for the good of everyone in society, gives a free airing of social and political issues where opinions differ. Not only that but they also act as watchdogs, criticising politicians and the powerful when they override the interests of ordinary people.

The Marxist view

This approach argues that the mass media are in the hands of a few people who impose their views on us. The role of the mass media is to distort reality, justifying the deep inequalities of wealth that exist, at the same time keeping the masses happy with pictures of attractive women and stories on sex and sport.

Before we can say which approach, if either, is nearer the truth, it may be helpful to look at patterns of ownership and secondly patterns of control of media output.

Ownership of the media

Who owns the mass media?

The evidence clearly shows that a few companies and owners dominate the mass media. The newspaper industry is dominated by just five companies, the cinemas by two, radio by the BBC, and television by the BBC and the five biggest independent companies. One man alone, Rupert Murdoch, owns newspapers which account for 40 per cent of all daily sales in England and Wales.

The trend of ownership is one of concentration, which means that the media of all types are coming under the ownership of fewer companies. Linked to this is the trend towards internationalisation, which means that companies owning the media have international links, so there will be fewer independent sources of information in the world. The recent development of satellite television transmissions means that one company can now broadcast to whole continents.

Ownership of the media

Owner	Main British press interests	Selected other media interests
British Electric Traction	Argus Newspapers Illustrated Publications Model and Allied Publications Industrial Newspapers Electrical Press (Total circulation: 1.4 million)	Capital Radio Thames Television Reditune GmbH (W Germany) Communication Channels Inc (USA)
Lonrho Owner: 'Tiny' Rowland	*Observer* George Outram and Co Scottish and Universal Newspapers (Total circulation: 1.3 million)	Radio Clyde Border TV Radio Ltd (Zambia) Times Newspapers (Zambia) Gramma Records (Zimbabwe)
Fleet Holdings Owner: Lord Matthews	*Daily Express* *Sunday Express* *Daily Star* *Standard* Morgan-Grampian Magazines (Total circulation: 7.1 million)	TV-AM Asian Business Press (Singapore) Specialist Publications (Hong Kong) Capital Radio
Associated Newspapers Owner: Lord Rothermere	*Daily Mail* *Mail on Sunday* *Weekend* Northcliffe Newspapers Associated South Eastern Newspapers (Total circulation: 5.3 million)	London Broadcasting Company Herald-Sun TV (Australia) Plymouth Sound Wyndham Theatres Harmsworth House Publishers (USA)
Pearson Longman (Cowdray)	Westminster Press Group *Financial Times* *The Economist* *Northern Echo* (Total circulation: 1.8 million)	Longman Penguin Goldcrest Films Yorkshire TV Viking (USA) Morie Channel
Pergamon Owner: Robert Maxwell	*Daily Mirror* *Sunday Mirror* *Sunday People* *Daily Record* *Sunday Mail* (Total circulation: 11.7 million)	Central Independent TV Rediffusion Cablevision Pergamon Press International Learning Systems British Printing and Communications Corporation
News International Owner: Rupert Murdoch	*Sun* *News of the World* *The Times* *Sunday Times* *Times Educational Supplement* (Total circulation: 10.2 million)	Satellite TV Collins (Fontana) News Group Productions (New York) Channel Ten – 10 (Sydney) *Daily Sun* (Brisbane)

Source: Adapted from J Curran and J Seaton, *Power without Responsibility* (Methuen, 1985)

1 Make a list of the national newspapers shown in the table opposite. Now list those which are not in the table (these are not part of large corporations).

2 Would you describe the pattern of ownership of national newspapers
  a) as concentrated?
  b) as widespread?

3 Look in the column 'selected other media interests'; can you find any radio and television stations? What about book

publishing companies? (You may need to go to the the school/college library to find the names of book publishing companies.)

4 Do many of the companies have international links? Might this affect the content of the media in any way?

5 Does the information we have extracted from the table tell us anything about the possible range of views that will appear on radio, television and in the newspapers?

Control of media output

Do the owners control the content of the media?

It is clear that the media are owned by very few people, but this does not mean that the owners totally control their contents. Publishers and broadcasting companies have to take into account that the medium, whether television or newspapers, must be commercial; that is, that it attracts a large (or at least affluent) audience and that the medium attracts advertising. Although the personal views of the owner are important, these can be overridden by the need to make money.

Broadcasters and publishers need to ensure a large audience with the sort of interests and income to afford the products of advertisers. On the other hand, they must be careful not to offend advertisers. An exposé on the dubious practices of a travel firm is unlikely to attract advertising from that firm! The result is that publishers and broadcasters choose between two options: to appeal to a very small audience with proven attractiveness to an advertiser – the specialist approach (such as specialist car magazines); or to appeal to as many people as possible – the mass market approach. Media which do not rely on advertising revenue, such as record companies and film companies tend to follow the mass market approach.

A second constraint on the owner publishing or broadcasting whatever he wants is the idea of newsworthiness. This means that there are only certain topics, presented in certain ways which make an event worthy of inclusion in a newspaper or television programme for instance. It must be dramatic, usually be 'bad news' and preferably have an air of mystery/sex about it. Different newspapers then select the different elements of the 'story' for the sort of readership they are aiming at.

Conclusion

Do owners control the content of the media? The answer is that they certainly do, and editors are fully aware of the owners' political views and will always try to reflect those in the viewpoint of the papers. However, owners and editors are slightly restrained by the fact that they must make money and this generally means that they have to attract an audience and advertisers. The result is a press that generally supports the Conservative Party.

Media content: The influence of the owners

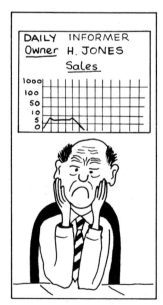

The power of an owner to influence people ultimately depends upon the sales

'By and large the editors will have complete freedom', promised Lord Matthews the ... proprietor of Express Newspapers since 1977, 'as long as they agree with the policy I have laid down'. 'I did not come all this way' (from Australia) declared Rupert Murdoch, owner of the *News of the World* and the *Sun*, 'not to interfere.' '... He (the owner) did this by persistent derision of them (opponents of Mrs Thatcher) at our meetings and on the telephone, by sending me articles marked 'worth reading', which supported right-wing views, by pointing a finger at head-lines which he thought could have been more supportive of Mrs Thatcher' – Harold Evans, former editor of *The Times* (owned by Rupert Murdoch).

But normally, editors and journalists have understood the sorts of news items and ways of presenting them that would be acceptable to the owners, which has made heavy-handed interference by them unneccessary (in other words that the paper is generally conservative and supports the views of big business, the law and the police – with only slight criticism of these institutions allowed). Owners have usually had a power over the appoint-ment of senior managers too.

Source: Adapted from M Grant, *The British Media* (Comedia, 1984)

1 Do editors and journalists decide exactly what sort of stories go into newspapers? Give one quote to support your answer.

2 Give two examples of how the owner of *The Times* influenced its contents.

3 Normally 'heavy handed interference' by owners is not necessary, according to the extract. Why not?

Types of mass media and variety of content

There are different types of media, including television, radio, newspapers and magazines. The content of the media varies mainly according to the audience that they are aimed at. This can be illustrated by the clear differences in content between the BBC radio stations. Radio 2 for middle-of-the-road entertainment (for middle-aged people) and Radio 1 for contemporary music (aiming at the younger audience).

The newspapers, too, reflect these divisions and in some ways mirror the class differences in British society, with the 'quality' papers (such as the *Guardian* and the *Observer*) and the 'popular' papers (such as the *Mirror* or the *Sun*). The contents of these papers vary considerably with the information in the quality papers being more detailed and less sensational than that in the popular papers. The focus of the quality papers tends to be on politics and economics, while the stress on the popular papers is on sensational stories often involving some sexual or criminal element.

Media audiences

1 Collect a cross section of daily newspapers. Suggest who they are aimed at, giving reasons for your conclusions.

2 Listen to BBC Radio 3 and 4, and to local radio stations. Suggest what audience they are aimed at. How does this influence their contents and presentation?

3 In one evening (starting at about 4 p.m.), check every two hours which programmes are on each channel and suggest their target audience. Give your reasons.

Two media views

The extracts from the *Sun* and the *Guardian* below are descriptions of the same event. In the *Sun*, it was the main front-page news, while in the *Guardian*, it was placed on page 2 and treated as a fairly unimportant piece.

Teachers act over 'racial tension'

Teachers in Liverpool last night suggested that a racially tense school should be closed 'from time to time' to allow talks between staff and officials to sort out organisation and discipline problems.

The call from the National Union of Teachers' branch came after seven white senior pupils at University Community Comprehensive said that they would boycott lessons unless they had pledges of safety from the headmaster.

One pupil is alleged to have said: 'There is one rule for the whites and another for the blacks. The teachers are frightened to do anything in case they are called racist.'

The pupils allege that attempts to create racial harmony have failed, even though, like the city's other new comprehensives, the school has a teacher with a brief to tackle race relations. They say that a blackboard must be called a chalkboard, discos must become reggae parties, the school held two minutes silence for a man hanged in South Africa, and that library books have been racially censored.

The pupils have complained to the headmaster, Mr Peter Fowler, about racial tension and a lack of discipline in the school, which was formed last September when three schools merged as part of the city's education reorganisation.

Education officials and union leaders, while admitting that there has been tension in recent weeks, said that most of it is the inevitable inter-school rivalry after the merger.

Fifteen pupils, aged about 15, yesterday put their case at a 75 minute meeting with Mr Kenneth Antcliffe, director of education. Also present were the chairman of the education committee, Mr Dominic Brady, the chairman of the school governors, Mr Tony Hood, and other governors, parents, and members of the Merseyside Community Relations Council.

Mr Antcliffe said afterwards that the incidents raised by the pupils were 'minor' and should not be got out of proportion.

Traditional rivalries between the schools had been heightened by their merger to produce a comprehensive of about 700 pupils, based on the old Paddingon school, which drew pupils from the ethnic community of Liverpool 8 and had a racially troubed past. Linked with it were the Liverpool Institutes for boys and for girls, while there were also said to be rivalries with a nearby Catholic girls' school.

The branch secretary of the NUT, Mr Jim Ferguson, which represents most of the school's teaching staff of over 60, said that pupils and parents had been told they would be able to continue courses, but there were not enough specialist teachers to go round.

'It has not been an easy merger but it is unfair to widen it in racial terms,' he said.

Earlier Mrs Josephine Campbell, a governor and chair of the parent-teachers' association, said: 'We had a parents' meeting and agreed that there is a lack of discipline. Black parents felt that staff were biased towards white children and white parents felt the opposite.'

Source: The *Guardian*, 13 February 1986

School of race hate

- Seven white kids quit over bullying
- The blackboard is called a chalkboard
- Two minutes silence for hanged African

Seven white boys quit their race-hate school yesterday because of bullying by black pupils.

They accused white teachers of turning a blind eye to the bullies for fear of being branded racists.

The boys claimed head-master Peter Fowler told them he could not guarantee their safety – so they walked out.

Four of the seven are prefects at Liverpool's Community County Comprehensive.

Worried education chiefs summoned the boys – all aged 15 and 16 – to a top-level meeting.

The boys claimed that at the troubled schools:

BLACKBOARDS have been banned – they are now known as chalkboards.

DISCOS are out – they are called reggae parties.

A TWO MINUTE silence was observed for a man hanged in South Africa.

AFRAID

One boy said 'it's like two different schools.

'There is one set of rules for the whites and another for the blacks.

'The teachers are frightened to do anything in case they are called racist.'

The seven boys were so afraid of being attacked that they sought protection in the girls' section of the school.

They claimed 45 other children have quit the school because of racial tension.

The seven spelled out their complaints at talks with school governors and Liverpool's education director Kenneth Antcliffe.

A PUPIL was disciplined for drawing Greenland bigger than Africa.

There are 700 boys and girls aged between 11 and 16 at the school. More than 250 of them are black.

The boys who quit used to belong to Liverpool Boys Institute High School, where Beatles George Harrison and Paul McCartney were educated.

They said the bullies came from the predominately black Paddington School, which merged with the Institute last year.

A council spokesman said last night: 'The director said there is no evidence of a black-white dimension.'

But Tony Hodd, chairman of the school governors said: 'Anyone who has watched Grange Hill on TV will know the friction gener- ated by merging schools.'

And Pat Brookes, leader of Liverpool's parent action committee, said: 'There has been an awful lot of racial tension bubbling for months – and it's only just under control.'

Source: The *Sun*, 13 February 1986

There are companies called 'news agencies' throughout Britain (and the world) which collect information, turn it into short articles and then pass them on to the newspapers who rewrite them for their own readership.

1 How can you tell that the information for both articles came from the same source (an agency)? Give two examples to illustrate your answer.

2 What sort of readership do you think
   a) the *Sun* has?
   b) the *Guardian* has?
   How can you tell this from the different styles in which the newspapers are written?

3 According to the *Guardian* article, is it true to say that the dispute was mainly over race?

4 What impression does the *Sun* give concerning the origins of the tension?

5 Which of the two articles do you think might lead to greater racial tension? Give reasons for your answer.

6 Suggest two different headlines for the story, one for a 'popular' newspaper (such as the *Sun*) one for a 'quality' newspaper (such as the *Guardian*), neither of which is racist.

News values

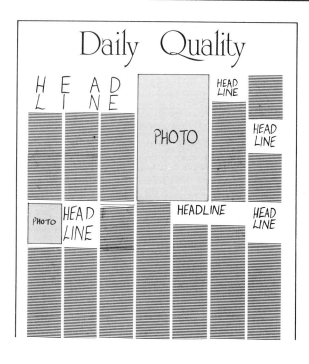

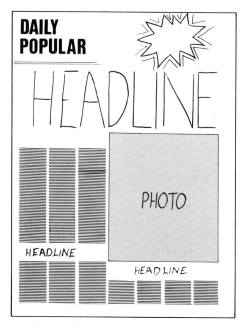

1 The friendly collie that saved the Jones family

2 Win one million pounds on our bingo

3 Liverpool run riot, defeating Arsenal 7 goals to 2

4 The United States invaded Mexico – Prime Minister expresses support

5 Fighting at rock concert, 13 injured, one person dead

6 The lady with the sexiest bust in Britain, brightens your day!

7 Bypass gets go ahead, Leigh church to be demolished

8 The wonder drug that keeps you young and virile – astonishing test results

9 Drought in East Africa, 1000s likely to die without aid

10 Unemployment reaches 4.2 million

11 Save our hospital cancer unit

Place the headlines from the list above on each of the front pages (on page 263) according to your view of importance/ interest for the readers of each type of newspaper.

Design the front page of a local newspaper and select suitable headlines.

Compare and explain any differences.

The mass media and . . .

What attitudes do the mass media promote on gender roles?

In this section, I want to look at the specific relationship between the mass media and a number of important areas of social life, in particular gender, race, politics, industrial relations and crime.

Gender

The media reflect (and help maintain) the two main roles of women: to be sexually attractive to men, and to be 'caring' mothers and housewives. The first of these two roles is to be found in the 'news' which is repeated daily on page 3 of the *Sun* that women have breasts! We are so accustomed to descriptions of women which describe them as 'attractive blonde, 25 . . .' and to comments on their clothes, that we think little of it. If similar comments were made about men, however, it *would* be noticeable.

As for the 'mothering' role, this is catered for by the large number of women's magazines on sale. These deal with recipes, household problems and romance stories. Those aimed at the younger, supposedly 'liberated' women (such as *19*) are largely concerned with attractiveness to men and, to a much lesser extent, careers (though usually in traditional areas of women's work such as secretarial and nursing work).

Ferguson in *Forever Feminine* found that there were certain themes which could be found in all women's magazines. These included the value of youth and beauty, female unpredictability and the importance of love in women's lives. She argues that these strengthen the lower-status position of women in society.

The media and gender

A nationwide poll has just revealed the secret behind sexual attraction. Women all over the country were asked just what attracted them most to a man. The result? Over 76 per cent put 'a good personality' which could 'make them laugh' as their first choice. As for the men, the number one choice was a women with a 'good bottom and legs'.

1 Examine a sample of recent newspapers and magazines (there will be some in the library) and make a list of the words used to describe men and women. Are there any differences? What sort of images of men and women do they present?

2 In what ways might the mass media be said to influence the different attitudes of men and women towards each other?

3 Collect pictures from newspapers and magazines showing the different images of men and women portrayed in the media.

Race

What attitudes do the mass media promote on racial divisions?

The attitude of the press towards race has been to see the whole topic in terms of a social problem. The general position of the press has been to stress the negative aspects of black Britons. Massive prominence is given in the 'tabloid' press to crime and riots, yet relatively little to the achievements of Blacks in sport for example, where the successful athlete is rarely described as 'black'. But the mugger, on the other hand, is. There are only two million Blacks and Asians living in Britain and most of these are concentrated in a few major cities, so the image of Blacks as a social problem, always causing trouble, as presented in the media has created a stereotype in the minds of the majority of Whites.

The media and race

The headline below suggests that Blacks are far more likely to commit crime than Whites. This is based on a very biased use of statistics. On examination the facts turned out to be very different from those the headline and article suggest. However, the stereotyped image of young Blacks was strengthened in many people's eyes.

Source: M Grant, *The British Media* (Comedia, 1984)

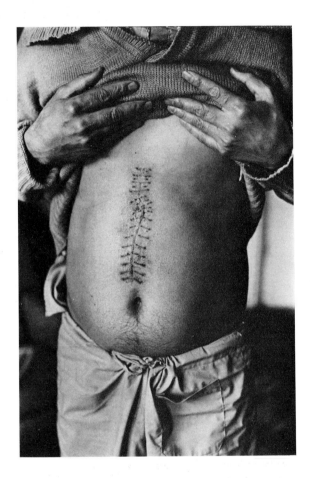

A black victim of a racial attack

The media stress the bad things done by the ethnic minorities and ignore the unpleasant aspects of their lives.

Have you read about the regular attacks on the ethnic minorities in the newspapers, or seen anything on television?

Politics

What political
attitudes do the
media present?

We have already discussed this in the section on the mass media and democracy (see pages 256–7). The point is that the press predominantly supports the Conservative Party, while broadcasting (television and radio) is generally liberal or conservative. Neither challenge the current society and rarely present alternatives. Only two of the major daily newspapers do not support the Conservative Party. However, it has been pointed out that there is nothing stopping radical newspapers: they fail because there is no public support for them.

Industrial relations

How do the media
report on individual
relations?

We have seen throughout this discussion of the mass media and its relationship to society, just how conservative it is. This reflects patterns of ownership and the expectations of the audience. The media is just as conservative too when it comes to strikes. It portrays workers on strike as 'greedy' and as 'standing in the way of technological advance and efficiency'.

The Glasgow University Media Group studied the television coverage of strikes in the late 1970s. They concluded that the news constantly over-simplified the issues, laying the blame on the workers. The views of the management were given greater support than that of the workers. The actual styles of interview for the news were different too, with managers being interviewed in their offices and workers outside on the picket line. The impression this gave to the viewer was that the manager's view was far more reliable and authoritative.

Strikes and the mass media

In the case of a strike . . .

The basic 'facts' of the case are taken from management – usually in a studio interview – while 'opinions' and events themselves are sought from the workers – usually outside the factory gates, even when they are not picketing. Interviews involving both sides often contain more 'supportive' questions to management:

'What will this strike cost your company?' or

'Do you think the workers have been misled by their leaders?' and more challenging or hostile questions to workers:

'After this strike will there be a job to go back to?'

'Aren't you cutting your own throats?'

'Do you realise the public hardship you are causing?'

Hardship to the public caused by strikes is news-worthy, but the hardship of low wages and poor working conditions of that same 'public' is not. The media tend to see their audience as consumers rather than workers, and strike-breaking is explicitly approved – the one train that does run is more newsworthy than the thousands that do not.

The 'cost' to the company of industrial action is very often stressed, usually in misleading terms of the total selling price of the goods and not simply lost profits. Savings to the company in wages, materials, fuel and other production costs are seldom taken into account. Nor is the fact that, sometimes, 'lost production' could not have been sold anyway: many strikes occur during periods of high production and low demand, and managers may then even push their workers into strike action (for example by cutting break times) precisely because this can save overall costs. The cost to the workers themselves in lost wages is rarely stressed, although because of the very real hardship involved workers will usually strike only as a last resort and only over a deeply-felt grievance.

Source: Adapted from M Grant, *The British Media* (Comedia, 1984)

1 Tape a range of interviews from the TV and the radio. As a group, compare the style of questioning.

2 Is it true what the author says in the extract?

Crime

Does the reporting of crime accurately reflect the reality?

False impression of the patterns of crime

Press and broadcasting coverage of crime tends to concentrate on certain areas and gives the impression that these sorts of crime are far more common than they are in reality. In order to give exciting headlines, the press concentrates on violent crime and sex cases, which are over-reported by a minimum of 20 times their actual occurrence. This creates stereotypes of crime and criminals in people's minds, so that older people, for instance, may be too frightened to go out.

Crime and the media

Just like prices, the amount of violent crime always seems to be going up.

However, ... when four sociologists examined the *Leicester Mercury's* reports of violence throughout Britain between 1900 and 1975 and compared this to the memories of retired policemen, they found that our times are not particularly violent and that people are less tolerant of street violence than they once were.

Why do people imagine that we live in a period of great violence? The authors suggest that the style of newspaper reporting of violent crime has changed and that it is now increasingly sensation-alised (made to seem more exciting than it really is), as this sells more copies. So, the authors think that newspapers are more likely to over-report violent disorders than ever before, thereby creating the impression of greater violence.

Source: *The Economist*, 1 March 1986

1 Do the media give a true impression of the extent of crime?

2 Why is this so?

The police viewpoint

Because the bulk of the information about crime and police activities comes from the police, reporters tend to give their viewpoint sympathetically. Although in cases where disputes arise over abuses of power by police, this often means that alternative views are not fairly treated in the press.

Scapegoating: The creation of folk devils and moral panics

What do we mean by 'scapegoating'?

Certain groups in society are often seen as posing a particular threat to the social order, for instance football hooligans. The media exploit the possibilities of a good story and sensationalise the issue. They focus so much on the area that public anxiety is whipped up and strong police action demanded. This results in a severe crackdown on the groups perceived to be dangerous, even if much of the material written and broadcast about them is not true.

In *Policing the Crisis*, Stuart Hall, through a Marxist perspective, analysed the way that a scare occurred over 'mugging' in the 1970s. Hall argues that in the 1970s the social problems of unemployment and of the inner cities led to a need by the State to crack down on possible trouble makers. In order to justify increased repression by the police and the courts, the issue of law and order had to be brought to the public mind. Hall argues that a campaign was whipped up against (black) muggers, with newspapers full of lurid details of vicious muggings against old age pensioners. The result was great public backing for the increased police presence in inner cities and the erosion in civil rights that took place.

'Ten policemen had to be taken to hospital today for intensive treatment after being viciously shouted at by strikers. Chief Inspector Plod has called for plastic bullets and nuclear weapons to be used so that law and order can be maintained.'

A moral panic

The media can help to create moral panics by labelling a group of people as deviant/bad and then creating a stereotype image of this group. The public are concerned and demand action by the police. Anyone who fits the public stereotype of this type of troublemaker is then under suspicion.

Using the model on the next page follow the history of any one moral panic.

There is usually at least one moral panic each year. In the past, they have concerned football supporters, inner-city black youths, drug takers (particularly glue sniffing) and the yearly 'peace convoys' to Glastonbury.

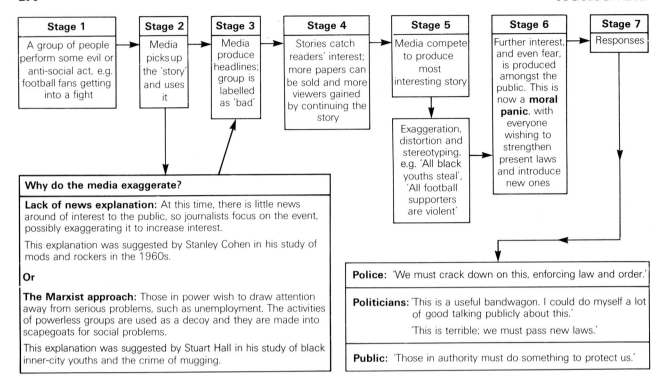

Stage 1	Stage 2	Stage 3	Stage 4	Stage 5	Stage 6	Stage 7
A group of people perform some evil or anti-social act, e.g. football fans getting into a fight	Media picks up the 'story' and uses it	Media produce headlines; group is labelled as 'bad'	Stories catch readers' interest; more papers can be sold and more viewers gained by continuing the story	Media compete to produce most interesting story	Further interest, and even fear, is produced amongst the public. This is now a **moral panic**, with everyone wishing to strengthen present laws and introduce new ones	Responses

Stage 5 (branch): Exaggeration, distortion and stereotyping, e.g. 'All black youths steal', 'All football supporters are violent'

Why do the media exaggerate?

Lack of news explanation: At this time, there is little news around of interest to the public, so journalists focus on the event, possibly exaggerating it to increase interest.

This explanation was suggested by Stanley Cohen in his study of mods and rockers in the 1960s.

Or

The Marxist approach: Those in power wish to draw attention away from serious problems, such as unemployment. The activities of powerless groups are used as a decoy and they are made into scapegoats for social problems.

This explanation was suggested by Stuart Hall in his study of black inner-city youths and the crime of mugging.

Police: 'We must crack down on this, enforcing law and order.'

Politicians: 'This is a useful bandwagon. I could do myself a lot of good talking publicly about this.'
'This is terrible; we must pass new laws.'

Public: 'Those in authority must do something to protect us.'

Advertising

In *The Hidden Persuaders*, Vance Packard exposed how advertisers were trying to 'ferret out' and then exploit our deepest needs – emotional security, 'reassurance of worth', status, sex and so on in attempts to sell products.

Market researchers are still using nearly all the strategies Vance Packard described, and new ones have been added. Peter Cooper, a psychologist who founded the Cooper Research and Marketing Agency, says, 'We want to attach *meanings* to brands,

ones appropriate to those different groups in society, to get people to buy those brands rather than other similar objects,' for example Lux lather on the face of a beautiful, mature women – soft skin, fewer wrinkles, youth, beauty, sexual attraction, or a Renault 5 surrounded by disco dancers – youthful, fun-loving, stylish.

Is the advertising expertise of decades now doing its deadly work and manipulating us unawares? Politicians have started hiring ad agencies,

which should be enough to make us re-examine the role of media persuasion.

But, research seems to show that we are not *that* gullible. A recent report 'Advertising, Brands and Markets' concluded that whether or not ads are successful depends on many other factors including, surprise, surprise, the quality of the brand. Price is also important, packaging, distribution, competition and so on.

Second, if advertising could

really 'dictate how our society must think, act and dream' as some critics claim, then heavily advertised products should grab an ever increasing share of the market at the expense of less heavily promoted products – 'but such trends cannot be identified'. Third, if advertising were such a powerful manipulator, the report says, the failure rate for new products backed by heavy advertising would not be anything like the estimated nine out of ten.

Source: Adapted from M Tysoe, 'Never give a sucker an even break' in *New Society*, 2 May 1985

1 Briefly explain how advertisers try to make us buy products.

2 What sort of 'meanings' do advertisers create concerning
   a) perfume?
   b) beer?
   c) jeans?
   d) cars (there could be more than one meaning here depending upon the 'market')?
   e) Coca-Cola?

3 According to the extract, are advertisers wholly successful in selling things? Give two reasons for your answer.

4 What other important factors are there?

5 What are the two most effective advertisements which have influenced you? Explain why they did so.

CHAPTER SEVENTEEN
RELIGION

The relationship
between religion
and society . . .

Secularisation: The
decline in religion . .

The growth of
sects . . .

Non-Christian
religions . . .

The relationship between religion and society

Does religion contribute to the well-being of the majority of people in society?

In every society people are frightened about the certainty of their deaths; they need some explanation for their brief stay here on earth. Surely it must all have some meaning? It is precisely this question that religion answers. Life does have meaning and there is a life after this one on earth.

The relationship between religion and society has been the subject of furious debate amongst sociologists. They agree on one thing only: that religion is important to society and *does* affect the way people act. Basically, there are three views on religion:

- that it is good for society, helping to draw people together and creating a sense of community;
- that it is a bad thing for the majority of people, stopping them complaining about the unfairness of society;
- that it can be important in bringing about social change.

Before we go on to discuss these viewpoints we ought just to note that sociologists are not concerned about the question of whether God exists or not, that is a question far beyond the powers of mere sociologists! They are only concerned with the *role* of religion in society.

Religion is good for society

This was the viewpoint of the nineteenth-century sociologist, Emile Durkheim. He pointed out that religion helps both society and individuals in different ways.

Religion: the opiate of the people?

For society

Religion provides the moral backing to the rules and laws of society, placing them beyond question. The result is a generally accepted way of behaving, which pulls people together in a shared morality. Those who do not share these basic values are regarded as outsiders and deviants. The result is that religion plays a major part in keeping societies stable and preventing abrupt change.

For the individual

Religion can provide a sense of purpose and meaning in life. We are here because God put us here and after our death we will go on to an after-life. Secondly, it gives us emotional support in times of crisis. So, death is not such a tragic event if we know that the dead person has gone to Heaven. Thirdly, for many people the church provides them with a sense of community. They feel they belong to something that cares about them.

Religion:
the opiate of the people?

Religion is a bad thing

This approach derives from the nineteenth-century sociologist, Karl Marx, who saw religion as a means by which people are tricked out of seeing the way they are being cheated and used by the rich and powerful. Although most people spend their lives working for the rich, they are comforted with the knowledge that if they cause no trouble and do their best to live a 'good' life (that is to do what they are told), then they will go to heaven after their death. Religion then prevents them from ever questioning society the way it is. For Marxists, religion acts as a form of social control.

A criticism of both the above approaches is that religion can also lead to social change, as well as maintaining stability, and can be used as a focus by the poor and underprivileged to challenge their position in society. The Iranian revolution which overthrew the Shah of Persia, was led by the Islamic religious leaders.

Religion as a cause of social change

Max Weber, writing at the beginning of this century, pointed out that the idea religion always plays a major role in maintaining social stability is not true. He argued that religious ideas are just as likely to bring about change as to prevent it.

Weber described how the ideas of a Protestant sect, the Calvinists, played a crucial part in bringing about industrialisation (production by machines in factories) in Britain more than two hundred years ago. Calvinists believed that working hard and not spending money on enjoying oneself was the way to win God's approval. To be successful was taken as a sign of approval by God and an indication that one was likely to go to Heaven. The result of the Calvinists' hard work (and no play) was considerable savings, which they were able to invest in factories. People with other religions which stressed giving money away to the poor, for instance, which resulted in them having only small savings would not have been able to finance the building of factories and machinery. So Weber concluded that the values of Calvinism led to savings which in turn led to industrialisation as we know it today.

It is important to remember that Weber was not saying that Marx and Durkheim were wrong, only that religion can bring about change as well as stability and that it is not always a way of manipulating people.

What is the relationship between religion and social control?

Religion and social control

The Ragged Trousered Philanthropists is a classic novel published in 1914 which tells of the lives of a group of workers of that period. The author uses the book for some very bitter criticisms of British society. Amongst the objects of his attacks was religion.

'Well the vicar goes about telling the Idlers that it's quite right for them to do nothing, and that God meant them to have nearly everything that is made by those who work. In fact he tells them that God made the poor for the use of the rich. Then he goes to the workers and tells them that God meant them to work very hard and to give all the good things they make to those who do nothing, and that they should be very thankful to God and to the Idlers for being allowed to have even the very worst food to eat and the rags and broken boots to wear. He also tells them that they mustn't grumble, or be discontented because they're poor in this world, but that they must wait till they're dead, and then God will reward them by letting them go to a place called heaven.'

Frankie laughed, 'Do they believe it?'

'Most of them do, because when they were little children like you, their mothers taught them to believe, without thinking, whatever the vicar said, and that God made them for the use of the Idlers. When they went to school, they were taught the same thing: and now they've grown up they really believe it, and they go to work and give nearly everything they make to the Idlers, and have next to nothing left for themselves and their children.'

Source: R Tressall, *The Ragged Trousered Philanthropists* (Granada, 1965)

1 Who is the author referring to when he talks about 'the Idlers'?

2 What does the vicar tell the workers?

3 Why shouldn't they complain?

4 Why do they believe it?

5 Why do sociologists call religion 'an agency of social control'?

6 Today the influence of religion has declined. Are there any other agencies which have taken over the job of social control? If so, what are they?

7 Can you suggest any ways in which these modern agencies help to control people? (It may help you to look at pages 203–5.)

Religion and revolution

The Iranians and Iraqis are at war. Iraq has superior weapons and, to counter this, Iran is prepared to sacrifice tens of thousands of young people who attack the Iraqi fortifications in 'human waves'. They overcome the Iraqis by sheer force of numbers, as the Iraqis cannot kill them fast enough.

Friday prayers in Tehran are the beating heart of the Islamic revolution, the power of Ayatollah Khomeini set out for the world to see, the reason the Iranians are advancing against a technically superior enemy. . . .

Ten thousand crowd the central area within sight of the prayer-leaders. Hundreds of thousands more pack all the roads and spaces around to follow the proceedings relayed by loudspeakers.

Long before reaching the central area, the chants can be heard punctuated by a rhythmic beat like the stamp of marching feet.

It is the sound of the vast assembly ritually beating themselves on the chest. In the front rows the leading mullahs (religious leaders) sit with the officers and visiting dignitaries. The war-wounded, in wheelchairs or with their arms in slings or their legs in splints, have their own enclosure. Next to them is a group of 100 Iraqi prisoners of war who have volunteered to fight against their own country – one of them weeps uncontrollably for much of the time.

The most chilling sight of all is the lines of boys – children – wearing red bands around their heads bearing the inscription *Labbayk* (We are ready for death).

Boys younger still . . . distribute sweets to the visitors. They are the *baseej*, the volunteers who will go to the front as soon as they are old enough. . . . Few of the *baseej* who set off for the war ever see their homes again.

To begin with, the carefully-segregated crowd is relaxed and cheerful, meeting friends and chatting on their one day off in the week. Then the microphones crackle into life and the mood soon changes. At times it is like a Billy Graham revivalist rally, at others like Nuremberg.

The slogans chanted so rhythmically vary, but the theme is the same. And that theme is war, death, victory at any price. 'War, war until victory; We are ready to go; We are ready to sacrifice; We will follow Khomeini's orders.' On it goes hypnotically, and the effect on the crowd shows.

From beating their chests with their right hands, many men now use both. Here and there men leap to their feet to shout their own readiness to die for their country, for their faith. Only the carefully-chosen guards remain calm, warily facing the crowd, not the speakers.

Source: *The Independent*, 31 January 1987

1 Why are the people gathered together?

2 Who are
      a) the mullahs?
      b) the baseej?

3 What does the extract tell us about the power of religion in
   Iran?

4 Do you think that the Marxist idea, that religion is a means of
   social control, is true in this situation? Give reasons for your
   answers.

Secularisation: The decline in religion

What does 'secularisation' mean?

One hundred years ago about 40 per cent of the population claimed to attend church each week. Today the figure is a little over 10 per cent. The obvious conclusion drawn by some sociologists is that people are less religious today than in the past.

The argument then continues that the churches have lost much of their influence in modern society. Fewer people believe in God, and use religious values as their guidelines on how to behave. For example, although the churches disapprove of abortion, today 17 per cent of all pregnancies are terminated by abortion, while contraception is accepted as normal. Indeed, it seems that the reverse is true today and the churches follow the general change in attitudes, an example of this is the Church of England's acceptance of the right of people to divorce.

The political influence of the Church of England has declined too and is rarely listened to by those in power. The importance of religious teaching in schools has slowly eroded so that it no longer has an important place in most schools' teaching programmes.

The functions of the churches have been lost to other agencies. Social workers, for example, paid by the State take the main responsibility for care of those with problems.

The status of the church has declined, particularly amongst the young. Church membership is seen by young people almost as an embarrassing thing to admit to. The rate of church attendance is far higher amongst the elderly than it is amongst the young.

All of this is summarised in the word 'secularisation'.

Reasons for the secularisation of society

The reasons given for this decline are that people now explain the world in scientific terms. Rather than understanding such things as the creation of man and women in terms of Adam and Eve, people now understand it as a result of evolution.

Why do people argue that Britain is a secular society?

In general then people look for natural explanations for events rather than supernatural ones. This has also influenced the idea of sin and morality. For example, illness was once seen as punishment by God and having done something wrong. Today, we see illness as a result of having caught some 'bug' and so we go to the doctor. Of course, this has also weakened the importance of the clergy in the community.

Along with the change in ways of explaining the world, there has also been a change in the values of society. Modern society stresses that success is the ownership of as many things as possible. For example, a successful married couple is one with a large house, car and all the consumer goods that their family wants. The traditional values of stress on community and mutual help, strongly associated with the churches have declined.

Churches: The changing membership

Church	Membership	
	1970	1985
Church of England	2 558 000	2 058 000
Roman Catholic	2 524 000	2 265 000
Presbyterian	1 890 000	1 483 000
Methodist	673 000	485 000
Mormons	80 000	102 000
Trinitarian sects	561 000	758 000
Muslims	400 000	900 000
Sikhs	115 000	175 000
Hindus	100 000	140 000
Jews	111 000	111 000

1 Which four churches have declined in numbers of their membership?

2 What do we mean by the term 'sect' (see main text page 279)?

3 What has happened to their membership?

4 What has happened to the membership of the Muslim, Hindu and Sikh religions?

5 Why has this change occurred?

6 According to the figures above, would it be entirely true to say that Britain is becoming a less religious (secular) society? Explain your answer with references to the statistics above.

7 Do you think that to be religious it is necessary to be a member of a church, or to attend church regularly?

8 Bearing in mind your answer to the last question, what problems can you see in measuring how religious a society is by church membership and attendance alone?

In defence of religion

It has been argued that the statistics, which so convincingly show a decline in religious belief, in reality only show a decline in attendance at church, which is a very different matter. After all, believing in God, does not mean attending church. For example, in a European survey taken at the end of the

1970s, 76 per cent of people said they believed in God. Furthermore, in a survey commissioned by the Bible Society in 1982, only seven per cent replied that they felt that they belonged to no church at all.

In the past there was great social pressure on people to attend church each Sunday, because it was a sign of social respectability. People may have attended but not really believed in God. Today, not attending church is perfectly acceptable. Those who do attend, do so for the right reason – that they truly believe.

British society is still based upon Christian values, with at least 80 per cent of people questioned regarding seven or more of the Ten Commandments as applying to them in their own lives. The importance of the church in the lives of people is still very strong. This is shown by the way that the major rites of passage (major points of change in our lives) are still marked by religious ceremonies. Baptism, marriage and the funeral service are all important church rituals for most families.

Finally, and most importantly, the decline in church attendance usually refers to the more traditional churches, such as the Church of England, or the Catholic Church. There has been a great growth in sects (as we discuss on page 279), such as the Moonies and Scientology, as well as in pentecostal churches, such as the Elim Pentecostal Church. Sects which are primarily attended by West Indians, for example, showed a growth in membership of more than 20 per cent, in the five years up to 1980. The Muslim faith has shown an increasing growth in membership, almost doubling its numbers between 1970 and 1980.

Is religion on the decline, or is it simply changing?

Conclusion

The death of religions does seem to have been exaggerated. Clearly there has been an overall decline in the importance of religion in British society, but to measure that solely in terms of church attendance is mistaken. However, much of the decline in attendance appears to be in the older-established churches, such as the Methodist, Church of England, Catholic, etc. Amongst the newer sects and the non-Christian faiths, such as the Muslims, there is significant growth and the rules of their faith seem far more important to them.

The growth of sects

What are sects?

When discussing religion, we people commonly talk about churches, meaning religious organisations that meet regularly to worship God. However, sociologists find this a little too vague and prefer to distinguish between three different types of religious organisations: the church, the sect and the denomination.

Basically, the more formal, the larger, the more tolerant and the more conformist a religious organisation is, the more likely it is to be a church. It follows then that the smaller, the more radical, and the stricter a religious organisation is, the more likely it is to be defined as a sect. In the middle lies the denomination.

- **A church:** a religious organisation with paid officials, usually fully integrated into the values of society. It has regular formal acts of worship in a special place put aside for that purpose. One of the major churches is generally linked to the State, and is known as the 'Established Church'; in England, this is the Church of England.

- **A sect:** a small religious organisation which is very strict in its beliefs and control of its membership. Usually they believe that only they have found the truth concerning God. There are rarely any paid officials. They are generally strongly opposed to the accepted values of society. An example is the Jehovah's Witnesses.

- **A denomination:** a religious organisation which is accepted by the wider society, although it has no connection with the State. It is smaller in size than a church and the running of the church is far more in the hands of the congregation than in a church. Often denominations are sects that have grown in size and have become less critical of other religious groups. The Methodists are an example of a denomination.

The most noticeable thing about the changing face of religion in Britain has been the decline of the older established churches, and the growth of sects. Sociologists have suggested the main reason for this is that sects are performing the functions that the older established churches are no longer providing. So the sects have taken their places. The small size of the sects, their discipline and stress on shared experience provides a home for those who are lonely, or searching for a creed full of certainty.

The membership of sects

Who joins sects?

Membership appears to be drawn from two very different groups, the rejecters and the rejected.

The rejecters are those who feel that the values of society are wrong and that the modern stress upon ownership of possessions as the one gauge of value ignores the need for inner harmony and contentment. These rejecters are usually younger people from well-off homes who are themselves not financially deprived, but feel they need a sense of purpose in their lives. Sects such as the Moonies and Hare Krishna draw their recruits from these sorts of people.

The rejected on the other hand are from the poorer, deprived groups in society who need comfort and explanation for their situation. In particular sects have arisen amongst those of Caribbean origin.

Sects

In the USA, as in Britain, a considerable number of sects developed from the 1960s onward. One of these was the Black Muslims. Kaplan argues that the growth of this sect amongst poor blacks was because:

It offers him a rebirth. He can shed his old despised identity. It offers him an emotional if not physical outlet for his hostility toward the white man. It offers him hope. Joining the highly moral and disciplined Black Muslims gives him the prospect of raising himself from his condition of poverty and frustration. It also provides him with the goal of building for a new glorious future in a united and powerful black society.

Source: Adapted from H M Kaplan, 'The Black Muslims and the Negro American's quest for communion' in *British Journal of Sociology*, 20 June 1969

1 Why was it more likely that the membership of the Black Muslims should have been amongst the poor Blacks, than amongst the better-off Blacks in the USA?

2 What sort of people generally are attracted to sects?

How sects can change into denominations

Over time the original founders of sects die and as the dominance enjoyed by them over everybody else (known as 'charisma') in the sect declines, so rules of behaviour replace the orders of the founder. New recruits may not be as fervent as those of the first generation and gradually, as the sect grows in size, the radical ideas become watered down to attract yet more members. So, over a considerable period, the sect takes on the characteristics of a denomination. Methodism is an example of this.

The rising tide of evangelism

While the more traditional churches are declining in membership, newer, more vigorous churches are rapidly expanding. The pentecostal and charismatic churches, for example, now claim a worldwide membership of 110 million people.

Non-Christian religions

When Asian immigrants began coming to Britain in the 1950s, they brought with them their religions. The values of these religions have provided the Asians with a sense of their cultural identities. They unite the various Asian groups from particular areas and help them to preserve their own values while living in Britain. The main religions are Islam, Hinduism and the Sikh religion. It is important to note that whereas each religion draws together those from similar backgrounds and origins, there is considerable friction between the different religions, reflecting the divisions in the Indian sub-continent, where Pakistan (Muslim) and India (Hindu) have fairly poor relations and where the Sikhs are trying to obtain an independent state from India by sometimes violent means.

The followers of Islam are Muslims and believe in the prophet Mohammed. They believe that Jesus was not the son of God (whom they call Allah), but an earlier prophet and that the preachings of Mohammed overrule those of Jesus. Their holy book is the Koran (Qur'an) and they are very strict in their interpretation of it. One of the main social differences is their stress on the role of women, who are expected to be extremely modest, covering all their bodies (including the face) and to be totally under the control of their husbands/fathers.

The Hindus believe in reincarnation, which means that after death they return again on earth in another form. What you return as depends upon your behaviour in your previous lifetime. They do not believe in one individual God (whom they call Brahman), but that God is part of everything, taking different forms. Socially, they too stress the importance of modesty and obedience by women. Traditionally they believe in the caste system, in which people are graded according to their holiness and 'inferior' people must accept the superiority of others. These social rules appear to be breaking down in Britain.

The Sikhs come from Northern India, they are instantly recognisable because of their turbans. They gather for worship, which consists of readings from their holy book, the Granth, and then listen and sometimes discuss sermons based upon it.

INDEX